BACK FROM THE
FAR FIELD

American Nature Poetry
in the Late Twentieth Century

Bernard W. Quetchenbach

UNIVERSITY PRESS OF VIRGINIA · *Charlottesville & London*

The University Press of Virginia
© 2000 by the Rector and Visitors of the University of Virginia
All rights reserved
Printed in the United States of America

First published in 2000

∞ The paper used in this publication meets the minimum
requirements of the American National Standard for Information
Sciences—Permanence of Paper for Printed Library Materials,
ANSI Z39.48-1984.

Library of Congress Cataloging-in-Publication Data
Quetchenbach, Bernard W., 1955–
    Back from the far field : American nature poetry in the late twentieth century /
Bernard W. Quetchenbach.
        p. cm.
    Includes bibliographical references and index.
    ISBN 0-8139-1953-3 (cloth : alk. paper) — ISBN 0-8139-1954-1 (pbk. : alk. paper)
    1. American poetry—20th century—History and criticism.   2. Nature in
literature.   I. Title.

PS310.N3 Q48   2000
811'.540936—dc21   99-089089

For Cara and Tom, and for my parents

Contents

Preface

IN THE LATE 1970s and the 1980s, a series of now-classic critical studies emerged concerning the poets who came to prominence in the 1950s and 1960s, and who have since become the senior generation of American poets. These were the poets who, according to James E. B. Breslin, M. L. Rosenthal, Charles Altieri, and others, had ushered in a new post-Modern generation, which was termed "contemporary" as a logical development from the Modern. The use of this term has become problematical in recent years, as it sometimes denotes any current or living poet, but sometimes, in a more limited sense, it refers to a particular period, roughly extending from the end of World War II until perhaps 1980, though these are approximate boundaries. This latter is what Breslin meant by "contemporary poetry," though he did not set an end date to the period (my end date is based on my own sense of changes in poetry and poetics that are only now becoming apparent). Contemporary poets, as the critics more or less agreed, were defined by a preference for free verse and by a propensity to identify, or at least be identified, with certain "schools," but mostly by a "poetics of immediacy" or "radical presence" in which the world of the poem revolves around the perspective and quotidian experience of the poet herself or himself, or at least of a persona difficult to distinguish from the poet. Breslin sums up the intentions behind contemporary poetry in Robert Lowell's decision to seek a "breakthrough back into life" (xiv),[1] that is, the life of the individual. Poets like Lowell, Theodore Roethke, Denise Levertov, and Allen Ginsberg typify the beginnings of contemporary poetry by "shifting" from the self-contained "autotelic" poetry of post–World War II America to the style that was to dominate American poetry for most of the remainder of the century.

It has often been noted that contemporary poetics, with its idiosyncratic focus, has proved unsuited to making political statements. The poetry of the Vietnam era has generally been pointed to as a case in point. Since the poet speaks only as himself or herself, the poetry lacks authority, a sense that the poet is addressing the entire culture from an agreed-upon perspective. In breaking through into the streets and houses of their own lives, contemporary poets have had to give up any claim to a position atop Parnassus.

The contemporary poet is therefore in an ironic situation. Forsaking the ivory towers of self-contained "academic" verse, the poet becomes "one of the people." And in the atmosphere of the 1960s, the people were perhaps even willing to accept the poet as a kind of cultural guide. Poets such as Ginsberg and Robert Bly became well-known counterculture figures. Ginsberg associated with and even toured with popular musicians like Bob Dylan. (Dylan, for his part, admired poetry, published some, and was widely seen as a "rock poet.") Bly attempted to parlay his role of poet into a position of cultural leadership, with this effort culminating in the public gesture of turning his National Book Award check over to draft resisters. Yet even as they found themselves in the public eye, the poets were working through an exploratory poetics based on the unfolding of individual experience, the "unpremeditated" nature of which virtually precluded making lasting statements of shared values. In contemporary poetry, truth is provisional and fleeting.

In the decades following the development of contemporary poetics, many poets have found strategies to combat the isolation inherent in contemporary poetry. In addition to the three contemporary poets central to this study, Ginsberg, Levertov, Amiri Baraka, and Adrienne Rich come to mind. Other poets who emerged somewhat later and might be said to represent an additional contemporary generation, such as Carolyn Forché, whose work includes political prose poems, have followed their examples. Though they were unable to take full advantage of the opportunity for a truly public poetry presented by the 1960s, it is true that many of the post–World War II poets, including the central figures in this book, are now regarded as unconventional elder statesmen and stateswomen of American poetry at the turn of the millennium.

This study considers strategies developed by three American poets of the contemporary generation—Robert Bly, Gary Snyder, and Wendell Berry—

to achieve a "public" voice capable of addressing societal values and concerns. The particular focus is on environmental issues, about which, despite much polarization, public concern has been widespread since the 1960s, as opinion polls have consistently shown. As Bly points out, even the disaffected "siblings" of the 1990s "are willing to accept that the earth's resources are limited, and many are passionate recyclers" (*Sibling* 243). Moreover, some of these younger people feel a "naturally ecological" connection with "the wren, the dolphin, the whale, the falcon in its threatened nest, the owl among the maddened loggers, and the mink standing in the snow" (243). To realize this potential connection between poet, subject, and reader, Bly, Snyder, and Berry must overcome significant obstacles. In their own ways and depending on their own lights, each has sought to "speak for" nature. But in doing so, they have had to discover ways to communicate what is essentially a privately held faith in the "meaning" of the natural world, and they have sought to do this through contemporary poetry, a vehicle designed more for introspection and individual experience than for public issues and shared values.

For this discussion, I have chosen to focus on three contemporary poets whose work features a range of approaches to nature and to reconciling private and public voices. Furthermore, each has actively wrestled with the question of the poet's place in society, so that not only do they exemplify the attempt to reconcile the private and public voices, but in fact they have been leading figures in an ongoing discussion of poetic authority and of the poet's responsibilities both to private vision and practice and to the culture as a whole.

In choosing the central figures for this study, I inevitably have had to focus on some figures and not on others. While this study is not meant to be comprehensive, I would like to acknowledge the contributions of three poets on whom I have chosen not to focus. Both Denise Levertov and W. S. Merwin are major figures of the contemporary generation, and both exhibit a "green sensibility" in their work. Although Levertov spent her early life in England, both she and Merwin could justly be termed contemporary American nature poets. Merwin, moreover, has written eloquently in defense of the earth, particularly concerning Hawaii, his adopted homeland. Levertov's importance in the development of the "contemporary shift" and her political activism make her a key figure in understanding the relationship between contemporary poetics and the public voice. Although the techniques they employ and the form their political activism has taken make them less appropriate for this study, both poets have made a mark on American nature poetry.

Another poet who deserves mention here, though one not usually thought of as a nature poet, is Adrienne Rich. Perhaps more than any poet of her generation, Rich has attempted to create a contemporary poetry that addresses large-scale social themes. She has in effect been labeled by Harold Bloom as a leader of the "enemies of the aesthetic" because of the political and social nature of her work (16). In his anthology *The Best of the Best American Poetry: 1988–1997,* Bloom makes a point of omitting any poem that appeared in the 1996 edition of *The Best American Poetry* series, which Rich edited. He announces his decision in the anthology's introduction, asserting that the 1996 edition "is of a badness not to be believed, because it follows the criteria now operative: what matters most are the race, gender, sexual orientation, ethnic origin, and political purpose of the would-be poet" (16). Though Bloom's appraisal is hardly complimentary, his singling out of her edition is evidence of Rich's unquestionable influence on the generation of poets that matured, or is still maturing, after the contemporaries.

Finally, in choosing to focus my attention on Bly, Snyder, and Berry, I have elected to consider three poets who for a number of years have been especially conscious of themselves as "spokespersons" for a constituency consisting in part of nature and the nonhuman. It is my belief that, among poets of their generation, these three have been most consistently conscious of the poet's role as a public figure in advocating for the earth.

Acknowledgments

LIKE ALL WORKS of its kind, this project would have been impossible without the assistance of many people. I would like especially to acknowledge the late Leonora Woodman of Purdue University. I would also like to acknowledge Marianne Boruch, Wendy Flory, Neil Myers, Robert Lamb, and Stan Goldman, all currently or formerly associated with Purdue. Acknowledgments are also due to the editors and staff at the University Press of Virginia, particularly to Cathie Brettschneider, Humanities Editor; Boyd Zenner, Acquisitions Editor; Ellen Satrom, Managing Editor; and Julie Falconer, Assistant Project Editor. Special thanks are due to Cara Chamberlain, Elizabeth Dodd, and Ann Welpton Fisher-Wirth, who read the manuscript while it was being prepared; Kathleen McKenzie of Radical X Editing; Christina Hughes, who assisted in research and editorial preparation of the manuscript; Jane M. Curran, who copyedited the manuscript; and Dina Jones-McKelvy, who assisted in research and prepared the index. I would also like to extend my appreciation to the faculties, libraries, and administrations of the University of Maine at Fort Kent and Northwest College, Powell, Wyoming. Many other colleagues, family members, and friends have also been patient and helpful as I completed the project.

Parts of chapters 4 and 5 appeared in my essay "The Search for Community in the Work of Wendell Berry and Gary Snyder" in the University of New Haven's *Essays in Arts and Sciences* 26 (October 1997): 27–40, edited by David E. E. Sloane.

Grateful acknowledgments are also due to the following presses and individuals.
    Berry, Wendell. "The Lilies," from *Farming: A Hand Book.* Copyright ©

1970 by Wendell Berry. "The Mad Farmer Manifesto: The First Amendment," from *The Country of Marriage*. Copyright © 1973 by Wendell Berry. Reprinted with permission from the author.

Berry, Wendell. "Requiem," "Setting Out." Reprinted from *Collected Poems 1957–82*. San Francisco: North Point Press, 1985. "Sabbaths 1979 (VII)." Reprinted from *Sabbaths*. San Francisco: North Point Press, 1987. Copyright © Wendell Berry. Reprinted by permission of Farrar, Straus & Giroux.

Berry, Wendell. "Sabbaths 1988 (IV)," from *A Timbered Choir* by Wendell Berry. Copyright © 1998 by Wendell Berry. Reprinted by permission of Counterpoint Press, a member of Perseus Books, LLC, and the author.

Bly, Robert. "Poem against the British." Reprinted from *Silence in the Snowy Fields,* Wesleyan University Press, Middletown, CT, 1962. Copyright © 1962 by Robert Bly. Reprinted with his permission.

Bly, Robert. "Fifty Males Sitting Together," and "Kneeling Down to Peer into a Culvert." Copyright © Robert Bly. Reprinted by permission of Doubleday, a division of Random House, Inc.

Bly, Robert. "Hunting Pheasants in a Cornfield," "Opening the Door of a Barn I Thought Was Empty on New Year's Eve," "Snowfall in the Afternoon," "Watering the Horse," from Robert Bly, *Selected Poems*. Copyright © 1986 by Robert Bly. "Dawn in Threshing Time," "Walking and Sitting," from Robert Bly, *This Tree Will Be Here for a Thousand Years. Revised Edition*. Copyright © 1979, 1992 by Robert Bly. Reprinted by permission of HarperCollins Publishers.

Jeffers, Robinson. "Love the Wild Swan," from *The Selected Poems of Robinson Jeffers* by Robinson Jeffers. Copyright © 1935 and renewed 1963 by Donnan Jeffers and Garth Jeffers. "Original Sin," from *The Selected Poems of Robinson Jeffers* by Robinson Jeffers. Copyright © 1948 by Robinson Jeffers. Reprinted by permission of Random House, Inc.

Jeffers, Robinson. "October Evening," "Oh Lovely Rock." Tim Hunt, ed. *The Collected Poetry of Robinson Jeffers, Three Volumes*. Copyright © Jeffers Literary Properties, © transferred 1995 to the Board of Trustees of the Leland Stanford Junior University. Published by Stanford University Press.

Roethke, Theodore. "Death Piece," "The Far Field," "The Lost Son," "Moss Gathering," "Root Cellar," "The Rose," "Weed Puller." Reprinted from *The Collected Poems of Theodore Roethke*. Garden City, NY: Anchor/ Doubleday, a division of Random House, Inc., copyright © 1975.

Snyder, Gary. "Logging," from *Myths & Texts*. Copyright © 1968 by Gary Snyder. "What You Should Know to Be a Poet," from *Regarding Wave*. Copyright © 1970 by Gary Snyder. "Pine Tree Tops," "Spel against Demons," "Toward Climax," from *Turtle Island*. Copyright © 1974 by Gary Snyder. Reprinted by permission of New Directions Publishing Corporation, and the author.

Snyder, Gary. "Elk Trails," "Mid-August at Sourdough Mountain Lookout," "Piute Creek." Reprinted from *No Nature*. New York: Pantheon, 1992. Reprinted by permission of Farrar, Straus & Giroux. World rights copyright © Gary Snyder, 1958, 1986.

Back from the Far Field

I · Contemporary Poetry, Nature Writing, and Nature

Speaking of (and for) Nature

IN HIS PREFACE to *No Nature,* his 1992 book of new and selected poems, Gary Snyder comments on the difficulty involved in defining nature, which "will not fulfil our conceptions or assumptions" and "will dodge our expectations and theoretical models" (v). Although nature includes human beings and human culture, "we do not easily *know* nature, or even know ourselves" (v). The relationship between humanity, especially urbanized and industrialized Western civilization, and nature constitutes something of a paradox; as creatures, humans are part of nature, yet in our effort to understand and manipulate our surroundings, we view nature as the "other" or "not me," the physical creation as a thing apart from the human "me" or "us." "Its separation from human society," says Bill McKibben, "at least in modern times, [has] defined nature for us" (64).

If nature is the "other" or "not me," then the work of the poets discussed here can be seen as an attempt to mediate between human and nonhuman, or between culture and nature. In this, they parallel prose nature writers. John Elder and Robert Finch, in their introduction to *The Norton Book of Nature Writing,* link the inception of modern nature writing as a literary type to the development of the detached, scientific, "objective" perspective of the natural sciences. Because nature writers depend on that perspective, although not always agreeing with or accepting it, they are seen by Elder and Finch as "the children of Linneaus" (19). Yet nature writers are not completely comfortable with the detached perspective of the scientist. As Stephen Trimble finds, "They see the natural world in a different way than scientists do, and 'naturalist' sounds a little too scientific for many of them" (5). Peter Fritzell identifies the tension between dependence on, or even enforcement of, the objective perspective and the opposing need to consider the human individual as part of nature, which justifies and requires a more personal response, as the definitive characteristic of the more "self-conscious" and "American" version of nature writing. Though this nature writing is conceived in various ways, there is something of a consensus that the blending of scientific, personal, and philosophical perspectives and the tension between those perspectives is intrinsic in and central to nature writing as it is currently practiced in America. Thomas Lyon characterizes the natural history essay as part of "a halting journey toward understanding the world, and ourselves within it, as one system" (*This* xv).

The attempt to find meaning in an individual's relationship with nature is a characteristic of nature writing but is also typical of the Romantic tradition in European and American culture. According to Lyon, "the Romantic movement in philosophy and literature . . . helped give the individual experience of nature, in all its intuitive and emotional vagueness yet penetrating insight, some credibility and standing" (19–20). He goes on to say that "Our literature of nature owes a great deal of its content and development, and its currency now, to the major contributions of Romanticism and science" (23). Robert Bly, Gary Snyder, and Wendell Berry have each acknowledged their place in the tradition of Romantic or post-Romantic nature poetry. In his 1980 anthology *News of the Universe,* Bly traces the "Goethe stream" of Romantic thought to the present, where he locates each of the three poets discussed here. Wendell Berry traces a similar history of nature poetry in "A Secular Pilgrimage," an essay in *A Continuous Harmony,* citing William Wordsworth and D. H. Lawrence, both of whom Bly includes in *News of the Universe.* Among contemporary nature poets, Berry includes Snyder, Denise Levertov, and A. R. Ammons (2), two of whom (Snyder and Levertov) have works included in Bly's *News of the Universe.* Snyder also includes Lawrence among his influences (*Real* 56), and, among contemporary poets, notes Robert Duncan, Michael McClure, Bly, Berry, and Robert Sund (123–24), each of whom appears in Bly's anthology.

According to Bly, what these poets have in common is their willingness to "grant consciousness" to "trees or hills or living creatures not of their own species" (210), that is, to consider other parts of the physical creation as significant not only as objects for study and use but in their own right as well. In Bly's formulation of Romanticism, the physical creation is peopled by distinct "authentic" entities linked by shared consciousness.

This chapter considers nature poetry in the context of contemporary poetics, but it is also revealing to consider Romantic and post-Romantic nature poetry as constituting a parallel development to nonfiction nature writing.[1] If contemporary nature poetry grows out of the Romantic tradition in European literature, as Robert Bly asserts in *News of the Universe,* then both contemporary nature poetry and American nonfiction nature writing are reactions against, or modifications of, the Enlightenment notion of the separation of subject and object.

In the *News of the Universe* essays, Bly considers Romanticism as an attempt to keep alternative channels of understanding open to augment the increasingly powerful scientific objectivity, which, isolated from other epistemological means, becomes sterile, manipulative, and ultimately wrongheaded. Others who have adopted this or similar criticisms of science range from Emerson in "Nature" to Carolyn Merchant and Neil Evernden. Elder and Finch differentiate between science as such and "the older term 'natural history' [which] has often been defiantly embraced by nature writers as they respond to the physical creation in ways that, while scientifically informed, are also marked by a personal voice and a concern for literary values" (22).[2] Fritzell agrees, citing nature writing as the "archetypification of that historic interplay between personal narrative and systematic science, perhaps even the perfection of it" (6).

Nonfiction nature writers and Romantic poets, in preserving the value of personal response to the physical creation by contextualizing the scientific-objective approach within a larger framework of understanding, combat what Bly calls the limited, rationalistic "Old Position" by combining new knowledge with still-older orders of awareness and response.[3] Each rebels against the rationalistic hegemony by which "A white-coated, passive, impersonal style became the established voice of 'objective science'" (Elder and Finch 22).[4] But it is not science itself against which they rebel. Like nonfiction nature writers, each of the poets considered here is aware of a profound debt to the scientific understanding of nature. Instead, both Romanticism and American nonfiction nature writing criticize the way in which scientific epistemology has intensified what Bob Steuding calls "the general drift of Western Civilization; that is, its unconscious desire to render the wild world tame and to bend nature to its will" (153). Science provides an incisive, perhaps even an essential, method for understanding, but when its objectivity becomes more than a necessary fiction in the service of the scientific method and becomes an assumption about the overall relationship between humanity and nature, then, as Neil Evernden points out, "the path to knowledge" becomes "that of the stranger" leaving nature "utterly devoid of human qualities" and eliminating "kinship" between ourselves and the natural world (89).

In "A Secular Pilgrimage," Berry defines nature poetry as poetry that "considers nature as subject matter and inspiration" (*Continuous* 1). This simple definition links Berry's notion of nature poetry with the American tradition of nonfiction nature writing. Fritzell describes American nature writing as balancing between two forms of response to the natural world and therefore as an interplay between two voices, that of the separate, "objective" observer and that of the intuitively responding participant. Berry's "subject matter" suggests nature as object of study, which in turn implies a separate perspective for the observer. "Inspiration," if considered carefully (and Berry would not use such a word without careful consideration) clearly involves a merging, a drawing together of subject and object, in an interchange like breathing. In "The Conservation of Nature and the Preservation of Humanity," an essay from *Another Turn of the Crank*, Berry concludes that "our relation to the world surpasses mere connection and verges on identity" (74–75).

Bly, Snyder, and Berry share with nonfiction nature writers a common history of insisting on what Elder and Finch call the "personal element— that is, the filtering of experience through an individual sensibility" (26). Not surprisingly, these poets acknowledge a debt to the nature writing tradition, particularly to Henry David Thoreau, since "What Thoreau affirmed as absolutely instructive," according to Lyon, "was his own experience of the particulars of nature" (*This* 51). Max Oelschlaeger also cites the importance of individual experience to Thoreau, concluding that Thoreau's "excursions" in the natural world constituted "the folding back of consciousness on his immediate experience" as well as the means by which he "gradually overcame the alienation of the person . . . from nature" (137). Bly has edited a collection of Thoreau's poetry and also went "out of genre" to include a passage from *Walden* in *News of the Universe*. William Scott McLean notes Snyder's debt to Thoreau, in the context of Romanticism, in his introduction to *The Real Work* (xi–xii), and Bob Steuding discusses how Snyder's reading of Thoreau at Sourdough Mountain informed his developing concept of wilderness (115–18). The last line in *Myths & Texts* echoes the final image in *Walden*. Thoreau's continuing influence on Snyder can be seen in his discussion of "Tawny Grammar" in *The Practice of the Wild*. Berry, too, points to Thoreau as offering a "quiet" alternative to the destructive attitude of Western civilization toward nature (*Long-Legged* 42) and writes admiringly about the avowedly Thoreauvian Harlan Hubbard.

It is no coincidence that both critical studies and anthologies devoted to nature writing pay close attention to Romanticism and to American transcendentalism in particular. For example, the first section of Ann Ronald's *Words for the Wild: The Sierra Club Trailside Reader,* entitled "The Nineteenth Century Transcendentalists," consists entirely of selections from Emerson and Thoreau. The transcendentalists, and Thoreau particularly, are known as Romantics with an appreciation of the details of natural history. Edward O. Wilson credits the New England transcendentalists with finding "science more congenial than did their European counterparts— witness the many accurate natural history observations in *Faith in a Seed* and other writings by Thoreau" (37). The central figure of Thoreau links the traditions of American Romanticism and nonfiction nature writing.

There are many reasons for poets such as Bly, Snyder, and Berry to seek a solid position from which to address their culture as a whole. One reason is the isolated situation of the contemporary poet, the subject of the next section of this chapter. Another has to do with the equally solitary position of the American nature writer. Nature writing, particularly in its American embodiment, has always sought what Aldo Leopold calls "a durable scale of values" (200), deriving its authority from attentive experience of and in the natural world. From the day that William Bartram picked up his backpack and notebooks and went off to "botanize," as Thoreau would say, his travels became an exercise in seeking meaning in an individual encounter with the nonhuman. The same can be said of Thoreau, John Muir, Aldo Leopold, and eventually Annie Dillard.

One of the benefits of "going to the woods" is the distance one can place between one's self and one's fellows. The pastoral convention has been studied in the context of American literature by many scholars, including Leo Marx. Lawrence Buell, Annette Kolodny, and Glen Love have been prominent in discussing the American pastoral from an ecocritical standpoint. Among other things, the movement into the woods has served to rid the mind of the distractions that come between one's self and the ability to see clearly and respond to what Bly figures, in "Watering the Horse," as "The white flake of snow / That has just landed in the horse's mane" (3–4). In the relative isolation of Walden Pond, Thoreau is able to produce writing remarkable for its blending of the objective and the subjective-personal voices, as when he finds himself "watching a barred owl (*Strix nebulosa*)," which, he observes, "would stretch out his neck, and erect his neck feathers, and open his eyes wide; but their lids soon fell again, and he began to nod." Thoreau follows this close and straightforward observation with a personal response: "I too felt a slumberous influence," and goes on to blend the two modes of perception in a metaphorical comparison, the owl figured as "winged brother of the cat" (*Walden* 266). Similarly, Muir finds his freedom from civilization to be a key to his hearing so well the "good tidings" of the mountains. He even attributes his only dangerous fall in the Sierras to a stay in San Francisco and Oakland, which not only made his woodcraft rusty but, more importantly, strained his usual rapport with the mountains (244–45).

This incompatibility of human and natural realms is shown in Annette Kolodny's insightful discussion of John James Audubon in *The Lay of the Land* (74–88). The accompanying ambivalent attitude of the American nature writer toward humanity is also evident in contemporary nature writing. One example is Richard Nelson's *The Island Within;* throughout the book, Nelson considers the contradictory desires for solitary exploration and for time spent with family and friends.

The path into the wilderness necessarily leads away from the domestic concerns of one's fellows. Even as non-wilderness-oriented a poet as Wendell Berry, for example, recognizes the pull that leads Daniel Boone, as "long hunter," away from the world of family and farm. In "The Peace of

Wild Things," he acknowledges, as Bly does in "Watering the Horse," that when one wants to step into the presence of nature, one has first, in Whitman's words, to "turn and live with animals" ("Song of Myself" 32.1). Similarly, Gary Snyder finds that one has to allow "Words and books / Like a small creek off a high ledge" to be "Gone in the night air" ("Piute Creek" 16–18) before one can experience the "Cold proud eyes / Of cougar and coyote" (27–28).

Both Berry's "The Peace of Wild Things" and Snyder's "Piute Creek" end with a movement away from the natural scene. This seems strange at first. Why would the poet choose to break off the sought-after moment in the "grace of the world" ("The Peace of Wild Things" 11) by reminding himself, and his readers, that the respite is only "for a time" (10)? The desire to "rise and go" ("Piute Creek" 29) back, however, is not really so surprising. Interpretation has always been part of the nature writer's commission. Like the survivors in Stephen Crane's "The Open Boat," Snyder and Berry feel that, by virtue of their intimate experience, they should act as "interpreters" of nature. The need to communicate full experience, including its "meaning," has been a source of considerable vexation to American nonfiction nature writers as well as poets; from Thoreau's excoriation of his farmer neighbors who fail to see the true worth of their land to Muir's exhortations to "Climb the mountains and get their good tidings" (311), there is an almost evangelical attempt by many nature writers and poets to reach an audience wrapped up in everyday personal and societal concerns, in what Bly characterizes significantly and disparagingly as "domesticity."[5] In discussing John Muir, historian of religion Catherine Albanese outlines the two parts of the nature writer's mission in religious terms. Muir must "go to the mountains and the sequoia forests . . . to engage in religious worship of utter seriousness and dedication" but must also fulfill an obligation by returning to society. "To come down from the mountains and preach the gospel of preservation," she concludes, "was to live out his life according to the ethic that his religion compelled" (101).

There are other reasons for contemporary nature poets to seek a public voice, but the reason most essentially endemic to their life's work is the nature writer's traditional desire to bring culture closer to nature, thus relieving culture of its habitual "domestic" dullness, narrowness, and arbitrariness, while still maintaining and benefiting from cultural interchange with others. This is why Thoreau finds it worthwhile to live a "kind of border life" (*Natural* 130) between the town and the woods, culture and nature.

Nature writers, in exploring the "otherness" of nature, have arguably been less willing to take that separation for granted than has their culture as a whole. Fritzell posits that an ambivalent or self-conscious sense of the separation (and the connection) between human and nature is characteristic of the best nature writing. Albanese notes the desire of Thoreau and Muir to achieve a state in which, as "once-confessed" by Thoreau, they are "nature looking into nature" (Albanese 99). In practice, however, the nature writer tends to echo the general conception of nature as "that which is not me." Even Snyder, who titles his selected poems *No Nature* to emphasize the illusory quality of any separation between the human and the nonhuman, nevertheless confirms the integrity of nature as the nonhuman. One definition of nature poetry is, therefore, poetry that considers the physical creation as significant in its own right, essentially independent of human culture.

Independence, however, does not necessarily entail the complete isolation of human consciousness from the rest of nature. In fact, Bly, Snyder, and Berry find their experience with nature rich in meaning that, though perhaps not totally understandable, can be evoked through language and, albeit imperfectly, communicated to others.

The Experiential Voice

In American poetry, a more-or-less distinct borderline exists between the late Modern or New Critical period and what, for lack of a better term, has been called the post-Modern or contemporary period. This border was crossed sometime after World War II with the publication of such works as Roethke's *"The Lost Son" and Other Poems,* Lowell's *Life Studies,* and Ginsberg's *"Howl" and Other Poems.* Critics agree that a salient characteristic of this new poetry is a rejection of the self-contained autotelic poetics developed in response to the New Critics. Poets attempted to break through into a new poetic style and, moreover, according to James Breslin's *From Modern to Contemporary,* to find a new source for poetic authority—not in the various forms of cultural history so favored by the "Great Moderns" but instead in the day-to-day phenomena of experience.

Breslin's work is central to the flowering of critical commentary about contemporary poetry that occurred in the late 1970s and early 1980s. In a 1996 address to the University of Maine's National Poetry Foundation, Charles Altieri confirmed the importance and essential correctness of Breslin's work ("Poetics"). Altieri himself, in his 1984 book *Enlarging the Temple,* sees the contemporary shift as a reassertion of "Romantic immanentism," particularly as a reformulation, or group of approximately equivalent reformulations, of Wordsworthian poetics and philosophy of poetry. Even those critics such as Christopher Clausen and Robert Pinsky, who are more concerned with tracing continuity and are therefore inclined to see the period as a time of variation rather than revolution, note a difference in method if not in ultimate purpose or philosophy. Moreover, the poets themselves are aware of the change and address it as such in their poetry and commentary. Marked by a move from tightly controlled lyrics that generally employ prescribed poetic structures to a more "organic" or "open" free-verse form, this shift is plainly visible in Roethke's *"The Lost Son" and Other Poems* and, later, in the works of poets as diverse as Robert Lowell, Denise Levertov, James Wright, Adrienne Rich, Allen Ginsberg, and Robert Bly, who, through his seminal *The Fifties,* sought, as Deborah Baker says, "to encourage a new imagination in American poetry" (49).

Nowhere is this shift more clearly demonstrated than in the work of Theodore Roethke. The formal quality of his first book, *Open House,* a title that belies, as Richard Blessing has noted (40), the tightly controlled nature of the poems, is exemplified by "Death Piece." The poem consists of two ballad or hymnal stanzas, rhymed quatrains of alternating iambic tetrameter and trimeter lines. The final stanza follows:

> His thought is tied, the curving prow
> Of motion moored to rock;
> And minutes burst upon a brow
> Insentient to shock.   (5–8)

In keeping with the poem's technical regularity, its thematic content is "poetic" and poetically rendered (consider, for example, the "curving prow" of moving thought), and the total effect is of a neat artifact. Even the more "progressive" *Open House* poems like the often-anthologized "The Premonition" are formally and thematically "worked out." In Roethke's initial volume, as William Meredith has observed, "The subjects were not tame . . . but the issues of the poems were resolved by poetic formulas" (37).

After *Open House, "The Lost Son" and Other Poems* is a radical departure. The "Greenhouse Poems" that begin the book are free verse, although there is some use of end rhyme and slant rhyme ("crates / bait" in "Root Cellar," or "roots / juice / boots" in "Old Florist," for example), and the line lengths vary greatly. The subject matter and images are much more idiosyncratic and personal than even in "The Premonition." The greenhouse may be an Edenic symbol, as Louis Martz has suggested (32–33), but it is certainly a somewhat private one, with roots in Roethke's personal history. "The Lost Son" sequence itself can be seen as completing Roethke's emergence into the contemporary idiom.

In the seminal *From Modern to Contemporary,* Breslin documents the manifestations of the shift indicated in his title in the various loosely defined poetic schools of the period: the confessionals, the deep image poets, the Beats, the New York school, and the projectivists, or Black Mountain school. Each group, in its own way, sought to change the source of poetic authority from the collective history of the culture to the quotidian experience of the individual. This exploration, no doubt, revitalized poetry in America, but it also, by its very nature, limited the poets' ability to invoke public values and idea structures, since the grounds for any attempt to do so while practicing a poetics based on individual experience can only extend to others through analogy. The daily personal anguish of the confessional poet, for example, becomes universalized when seen as representative of the age. Yet, despite the successes of confessional poets and the poets' attempts to provide historical context (Sylvia Plath's characterization of her injured thumb as a seventeenth-century Puritan in "Cut" is a characteristic example, as is the genealogical content of Lowell's *Life Studies*), the analogical process lacks a clear cultural grounding, as the defining critics of contemporary poetry have recognized. Geoffrey Thurley notes "a certain baselessness" (49) in American poetry and links it to the lack of a clearly defined social and cultural role for poets and poetry in America. Altieri finds the lack of cultural authority to be the source of the failure of the Vietnam-era poets to produce a public art of lasting significance (*Enlarging* 231–33). In his review of John Haines's selected poems, Robert Richman dismisses contemporary political poetry, saying of Haines's poems from "the late 1960s and early 1970s" that "deal with national and international political events" that "These, one is thankful, are . . . relatively few in number" (196). Concerning Gary Snyder, Helen Vendler also prefers "the elegantly arranged cinematographic poems . . . to the heavy-handed protest poems" (121), which she calls "political-tract boilerplate" (122).

Dana Gioia, in considering Robert Bly, disagrees with this predominant viewpoint, calling Bly's antiwar poems his best work and even "a few of the most stunning political poems in American literature" (179). About these poems, Bly himself says, in a *Bloomsbury Review* interview, "Now I go to universities and people say to me, 'How do you feel about your antiwar poems?' They want me to apologize. And I say, 'I really regret that I didn't write more of them'" (Estés 12). Even so, Bly recognizes contemporary poetry's essential privacy. In fact, he once dismissed Modernism as a "Wrong Turning" (*American* 7) because of its lack of "inwardness." Bly's attempts to reconcile inwardness with the public voice are discussed later, but it is easy to see how inwardness and the reliance on individual experience and impression can lead to an obscurity as opaque as that of the most erudite Modern. Roethke, for example, is certainly open to charges of obscurity in the "Lost Son" and "Praise to the End!" sequences. The inwardness of contemporary poetry places the poet in a position essentially withdrawn from what might be characterized as a public speaking voice, that is, a voice that can access publicly shared images, values, and, ultimately, concerns.

The inward focus has led to a poetry that adheres in principle to Archibald MacLeish's famous maxim, "a poem should not mean / but be" ("Ars Poetica" 23–24). Much contemporary poetry tends to concentrate on the way in which an individual perceiver is exposed to and ultimately conceptualizes experience. Bly's "Watering the Horse" from *Silence in the Snowy Fields* shows how, in practice, this focus tends to isolate the self, with the broader cultural perspective becoming a distraction, so that the poem's speaker must give up "all ambition" (1) to see "with such clear eyes" (2).

"Ambition" is, of course, a loaded word, implying a wide range of personal and social goals and desires. One could substitute Isaac McCaslin's "ownership" (in Faulkner's "The Bear") or the American standby "success" to capture some of the specific meanings that could attach to it. But what clouds the poet's eyes here is *all* ambition, any desire to do anything but experience the act of seeing. The poem can be seen as an answer to Robert Frost's "Stopping by Woods on a Snowy Evening." Frost's moment of indecision is followed by his resolution, albeit a reluctant one, to return to the conscious world of his fellows, to the "promises to keep" (14). For a poet, this responsibility includes not getting mesmerized by one's ability to see "the white flake of snow," which can have an ultimately arresting effect on the discovery or assignment of meaning in experience.[6] Even MacLeish, after all, must abandon his own instructions to deliver the final lines of "Ars Poetica." By concentrating on the individual "epiphany," the poet runs the risk, as Robert Pinsky claims in *The Situation of Poetry*, of cutting himself or herself off from the discursive elements of language used to communicate value and meaning. As Christopher Clausen points out, one of the things that poetry has traditionally done is communicate general truths and "significant ideas" (21). The poet Dave Smith concurs, opposing MacLeish by asserting that "Art, if it is art, makes a point. It means" (8). Almost simultaneously with the initial critical characterization of contemporary poetry, in fact, both poets and critics began to call for the reintegration of narrative and discursive elements into American poetry.

Contemporary poetry's experiential quality, its tendency to focus on individuals discovering their way through the everyday happenings of their lives, is close enough to the experiential basis of nature writing for Pinsky to characterize the urban notation poems of Frank O'Hara as a kind of nature poetry (102), and for Altieri to see the whole post-Modern poetry project, including such ostensibly non-Wordsworthian writers as O'Hara and Olson, as basically Wordsworthian in essence (*Enlarging* 17–18). For contemporary nature poets, this experiential quality is compounded by that traditionally associated with nature writing, producing an even greater isolation. A key case in point is Theodore Roethke, who characterizes his connection to the natural world in "Some Self-Analysis," an essay he wrote while attending the University of Michigan: "I can sense the moods of nature almost instinctively. Ever since I could walk, I have spent as much time as I could in the open. A perception of nature—no matter how delicate, how subtle, how evanescent,—remains with me forever" (*On the Poet*

4). In the same student paper he also indicates his familiarity, as well as his sympathy, with American nature writers: "I know that Muir and Thoreau and Burroughs speak the truth" (4).

Roethke's natural imagery recalls Peter Fritzell's characterization of nature writing in *Nature Writing and America*. According to Fritzell, "self-conscious" nature writers suspend themselves, or are suspended by circumstances, between two poles of language reflecting two approaches to nature. The nature writer is, on the one hand, a detached and scientific observer, like the "botanizing" Bartram or Thoreau. On the other hand, there is the desire to acknowledge and explore an intimate connection with nature, not as object of study, but as matrix in which the writer partakes and from which he or she is inseparable. Roethke's writing reflects this tension; his descriptions of birds in particular suggest, if not the scientific monograph, at least the popular field guide. Thus, the bluebird is characterized as the "lover of holes in old wood" ("The Rose" 3.9), the catbird appears in appropriate habitat in the overgrown corner ("The Far Field" 2.1–3), and the warblers appear, as they do later in Wendell Berry's poetry, carrying their occasionally poetic ("Cape May, Blackburnian, Cerulean"; 2.8), but just as commonly descriptive and awkward designations. In "Some Self-Analysis," Roethke fears that he has "become a mere reporter" of the objects and "prosaic people" around him (*On the Poet* 4). But Roethke does not remain simply a reporter in his poems. His desire for a kind of mystical, responsive interchange between self and nature has been amply demonstrated by numerous observers, as has his familiarity with contemporaneous sources on mysticism and mystical traditions such as Evelyn Underhill, Nijinsky's notebooks, and P. D. Ouspenski.[7]

Roethke the nature writer is also Roethke the pioneer of contemporary poetics, and the similarity between nature writing and contemporary poetry is evident in his work. Both rely on ongoing experience as the basic source of authority, contending that previous experience, as well as "book knowledge," significant as they are, must yield to the authority of continuous discovery. Just as Thoreau, in leaving Walden Pond, concludes that there are other lives and "more day yet to dawn" (*Walden* 351), Roethke, in his famous response to Eliot's "East Coker," makes his "old" speaker in "The Longing" an "explorer" (3.19). Although Breslin credits texts such as Lowell's *Life Studies* with opening up the contemporary "poetics of immediacy" (70), and Thurley considers Ginsberg's "Howl" to be the central text in *The American Moment,* Roethke's *"The Lost Son" and Other Poems,* as Peter Balakian notes, preceded these works by nearly a decade (3).[8]

One of the most persistent contemporaneous and retrospective criticisms of Roethke is that, in focusing on the individual's relationship to nature and experience in nature, he somehow cut himself off from the experience of his time and his society. This is reminiscent of Emerson's belief that Thoreau "had no ambition. Wanting this, instead of engineering for all America, he was the captain of a huckleberry-party" (260). Karl Malkoff asserts that "Roethke was never able to write very good poetry about society, or even about the individual's relationship to society in a general sense" (30). Rosemary Sullivan notes Roethke's inability to fulfill the public role he admired in Yeats, concluding that Roethke "felt more than is generally supposed the pressure toward a poetry of social concern" (91). She perceptively links this apparently unfulfilled and unfulfilling aspect of his work to the American "visionary tendency" (197) that leads toward "the wounded self withdrawing from human society in search of renewal" (196).[9]

In general, however, contemporary poetry locates its central authority in the self and experience. Therefore, criticism based on "Roethke's instinctive inability to admit the value of social criteria with reference to the self" (Sullivan 196) could just as easily be leveled at, say, Frank O'Hara. In fact, criticism of Vietnam War poetry, such as Altieri's concerning Denise Levertov, cites the failure to find an effective link between society and the self (*Enlarging* 231–36). However, criticism of this kind has been leveled with particular frequency and persistence against Roethke, has been directed toward his poetry's lack of social content rather than the ineffectiveness of its attempts to engage politics, and has included observers informed about and sympathetic to contemporary poetics, such as M. L. Rosenthal. The significance of the contemporary poem depends on the ability of the reader to identify the experience of the poem's speaker as somehow representative. Rosenthal's criticism of Roethke, and his dismissal of him as a talented but ultimately uninteresting confessional poet, is that his experience is too atypical, too far removed from "the concerns of his age" (118). Harry Williams addresses this point in *The Edge Is What I Have,* finding that "It is not usual to stress the social aspect of Roethke's poetry; indeed his ostensible neglect of the social theme has caused critics to assume that his range is limited, even as Robert Lowell seemed to do in a rather glib remark for *The Paris Review* (1961): 'the things he knows about I feel I know nothing about, flowers and so on'" (33–34).

By the mid-twentieth century the American experience had changed, and "nature's nation" had become urban and suburban. An increasing number of Americans have been exposed to nature primarily through the rarefied suburban lawn, the stereotyped portrayals in "nature shows," and perhaps a driving tour of a national park. The nature poet who depends on the kind of analogical process that characterizes contemporary poetics cannot count on the analogy to resonate for readers who do not share comparable experiences as a significant and familiar part of their lives. Even in the current age of environmental concern, it is still difficult for a nature poet to overcome the inability of the traditional poetry audience to connect with the subject matter. Helen Vendler chides Snyder's publishers for including on a book jacket a "heavy-handed pitch to the ecologically minded sector of his audience" (117). It is hard to imagine such a glib dismissal of any other social issue in a non-ironic context. For example, it would be unlikely for Vendler to note that a book tried to appeal to the "racially minded sector of its audience," at least without resorting to "politically correct" with its implications of insincerity and opportunism. Vendler goes on to establish that Snyder is an important poet not so much because of his ecological advocacy but because "he has also changed what we consider the lyric self to be" (117), as if this latter, purely aesthetic issue were automatically more important to readers of poetry. Lars Nordström notes that Oregon poet Vi Gale quotes an "Eastern editor" who rejected her poems out of hand since "We don't use nature poetry. Ours is an urban society" (141).

Almost since the initial critical characterization of contemporary poetry by Breslin and others, some poets and critics have called for a new, more discursive, less experiential poetics. Among these voices have been Robert Pinsky, whom Bly has called a "neoclassical critic" (*Talking* 298), and Robert von Hallberg. Questioning the possibility of a directly experiential poetry, Pinsky and von Hallberg provide convincing examples to illustrate how "experiential" language actually draws upon a vocabulary of conventional images and phrases and an equally conventional underlying set of questions and assumptions (Pinsky 13; von Hallberg 19–21), a position with which Altieri comes to agree in *Self and Sensibility in Contemporary American Poetry* (41). Alan Williamson argues that the entire Romantic project has reached a decadent phase in the "new surrealism" of such poets as Charles Simic and Mark Strand, in which the self in the privacy of its experience becomes the sole reference point in the poem, thus resulting in a minimalist poetics at least as confining as the autotelic poetics inspired by the New Critics. Following Christopher Lasch, Williamson asserts that "the dominant emotional malaise of our time is a narcissism whose hallmark is not that it finds the self exciting, but that it never finds anything beyond the self exciting enough." The "new surrealism," he concludes, "is the poetry of that narcissism" (95).

Williamson's concern that the Romantic preoccupation with the self can lead to an exclusive, rather than inclusive, poetics is reminiscent of Malkoff's and others' criticism of Roethke, and also calls to mind the individual focus of the traditionally Romantic prose nature writer. Thoreau, after all, says at the beginning of *Walden* that he "should not talk so much about myself if there were any body else whom I knew as well" (3). And though Williamson's most serious criticism is reserved for the new surrealists, he sees their work as the ultimate expression of the Romantic desire to isolate and explore the self in contemporary poetry. "The question remains," he says about contemporary poetics, "how such a style can move beyond the moment of attunement to a fuller spectrum of psychic life, not to mention social and political life" (73). Pinsky agrees, asserting in a critique of A. R. Ammons that "The limits of such material and such a style are severe; the poet cannot in good faith go very far from natural phenomena, and his own relation to reality" (155).

Emerson criticized Thoreau's lack of ambition in settling to lead a "huckleberry-party" rather than contributing in a more meaningful way to the development of American culture. But Thoreau himself would not have questioned the significance of huckleberries. Among nature writers in all genres, perhaps the most universal and unshakeable principle is the importance of their subject matter. The question posed above by Williamson could be rephrased by the nature writer as how to come near to expressing the fullness of the "spectrum of psychic life" involved in the basic relationship of the individual to the large community that is nature. Wendell

Berry's characterization of nature poetry as "A Secular Pilgrimage" indicates that nature and the human response to it are more than simply subject matter for poetry. Like Thoreau, the contemporary nature poet sees writing as a way in which to "front only the essential facts of life" (*Walden* 90). Furthermore, as nature keeps presenting itself in new ways, it is as unlikely to run down in exhaustion as any other of the large themes of literature. As A. R. Ammons notes at the end of "Corson's Inlet," "tomorrow a new walk is a new walk" (128).

The critiques by Pinsky and Williamson delineate common ground between nonfiction nature writing and contemporary poetry. In a purely literary context, the incompatibility between Romantic and anti-Romantic concepts of poetry defines a critical impasse that shows no sign of reaching anything more than a temporary and superficial kind of resolution. And no matter how radical a departure a work or movement of literature may seem, it often, in retrospect, is revealed as a continuation of its predecessors. But the contemporary nature writer, and the contemporary poet who is a nature writer, are faced with an additional pressure and an additional opportunity, both resulting from the current state of the relationship between humanity in general, and Western civilization in particular, and nonhuman nature.

As noted earlier, one of the reasons for the seeming irrelevance of Roethke's poetry—Rosenthal's sense of confession without cultural universalism—is that most readers have moved away from close contact with wild nature. This has made it increasingly difficult for many poetry readers to understand and experience the poet's experience. David Perkins, for example, sees a Snyder poem set high in the Western mountains as exotic, "strange and wonderful," because, he maintains flatly, "most readers of poetry live in cities" (564). For these readers, the way in which nature poetry, as John Elder says, "arises from the fever of cultural dividedness—man against nature, past against present, intellect against senses—but discovers grounds for reconciliation in the inextricable wholeness of the world" (1) becomes, ultimately, unsubstantiated and unsubstantiable.

In recent years, however, concern over the strained relationship between humanity and the natural world has resulted in an increasingly widespread if often unfocused awareness that the experiences of poets such as Bly, Snyder, and Berry are important, perhaps even crucial. For these poets, the environmental crisis has brought both an opportunity and an urgent need to overcome the distances between poet, reader, and nature.

Contemporary Nature Poetry and the Public Voice

It is useful at this point to ask why environmentally concerned poets such as Bly, Snyder, and Berry are implicated in preserving what is clearly an illusory separation between human and nonhuman nature. This is, after all, the essence of Pinsky's and Williamson's criticism—that it is, or has become, self-indulgent and conventional to envision a canyon only to gaze wistfully across it. Furthermore, from an ecological standpoint, is it not exactly that sense of separation, that perceived qualitative gap between human and nonhuman life, that nature poets should be attempting to bridge? As Neil Evernden argues, the gap between human and nonhuman has become a moat, leaving us at risk of being "imprisoned by self-worship" (87).

From the Western perspective, however, to ignore the gap, to assert, truthfully enough, that all the works of humanity are no less natural than a termite mound or anthill is to risk withdrawing, as Bly warns in his *News of the Universe* essays, into a world view in which "The proper study of mankind is man." [10] In *Turtle Island,* Gary Snyder quotes a friend as exclaiming on a Northwestern mountain, "You mean, there's a senator for all this?" (106) But, as Snyder realizes, the senators from Washington State only represent one small portion, the human part, of that which is Washington. From his more psychologically oriented viewpoint, Bly fears that, by not considering the nonhuman as significant and authentic in its own right, humans become self-absorbed, disconnected from vital energy sources that permeate the human psyche as well as nonhuman nature. Wendell Berry identifies as a source of social disorientation the illusion-haunted quality of contemporary American culture, which, quite literally, does not know where its bread comes from. If nature poetry is seen as an attempt to erect a bridge between human and nonhuman, then one of the prerequisites for such an attempt is to test, determine, and believe in the firmness of the ground on the other side.

Bly, Snyder, and Berry consider nature itself as the authenticating framework on which their experience stands and from which it receives its validation. For Bly, the authenticity of poetic intuition can be measured by how much psychic weight or energy it taps into. The primary source of this energy is the body, often approached through animals or a close examination of the earth itself, as in "Kneeling Down to Peer into a Culvert" or "A Hollow Tree." Snyder, intellectually eclectic as he is, consistently tests his ideas, and the applicability of the philosophical notions he encounters, in the world of nature as he experiences it. A reader of Snyder must get used to the juxtaposition of Buddhist or American Indian philosophy with the gritty realities of life at sea or in camp, homestead, or forest. Berry applies an Aldo Leopold–like standard when he measures the value of a culture by its ability to sustain itself on the earth and an idea by how true it proves itself in practice. Just as, for Whitman, the "look of the bay mare shames silliness out of me" ("Song of Myself" 13.20), for Berry, as he says in "Writer and Region," "The test of imagination, ultimately, is not the territory of art or the territory of the mind, but the territory underfoot" (*What Are* 83–84).

Such an authorizing role for nature depends on the ability of the poet to maintain a sense of nature's independence from human culture. Bill McKibben's *The End of Nature* considers potential effects of a projected wholesale breakdown in the self-maintaining character of natural systems on the conceptual viability of nature as ordering context and underlying "reality." McKibben's nature can be defined as a self-regulating and continuous amalgam of phenomena and processes of which humanity is a part but that functions independently of human culture. This sense of nature as "other" is one of the poles between which Fritzell finds nature writing alternating (the other is the self *as* nature). It is the basis for Thoreau's famous linking of wildness with the "preservation of the world" (*Natural* 112), Bly's identification of the authentic with "wildness," and Aldo Leopold's argument that wilderness functions as a "norm" for measuring the effects of human activity on land and natural systems (194–98).

One could argue that all of contemporary poetry relies on a dynamic interaction between the self and the world experienced, but in the work of Bly, Snyder, and Berry, this interchange is accompanied by an insistence on the authenticity, or even the primacy, of the "other." In their work, the immanentism that Altieri identifies is accompanied by and contingent upon the central belief that "out there" is ontologically real and forms a true context by which both individual and culture can be measured. In *The*

Sibling Society, Bly offers a Berry-like critique of contemporary artists who turn to "eclecticism" and away from "the authentic," and compares John Ashbery's "fantasy poems" to the "fantasy deer" of Disney films (82).

McKibben predicts that the loss of the functional independence of global natural systems will result in a corresponding loss of nature as a cultural concept, concluding that "Soon Thoreau will make no sense. And when that happens, the end of nature—which began with our alteration of the atmosphere, and continued with the responses to our precarious situation by the 'planetary managers' and the 'genetic engineers'—will be final. The loss of memory will be the loss of meaning" (213).

This is a dire prediction. Yet even now, certain passages from Thoreau seem curiously distanced from the contemporary perspective. His assertion that "things do not change; we change" (*Walden* 328) is strained in a world in which we are already conscious that we cannot change without changing everything else. And his escape to a huckleberry field where "the State was nowhere to be seen" in "Civil Disobedience" (239) is far removed from our current society with its ubiquitous and inescapable technologies. Even as Thoreau's connection between wild nature and personal freedom is echoed by writers such as Edward Abbey, the increased inroads into nature and natural systems by government and industry have led to the wholesale re-placement of Leopold's "blank spots on the map" with officially designated wilderness and lands "released" to industrial use.

McKibben's linkage of cultural memory with nature writing suggests that nature writing, and by extension nature poetry, serve as a kind of record of the culture's attempts to comprehend and coexist with nature. Poets such as Bly and, especially, Snyder and Berry have become aware of the impor-tance of this role, and it has provided them with a new and urgent impetus to make their experiences accessible to the members of the culture at large, as a way of preserving the meaning that nature has held for them in a world where that meaning is becoming more tenuous.

Each of the three poets central to this study has long been interested in cultural memory. Bly's efforts as an editor, translator, and popularizer of often obscure poets and poetic traditions reflect his concern for neglected areas of cultural history. Berry has consistently voiced his commitment to vanishing local cultures and his belief that the "margins" inhabited by "mad farmers" serve a vital function in keeping those cultures alive and perhaps available for future use. Berry is hardly one to hope for a golden future when man and nature would be correctly reassociated,[11] but he sees much of value in the margins, and valuable things, for Berry, are always worth saving. Furthermore, the sacredness of nature is clearly the basis for the value Berry puts on life, "a mighty blessing which we cannot bear for long" ("The Old Elm Tree by the River" 18), and to act in a way that damages life is not only dangerous but morally inexcusable. Cultural memory, for Berry, is a way of continually reestablishing durable and practical moral principles. One of Berry's most prominent themes is the passing on of effective moral standards from one generation to the next. Snyder also values the collective memory of cultures, and his interest in and dedication to American Indian tradition, myth, and knowledge is an expression of an enduring faith in the overall worth of cultural memory. Snyder maintains some hope that literature may serve as a catalyst for the eventual "reinhabitation" of the earth, by embodying bioregionalist principles intended "to help our human, cultural, political, and social structures harmonize with natural systems" (qtd. in Nordström 134). In *Imagining the Earth*, John Elder observes that "Snyder expects his archaic values to prevail eventually in the social and political realms, as well as in the present pattern of his art" (45).

Snyder's interest in Native American peoples is no accident, as many traditional Indian cultures have shown a remarkable resilience in keeping traditions of right living alive even in the most difficult of conditions, in which their immediate viability is tenuous at best. Thomas Berry finds Indian societies inspiring for their ability to maintain a nourishing cultural base that has proved remarkably able to "sustain life in its moment of high tragedy" (184). Despite his sensitivity to the exploitative aspect of appropriating indigenous beliefs into white society, Bly too comes to see Native American examples as a "great help" in overcoming the disruption of the "Sibling Society" (*Sibling* 239). Snyder sees Euro-American society in North America as ultimately evolving "an Indian identity truly in touch with the land" (Nordström 135).

Starting with the "Native American Renaissance" of the 1970s, Native American poets have become prominent in the poetry of ethnic identity that has followed the contemporary generation and that may be in the process of creating a poetics to succeed it. Kenneth Lincoln finds that Native

American communities afford a "potential for distinguished literature, and even more importantly, a supportive literary tradition" that is "perhaps higher than in any other enclave of American culture" (12). That this growth in influence is related to the increasing concern for the well-being of nature is noted by the historian Christopher Vecsey, who believes that the environmental crisis has resulted in a new sense that Indian traditions may offer something that white Americans need, a relatively stable relationship with nature (7). Similarly, in his study of Roethke, William Stafford, and Snyder, Lars Nordström locates the source of these poets' interest in American Indian cultures in their accordance with the "ecological metaphor" as well as in the more traditional attraction to the indigenous sense of place (25–26). He concludes that "In poetry, another dimension of the environmental ethic must also be mentioned: the use of early Native American life and values as a primary example of a vast and varied culture in harmony with its environment" (25).

The identification with Indian cultures by white Americans is problematical and is questioned both by Native Americans such as Ward Churchill and Wendy Rose and, for different reasons, by whites such as Louis Simpson. Churchill's objections, specifically, are discussed later. But it is clear that, since Rosenthal's dismissal of Roethke's experience as irrelevant, much has happened to increase public awareness of the importance of the human experience in nature. Vi Gale quotes the same "Eastern editor" who once rejected "nature poetry" in general as asking to "see some more of your ecology poems" fifteen years later (Nordström 141). Furthermore, the current audience for nature poetry extends beyond the universities and the "poetry community" because its interest is first engaged through a concern for the environment, that is, for the subject matter of the poetry rather than for technique or literary significance.

In this atmosphere, contemporary nature poets, particularly Berry and Snyder, have found their essays and even their poems appearing in publications ranging from agricultural trade journals to *Look* to *Sierra*. Additionally, activist poets such as W. S. Merwin and William Heyen have published "ecology pieces" in such specialized poetry publications as *The American Poetry Review*.[12] Robert Bly also has participated in this broadening of audience and of the concerns open to poetry or, more correctly, the way in which the poet is involved with the subject matter of the poem. *News of the*

Universe, published and recently reissued by Sierra Club Books, provided him with a forum to present a collection of poems and critical commentary focusing on consciousness in nature and designed to advocate for a more organic, less mechanical or "dead" sense of nature.[13] As Christopher Clausen notes, "Even Robert Bly's sometimes eccentric blend of nature-mysticism and new-left politics is, at its best, a constructive attempt to reinterest a contemporary audience in poetry by maintaining traditional kinds of poetic significance" (132). The nature poet in contemporary times may find herself or himself in a position to adopt the role that Emerson thought the poet should embrace, that of repairing "the decays of things" (130).

Bly, Snyder, and Berry, therefore, have personal, literary, and social reasons for developing strategies by which to reconcile the need to locate meaning in individual experience with the need to reach a reasonably broad audience, at least to formulate shared concerns in a way that such a broad audience could accept. In addition to the traditional desire of the nature writer to explain the "good tidings" of the natural world to distracted and unreceptive readers, contemporary nature poets, as discussed earlier, are faced with an increasingly tenuous analogical relationship between their experience and that of their audience. Recently, however, there has been a resurgence of concern for and interest in the subject and the issues, both personal and cultural, raised by nature poets and even in the role that poetry might play in forming and maintaining a stable and reasonably harmonious relationship with nature. According to Deep Ecology advocate Bill Devall, "Music and poetry which express the power of nonhuman nature, as well as our own wild nature, affirm our integrity and relationship with all living beings" (73). It is perhaps for this reason that environmental magazines often publish poetry, and several, including *Amicus Journal, Orion,* and *Wilderness,* even employ poetry editors.

By finding a way to address public values from an experiential perspective, nature poets such as Bly, Snyder, and Berry attempt to resolve both an old problem of nature writing and a newer problem of contemporary poetics, the "baselessness" of a poetics of individual experience. Each of the three poets central to this discussion has developed strategies to achieve a public voice while retaining the experiential quality of contemporary poetics. One of these strategies involves enlisting other genres, mainly prose, and nonliterary sources of knowledge, such as natural and social sciences.

Bly, Snyder, and Berry are prolific and ubiquitous prose writers as well as poets. As Elder and Finch note, due to its "extraordinary range of voice and achievement" (24), prose nature writing has appealed to poets, among them Wendell Berry. Like Berry, though not quite so prolific, Snyder has published collections of prose, among them *Earth House Hold, The Old Ways, The Practice of the Wild,* and, most recently, *A Place in Space.* Bly's prose works include *Leaping Poetry, Iron John, The Sibling Society,* and countless essays, articles, reviews, and forewords, a sampling of which is collected in *American Poetry: Wildness and Domesticity.* Furthermore, each has sought to blend the two genres. Berry's poems, essays, and novels form a web of characters, ideas, and settings. Charles Molesworth locates Snyder's *Earth House Hold* in the poetic-prose tradition of *Walden* and William Carlos Williams's *In the American Grain* (*Gary* 65), and Steuding has compared the prose that accompanies the poems in *Turtle Island* to Thoreau's "Walking" (118). In addition, Snyder's poems themselves have become increasingly instructional and didactic and have often "lapsed" into prose-like statement to do so. Nordström has observed the increasingly didactic tone of Snyder's poetry as he becomes more aware of his role as a "spokesman," and notes Richard Tillinghast's and William Stafford's criticism of the direct instructional quality of Snyder's later work (155). Snyder himself begins his answer to Nordström's question about the instructional nature of his poetry by asserting that instruction can be every bit as organic as more ostensibly poetic uses of language, seeing "instruction as a continuance, as biological almost" (138). Bly has been, perhaps, the most subtle blender of prose and poetry of the three, both in *News of the Universe* and in his devotion to the prose poem as an accessible and unpretentious way, as he quotes Francis Ponge, to "nourish the spirit of man by giving him the cosmos to suckle" (*News* 214).

The role of prose in overcoming the isolation of the contemporary poet is twofold. Because of its accessibility, prose can clarify ideas and images in the poetry and can flesh out the autobiographical and intellectual world of the poems. Bly and Snyder have written about their own poems and included explanatory prose essays in books like Snyder's *Turtle Island* and Bly's *Selected Poems.* All three have provided contextualizing details in their prose. Much of Berry's biography and thought is revealed through his essays and novels, and reading the prose can certainly deepen one's understanding and appreciation of a book of poetry like *The Wheel.* The prose also attracts readers who would not normally read poetry at all. The general community of intelligent readers identified by Dana Gioia in his important essay "Can Poetry Matter?" is reading "quality fiction and biographies" (18) but generally is leaving poetry to a specialized coterie of practitioners and fans. That at least some of these readers will turn to the poetry of Bly, Snyder, and Berry from the prose and that exposure to the prose will make them more receptive to the poetry seem inevitable. Patrick D. Murphy says the essays in Snyder's *The Practice of the Wild* are "attracting an entirely new set of readers, readers who will explore the poetry in order to learn more about Snyder and the ideas" in the essays (*Understanding* 167). At a conference of organic farmers held in Billings, Montana, in the early 1990s, Berry's talk was followed by questions about agriculture but also by requests for favorite poems, which Berry honored by reading them.

Each of the three poets has been informed by, and seeks to inform about, nonliterary sources of knowledge. Like Robinson Jeffers before him, Bly has used the natural sciences as a kind of objectifying lens for studying the human psyche. His use of Paul MacLean's "three brains theory" is a notable example of his borrowings from science. He has also become a kind of lay expert in Jungian and more recently Freudian psychology (in *The Sibling Society,* he honors Freud as "the most courageous and disturbing thinker since Galileo"; 163), and he punctuates his poetry readings with performances and psychological explications of stories and fairy tales. Ironically, considering Wilson's lionization of Enlightenment, or, as Bly sees it, "Endarkenment" (*Sibling* 198) figures like René Descartes, Bly could be seen as a purveyor of Edward O. Wilson's notion of "consilience" between the disciplines. Snyder studied anthropology at Reed College in Portland and at Indiana University and is also well versed in biological concepts and processes. In *Turtle Island,* for example, he cites Eugene Odom's description of biomass as a kind of intelligence, as a means of establishing consciousness in nature (107). Berry's knowledge is practical and historical, coupling a farmer's awareness of soil and natural processes with a championing of Jeffersonian agrarianism. Berry sees literature as a useful and necessary part of a broad-based culture, essentially connected to other functioning parts of that whole. He has been known to require an opportunity to speak on agricultural topics as a condition for accepting an invitation to give a poetry reading, and his collections of essays "cultural and agricultural" are further evidence of his belief in the holistic nature of cultural pursuits. The breadth of their knowledge and their awareness of ecological as well as literary interconnectedness have helped all three poets sharpen their sense of the relationships that intertwine the human and nonhuman parts of the creation. Each has recognized that a culture's treatment of the natural world and its treatment of human beings are inextricably tied together.

Despite the considerable efforts of all three in prose, only Berry is arguably thought of first as a prose writer. It is in contemporary poetry that the problem of blending private and public voices is most problematical and pronounced. And as poets, they are very different. Berry is formal, meditative, and frankly old-fashioned, as apt to view himself in the tradition of Marvell as of Thoreau. Snyder's style draws on his considerable knowledge of other cultures, the Pound branch of Modernism, the "field composition" techniques of the Black Mountain poets, and his early association with the Beats. Bly, a founder of what has come to be called the "deep image school," is more aesthetically inclined toward continental Europe and is likely to view anglophonic technique such as Berry's as lacking poetic excitement and primitivism such as Snyder's as an affectation.[14] They share, however, an approach to the poetic image that is accessible and essentially objective. Like that of Jeffers, Bly's imagery is archetypal rather than symbolistic. It depends on the Jungian idea of an underlying shared consciousness that incorporates the subjective perceptions of the individual into an encompassing pool of objective meaning that the imagery taps into. Furthermore, in Bly's poetry, surrealist-influenced deep imagery is presented in a more openly communicative and less idiosyncratic manner than similar material in Roethke's poetry. As Alan Williamson observes, Bly's deep image syntax is generally straightforward (68–69).

Like Bly, Snyder sees poetry as a way of "fiddling with the archetypes and getting at people's dreams" (qtd. in Nordström 156). Whereas Bly's image vocabulary depends on psychological resonance, Snyder's is totemic and mythic. Berry's approach to imagery is metonymic and democratic, evoking a shared landscape. Berry also openly engages Western poetic traditions (*Sabbaths* is introduced on its back cover as "his most formal poetic work to date"). In keeping with Berry's belief in the value of long usage, this openness to formal tradition also results in a poetry that is generally more easily accepted by a broad audience than Clausen's "ever-new poetic models" (96) because it speaks in a less idiosyncratic, more public manner.

Finally, each of the three poets has actively sought to make poetry, and the poet, an important part of an often-unresponsive culture by addressing significant issues and public concerns. Bly's involvement with the public voice dates to the Vietnam War years, when he was extremely critical of those poets who saw their art as a kind of insulation from world events. In poems like "The Teeth Mother Naked at Last," Bly forges a connection between the experience of the individual and the actions of the culture as a whole.

Both Bly and Snyder have been characterized as poet-shamans, a role that Snyder, for one, has at times welcomed and has defended even against charges of cultural imperialism from Native American sources.[15] They have also been instrumental in bringing poetry to audiences through poetry readings and through a willingness to recognize poetry's value as a way of communicating with other people. In "Poetry, Community and Climax," Snyder claims that "One thing that was clearly an error in the mentality of the early fifties literary world was the idea that poetry cannot have an audience, and indeed that it was a little shameful if a poem was too popular. There are people who still believe that, incidentally. There was also the defeatist attitude that 'we live in a philistine culture' and 'no one is interested in art anyway, so we'll just write to each other.' My generation found that boldly, to put it bluntly, having something to say helped with audiences" (*Real* 163).

Wendell Berry is a much more private individual than either Bly or Snyder. The abandonment of an active urban "writer's life" to return to the quiet Kentucky farmland of his youth is, perhaps, the major event of his life, and his discomfort with "group morality" has been clear since he cautioned against self-righteousness and specialized activism while making "A Statement against the War in Vietnam" in *The Long-Legged House* (74). Nevertheless, Berry is as acutely aware of the relationship between individual and culture as either Bly or Snyder. The small-scale social and economic organizations on which he depends and in which he is a firm believer are threatened by, and provide a meaningful alternative to, the destructive large-scale and abstract orders that envelop them, a situation that much of his work addresses. And like Bly and Snyder, Berry sees literature as basically instrumental, as something that "can and does affect, even in practical ways, the life of a place" (*What Are* 84).

As nature poets, Bly, Snyder, and Berry have had, by definition, to pay close attention to their surroundings. This has perhaps allowed them to "turn inward" without falling into what Charles Molesworth calls "the traps of autotelism and excessive self-consciousness." One way to avoid these pitfalls, says Molesworth, "is the insistent affirmation of some indisputable 'signified,' a 'beyond,' a realm where value is generated and confirmed" (*Fierce* 131). By reaffirming the integrity and authenticity of the nonhuman creation, these poets find such a realm. But as McKibben and Fritzell have pointed out, that realm is safe neither literally nor conceptually from human social orders and systems of thought. Since the birth of contemporary poetry in 1948, the year Roethke published *"The Lost Son" and Other Poems,* the relationship between the individual human life and the environment has gone from an idiosyncratic hobby to a matter of clear societal importance. By helping to preserve and modify the cultural sense of the integrity of nature, contemporary nature poets such as Bly, Snyder, and Berry have the potential to reempower poetry by giving it an essential and unquestionable purpose and perhaps even to contribute in a significant way to human survival on the earth.

2 · From Jeffers to Roethke

Robinson Jeffers as "Modern" Nature Poet

THE SHIFT FROM the Modern to the contemporary in American poetry can be seen by contrasting the work of poets from the two periods. However, the inability of critics and scholars, or of writers themselves, to agree on an exact border between the two periods suggests that significant overlap occurs, and that, although there are key publications, Lowell's *Life Studies* and Bly's journal *The Fifties,* for example, there is no exact moment when the Modern becomes the contemporary. Indeed, Breslin's title, *From Modern to Contemporary,* and his location of the transition between early and later books of Roethke, Wright, and others suggests that the liminal area between the two is uncertain and various. Roethke, after all, "became contemporary" with *"The Lost Son" and Other Poems,* which was published a decade before Wright's pretransition *The Green Wall.* Even the categorization of a transitional middle generation is problematical. Denise Levertov and James Wright are normally thought of as leading contemporary figures, yet, like Roethke, who is considered a middle-generation pioneer, their earlier works are in the New Critical tradition. Generally, however, it is safe to say that contemporary poetry is a product of the mid-1950s, with Roethke's *"The Lost Son" and Other Poems* as a "prototype" appearing in 1948. By the time Bly began his influential *The Fifties,* poets had begun to think of themselves as involved in a stylistic revolution.

It is important to acknowledge that, although the shift between the two periods is a recognizable phenomenon in twentieth-century poetry, it would be incorrect to characterize contemporary poetry as a complete rejection of and departure from Modernism. Contemporary poets, perhaps nearly universally, recognize Modernism as a direct ancestor. Roethke, for instance, finishes his "A Rouse for Stevens" by proclaiming "Brother, he's our father!" (20). Even Robert Bly, despite his famous statement that Modernism constitutes a "wrong turning," also locates the last American period of "new imagination" in the early twentieth century. What the contemporaries rebelled against was the autotelic poetics resulting from the New Critics' reading of Eliot and other Moderns. But as for the "Great Moderns" themselves, their influence is nearly universally acknowledged, particularly in the matter of experimentation with form. William Carlos Williams may be the most influential poet in the formal development of contemporary poetics, and he is also, not coincidentally, the most personal of the Moderns. Altieri figures the shift from Modern to contemporary poetics as a change from symbolistic to Wordsworthian notions of poetry, but it could also be seen as a movement away from a poetics based on a New Critical interpretation of Eliot toward the poetics practiced by Williams.

As discussed in chapter 1, one distinguishing feature of contemporary poetry is its emphasis on individual experience and a consequent private quality of the contemporary poetic voice. As Altieri says, preshift poetry was more able to concern itself with the values and ideas of the culture as a whole (*Enlarging* 236). Before discussing how Bly, Snyder, and Berry began to reach out from the world of their own isolated experience, it is appropriate to examine the effect that the contemporary shift had on the two aspects of poetry most central to this study: the ability of the poet to speak to public concerns for a public audience and the relationship between the poet and the natural world.

The second of these concerns has led me to select Robinson Jeffers as an example of a pre-shift poet and Theodore Roethke as an example of the transitional middle generation. Jeffers is clearly a poet of the natural world, so much so that his reputation has been kept alive and his books in print primarily as a result of his early advocacy for wild nature. An example of the esteem in which Jeffers is held can be seen in Max Oelschlaeger's *The Idea of Wilderness,* in which an entire chapter is devoted to Jeffers and fellow poet Gary Snyder. Dana Gioia crowns Jeffers "the unchallenged laureate of environmentalists" (49). Gioia also points to Jeffers's neglect among scholars and other poets, the usual poetry audience. Despite Jeffers's distance from the New Criticism and High Modernism, the scope of his themes is in line with the Modernist view of poetry. He can be considered, as Gioia does, as a poet of the Modern period, but one deeply at odds with some of Modernism's central tenets. And he is clearly the most significant American nature poet of the first half of the twentieth century.

Although he does not have the standing among environmentalists that Jeffers does, Roethke is the most significant nature poet among the middle generation figures. As with Jeffers, his subject matter put him at odds with the literary climate of his day. If, as Gioia points out, the New Critics were repelled by the directness of Jeffers's pronouncements, critics of the emerging contemporary generation often found Roethke's personal perspective too obscure, too far removed from contemporary urban American life. In a sense, each poet was branded too extreme in the use of the poetic idiom of the day. Modernism allowed for the addressing of "large" themes, but they were generally approached ironically or indirectly, not in Jeffers's straightforward way. On the other hand, the contemporary idiom required an individual focus, but the individual was supposed to be representative of the urban or suburban 1950s.

Jeffers's poetics illustrate the "public" quality of the Modern period both in form and content. In his poetry's form, Jeffers is noted for his adaptation of accentual verse. Karl Keller quotes a Jeffers letter in which the poet describes his characteristic line as "Eight feet to the line, that is, eight accented syllables, each with a certain weight of unaccented syllables, or of pause, to make it more or less equal in quantity to its neighbors. . . . The phrases are formed with regard to the pauses and cadences of the meter [so that] even the meaning appears clearer" (8) [brackets are Keller's].

Keller goes on to consider Jeffers's purpose in developing and using his accentual line, noting that the Jeffers line is primarily a pacing technique, particularly useful in slowing the reader, thus "making ideas clearer and more emphatic" (8). The Jeffers line, concludes Keller, "is rhythm put to the service of the didactic" (8).

Keller connects Jeffers's desire to communicate ideas clearly to his desire to reduce as much as possible the mediating effect of language, which can separate the writer not only from the reader but also from the subject matter, nature itself, observing that "Jeffers saw in the accentual, as he said himself, the opportunity for poetry to come closer to the subject matter, closer to those forms by which men communicate most easily and most effectively, closer to the vestiges of Nature that remain in man's culture" (11). Jeffers's accentual verse straightforwardly communicates unambiguous statements of values and ideas, as the poet himself said that poetry must, to "reclaim some of the power and reality that it has so hastily surrendered to prose" (qtd. in Keller 7).

In his poetry, Jeffers employs blunt declamatory statements in which the didactic quality noted by Keller is apparent. These assertions are sometimes imperative, as in the final line of "Love the Wild Swan," or judgmental, as in "Boats in a Fog," or simply obvious, as in the final line of "The Purse-Seine," but in each case they are intended as instructive vehicles for the poet's ideas, which, as William Nolte indicates, Jeffers believed that poetry should help its readers understand (34). Accordingly, the imagery in a Jeffers poem tends to demonstrate the verity of the accompanying philosophical statements. In "The Purse-Seine," for example, Jeffers uses the image of the fishing net to illustrate the idea stated straightforwardly in the last line. By contrast, in contemporary poetry blunt declarations tend to have a different purpose and, consequently, a different relationship to the accompanying imagery. For example, Robert Bly's "In a Train" from *Silence in the Snowy Fields* ends with the statement "I have awakened at Missoula, Montana, utterly happy" (4). In this, as well as in other contemporary poems, such as Lowell's "Skunk Hour" or Wright's "Lying in a Hammock at William Duffy's Farm in Pine Island, Minnesota," that utilize similar statements crystallizing or incorporating the poet's psychic state, the declaration functions not as a vehicle for an idea that the poet wishes the reader to accept, but as a method of interiorizing the poem's dramatic situation. Whereas the imagery in Jeffers serves to demonstrate the verity of a general truth embodied in a conclusive assertion, in contemporary poetry declamatory statements, when they are present, usually appear as the result of the imagery, that is, as the culminating expression that follows, apparently inevitably, from the experience of the imagery. When Bly, for example, says, at the end of "In a Train" that he has "awakened at Missoula, Montana, utterly happy," the line derives its meaning from the imagistic lines preceding it. It is not "true" until the reading of the poem has been completed. Even when the assertion comes at the beginning of the poem, as in

Bly's "Watering the Horse," its meaning is dependent on the context that follows. Such statements are essentially nonrhetorical, as Charles Molesworth recognizes when he says, "Far from reluctant to address ideas in prose argument, Bly makes his own poetic statements turn aside from the ease of identifiable cognitive patterns and plunge instead into dense, pathless areas of experience and darkly associative pools of feeling" (*Fierce* 116).

Thus, Bly's assertion that he has "awakened at Missoula, Montana, utterly happy," does not bear a direct logical or philosophical relationship to his description of the snow and the tracks. It does, however, involve the reader in the poet's individual response to the described landscape. This response is both emotional and intellectual. In "Walking and Sitting" from *This Tree Will Be Here for a Thousand Years,* "that's odd—I am trying to sit still / trying to hold the mind to one thing" (1–2) is more of an intellectual and aesthetic reflection than an emotional reaction, but it is clearly individualized, a "psychic snapshot" rather than a philosophical equation. In contrast, when, at the end of "The Purse-Seine," Jeffers declares "surely one always knew that cultures decay, and life's end is death" (27), the declaration is intended to be universal, with the speaker of the poem even sardonically expressing some surprise that the "lesson" in the metaphor of the net should not have been more obvious. The impersonal nature of the conclusion is heightened by the use of "one" instead of "you" or "they" and by the openly "public" quality of the preceding lines, concerning "our verse" (24) and "the recent young men" (26). The image of the purse-seine itself demonstrates, rather than determines, the meaning of the general philosophical statement.

Like nearly all prose nature writers, Jeffers believed, as Nolte says, that there was "permanence and meaning and hence value in the nonhuman world" (65). Like them also, he was motivated by the twin desires of gaining access to the intersection of culture and nature, and of communicating his experience to others. His misanthropy and tendency to see himself as isolated and embattled make it seem unlikely that Jeffers was consciously trying to win over political or social converts (although in Brother Antoninus he won over at least one), but Jeffers never abandoned the communicative, even blatantly didactic, function of poetry. Eric Paul Shaffer links Jeffers's surprisingly communicative verse with his "modern" ecological sense, noting that "Jeffers passes along accurate information and observations, and he is one of the first American poets to show concern for the planet on a global and geological time scale while examining humanity from the same perspective" (32).[1]

As Snyder would after him, Jeffers, who had studied medicine and forestry, often used his knowledge of natural science to determine what "accurate knowledge" to "pass along." Oelschlaeger, for example, counts thermodynamics and the expanding universe theory among Jeffers's scientific borrowings (255). Jeffers saw the empirical methodology and conclusions of science as a kind of objectifying lens, particularly useful in burning through both humanity's self-aggrandizement and art's tendency toward self-referentiality. William Everson, or Brother Antoninus, whom Bly calls Jeffers's "fierce student" (*News* 128) comments on Jeffers's use and acceptance of the methods and assumptions of the natural sciences in his foreword to *The Double Axe and Other Poems:* "it was science that provided him with the objectivity, and hence the authority, to effect the religious mission he claimed for his own—particularly the sciences of astronomy and physics. Between those two millstones, the galaxy and the molecule, he pulverized human complacency to reveal man's insignificance to man. Whereas religious humanists like T. S. Eliot resisted the tendency of science to displace humanity from the center of things, Jeffers welcomed it and, moreover, celebrated it" (viii).

Like Everson, Dana Gioia believes that Jeffers's scientific perspective was unique among the Moderns. In his review of *Rock and Hawk*, a selection of Jeffers's poems edited by Robert Hass, Gioia states that "Alone among the Modernist poets, he challenged scientists on their own territory. . . . He accepted the destruction of anthropocentric values explicit in current biology, geology, and physics, which humanists had struggled against since the Victorian age" (50).

Frederic Carpenter notes that though Jeffers's use of scientific language can sometimes be distracting in practice, at other times "it makes vivid the emotion and enlarges the horizon . . . [just as] in actual life the study of medicine served to draw him out of the aestheticism which characterized so many of the poets of his time" (29). This enlarging of horizons is a key to understanding Jeffers. Carpenter calls Jeffers's "emphasis upon perspective, or extreme distance," the cornerstone or "characteristic technique by which Jeffers expresses his criticism of life" (97). Robert Zaller marks Jeffers's adoption of "a perspective outside man," claiming that "To attain such a perspective and hold fast to it was . . . the core of Jeffers' poetic strategy" (87).

This strategy reflects and enables Jeffers's "Inhumanist" aesthetic. In his preface to *The Double Axe,* Jeffers defines Inhumanism as "a shifting of emphasis and significance from man to not-man, the rejection of human solipsism and recognition of the transhuman magnificence" (xxi). William Van Wyck claims that Jeffers "can analyze human conduct with that sense of detachment that a scientist has when he examines the behavior of an insect or regards one through a microscope" (16). Without the objectifying lens of natural science, the vantage point of the Inhumanist, with its implications of moral superiority and isolationism, would not have been possible.

Jeffers's poem "Oh Lovely Rock" illustrates the poet's use of science to achieve a distanced perspective. The poem's situation is simple, with the archetypal sense of imagery that is so typical of Jeffers. The poet-speaker is in a wilderness setting, the "pathless gorge of Ventana Creek" (1) with others who will later be identified as his son and his son's "companion" (8). The Pacific forest surrounds the small fire protecting and illuminating the sleepers, and the watchful poet-speaker. For Jeffers, as for John Muir, the rock is "living" (13), and for the same reason. Muir theorized that such seemingly inanimate objects as glaciers and mountain ranges might be regarded as living things, if one allowed for a great difference in "speed" or scope. The geological scale of activity is simply too slow for our perception, contained as it must be within a human lifetime. Jeffers sees that, for the rock wall, the span of human years is so brief that the rock itself takes on a childlike aspect, its "maturity" far removed from our own time scale. To make this point, Jeffers includes in the poem rather technical phrases drawn from the natural sciences, specifically geology, identifying the rock as a "light-gray diorite with two or three slanting seams in it" (10). After adopting the impersonal viewpoint and language of the scientist ("tree-trunks were seen"; 9), he describes the rock as a physicist might, as "not passive: the energies / That are its atoms will still be bearing the whole mountain above" (17–18).

"Oh Lovely Rock" also illustrates Jeffers's sense of isolation. The rock, though personified as a "grave smiling child" (15), faces the weathering elements essentially alone. He sees the rock face as "pure" and "naked" (11), its "passion" as "silent" (14), and its "fate going on / Outside our fates" (14–15), implying not only that the rock is eternally alone, but that each of our "fates" must be also. Even though the poet-speaker approaches the rock with "love and wonder," it remains "lonely" at the poem's end (19).

Jeffers's personal and philosophical isolation is perhaps reflected in his somewhat naive acceptance of scientific objectivity. For Jeffers, an essential role of scientific methodology is to extend perception beyond the distortions of the human perspective, to give people "hope to live without lies" (1), as he says in "Curb Science?" From the distanced perspective provided by the natural sciences, Jeffers believes that the poet can begin to apprehend an impersonal but "objective" role for humanity and, ultimately, a kind of harmony with nature, similar to that of an algae bloom, which, seen close-up, is an anomalous and potentially destructive event but, seen from a perspective far removed in time and distance, becomes a part of the natural pattern. Jeffers is often criticized for his contention, in *The Double Axe*, for example, that the events of human history are not worth the disruption they cause, but for Jeffers, the point is not that human activities are not important from within the human perspective (he did, after all, make his opinions on social issues known), but rather that the larger context of nature is necessary for a full understanding of the actual import of human events. Thus it is only from the anthropocentric perspective that Jeffers in *The Double Axe* appears unmoved by the human tragedy of World War II; from his distanced viewpoint the war becomes less an historical event affecting nations and more a natural event involving other species, landscapes, and energies as well. The enlarging of perspective, therefore, makes the war more tragic in Jeffers's view and tragic on a larger scale. In *The Cliffs of Solitude,* Robert Zaller claims that "Such effects [of enlarged perspective] were not intended to dwarf or diminish human actions; on the contrary, they often lent them a grandeur they sadly lacked in themselves" (87). Ironically, through attempting to free his perspective from being centered on humanity, Jeffers comes, in "The Beginning and the End," to see humans, along with the other animals, as "sense-organs of God" (114), a role for which humans are particularly well suited, since "The hawks are more heroic but man has a steeper mind" (130).

Jeffers's belief in the scientific "objectifying lens" is, however sincere, at odds with the emotional quality, the tone, of the poems. Jeffers's poems are not really those of a distanced observer, even though they utilize distancing techniques and though the poet himself may have attempted to achieve a liberated perspective by assuming a scientific point of view. Jeffers's voice is often emotionally charged, so that, even as he embraces objectivity, he does so in a notably subjective manner. For the isolated Jeffers, the objectivity that has provided scientists with the necessary fiction that the observer is not a participant in the observed pattern is understood as detachment, a practical impossibility that sometimes seems to make Jeffers blind to his own involvement in the natural pattern he sees.

The poem "Science" provides an example of Jeffers's highly emotional handling of the assumed objectivity of empirical science. Typically, Jeffers views the scientific method as a way for humanity to break away from "edgeless dreams" (5) and face reality, "the nature of things" (2), free from the illusion of humanity's primary importance in the universe. But the result of this breakthrough is also typical of Jeffers. Instead of accepting the revelation, humanity is overwhelmed by it, destroyed by it, as Actaeon was killed by his dogs. More problematical is the attitude the poem's speaker adopts toward the human. The tone of the poem is not one of humble acceptance of a tragic fate, but rather of a bitter rejection of humanity, described as maniacal, habitually driven by "self-love" (4) and deception, and unable to accept science's unveiling of a reality that contradicts a habitually elevated sense of self. The phrase "has begot giants" (3) is clearly sarcastic.

In a later poem, "Original Sin" from *The Double Axe,* Jeffers shifts immediately from a paleontological portrait of "the man-brained and man-handed ground-ape" (1) to the subjective judgment that the creature described is "The most repulsive of all hot-blooded animals / Up to that time of the world" (2–3). He concludes the poem with one of his most evidently misanthropic passages:

This is the human dawn. As for me, I would rather
Be a worm in a wild apple than a son of man.

But we are what we are, and we might remember
Not to hate any person, for all are vicious;
And not be astonished at any evil, all are deserved;
And not fear death; it is the only way to be cleansed.   (20–25)

If Jeffers's tone is incompatible with the ideas he so earnestly tries to communicate, this incompatibility reflects the paradox Fritzell says is typical of the self-conscious nature writer, who must somehow blend the objective and the subjective, the scientific impassivity with the personal quality of one actively engaged with the subject matter. But where *is* Jeffers, or the speaker of the Jeffers poem? Fritzell considers an awareness of one's own position as observer and an inability to completely separate one's self from the subject to be characteristic of the less naive and more worthwhile form of nature writing. Jeffers's subjectivity qualifies him for inclusion only if it is his *own* role of which he is conscious. At times, Jeffers seems unconcerned about or even unaware of his own complicity in the things he criticizes. In "Boats in a Fog," for example, Jeffers criticizes the arts as childish even as he practices as an artist himself. And his statement that "I'd sooner . . . kill a man than a hawk" (2.1), in "Hurt Hawks," seems to place the poet beyond both categories of beings. Similarly, in "The Purse-Seine," the speaker considers the metaphorical envelopment of his own civilization from a vantage point seemingly as distanced from this event as he is from the fishermen. Conceivably, although many of Jeffers's poems, "The Purse-Seine" among them, have an evident "environmentalist" theme, Jeffers, like most of his contemporaries, had not fully grasped the implications of the developing science of ecology, which provides Bly, Snyder, and Berry with a model of nature in which all things, even poets, are connected to all others. More likely, the poetics of the time allowed for Jeffers to sidestep his own personal identity, an option that contemporary poets would not have.

Along with his own statements concerning Inhumanism, Jeffers's assumed separation of poet from humanity is the source of his reputation as a misanthrope. To Helen Vendler, for example, Jeffers's penchant for remaining outside the realm of poetic investigation constitutes a kind of "moral timidity" (54) and leaves his own sadism and brutality unexamined. Even Bly, who respects Jeffers enough to anthologize him, notes "his freaky dislike of humans" (*News* 82).

The problematical nature of the separation of speaker and species and, on a larger scale, of species from "nature" is one that Jeffers does recognize in some poems. Although the arts are excoriated in "Boats in a Fog," the equally human fishermen are accepted with equanimity, suggesting that at least some human activities are "natural." And the time-blocked attempt to "participate in" nature in "Oh Lovely Rock" is countered by the "naturalness" of the Chinese gatherer in "Point Joe." In this poem, Jeffers's characteristic desire to broaden the scope, as well as his didacticism, is evident in his statement that "Permanent things are what is needful in a poem" (11). In "Oh Lovely Rock," it is only through the knowledge of natural science, of geologic time in particular, that the human observer achieves the necessary distance. This is consistent with Jeffers's statement in "Science" that humanity has only begun to apprehend "the nature of things this latter century" (2). In "Point Joe," however, the human achieves a state of natural harmony and "permanence" through repeated and essential actions, presumably across generations and despite the ironic shipwreck of "better men" (16), much as a kind of permanence is achieved in Berry's *The Wheel.*

The similarity between "Point Joe" and "Boats in a Fog" is obvious. In each case, it is the essential, "earnest" ("Boats" 23) action that is praised, that achieves a beauty comparable to that found in nature. "Point Joe" differs, though, in that it does not disregard art. As in "To the Stone Cutters," poetry is seen as a fitting response to the natural scene, any element of which would be suitable for a poem.

Jeffers deals explicitly with the relationship between art and nature in the later poem "Love the Wild Swan." In this poem, he concludes that the value of making art is not so much predicated on an ability to improve upon or even duplicate natural beauty as it is on the act of apprehending and praising the beauty itself:

—This wild swan of a world is no hunter's game.
Better bullets than yours would miss the white breast
Better mirrors than yours would crack in the flame.
Does it matter whether you hate your . . . self? At least
Love your eyes that can see, your mind that can
Hear the music, the thunder of the wings. Love the wild swan.   (9–15)

Jeffers does not here "repent" for his earlier stance (the theme of humanity's blind self-love would follow him into *The Double Axe*, for example), but in "Love the Wild Swan" the fact that the arts may not be up to the task of equaling nature, as he has them attempt to do in "Boats in a Fog," is made irrelevant by the assertion that the value of "verses" (1) rests in their status as an act of "love." Jeffers implicates himself, as a writer of poetry, in the process here also. Interestingly, Jeffers resolves the question of misanthropy in this poem by isolating the "self" as only a part of the human being, emphasizing its partial character by the ellipsis interjected in the word "your . . . self" and by contrasting "self" with "eyes" and "mind." As with the Chinese gatherer in "Point Joe," the human is valued as essence rather than as individual. The "typal" quality of the people depicted in the poems is, perhaps, one way in which the poems are Modern, but it also presages Robert Bly's later separation of the subjective personality from the "objective" deep mind. In each case, the "self" is circumvented by a direct connection between the human organism, including the mind, and nature. In "Love the Wild Swan," the *act* of writing poems, if not the result, is aligned with the organism and not with the limited, ego-centered self. As they do for Bly, Snyder, and Berry, poems achieve authority by involving a kind of natural act, functioning as a conduit through which the individual human being can achieve a measure of direct contact with the larger natural community, including, at an elemental, even biological level, other humans and human societies.[2]

"Love the Wild Swan" is perhaps the Jeffers poem that is most clearly recognizable as an example of what Fritzell might call "self-conscious" nature poetry. But although the poem was written later in his career, and although some observers, the generally unimpressed Vendler among them, have noticed an increase in "grace" later in his life (60), it would be an overgeneralization to say that Jeffers ever evolved any more systematically self-conscious notion of the role of the human in nature. "Point Joe" and "To the Stone Cutters," with their apparent recognition of the role of art in the human experience of nature, both predate "Boats in a Fog." Furthermore, in later poems such as "The Coast-Road," as Elder points out (8–10), Jeffers is as uneasy with, and as apparently isolated from, the civilization he criticizes as he is in "Boats in a Fog." He remained, as he says in "People and a Heron," "Well reconciled with the world but not with our own natures" (9).[3]

Jeffers's use of blunt declamatory statements is not unique among American poets of the first half of the twentieth century. Other Modern poets made pronouncements of entirely different sorts in the course of their poems. Poets as different as Frost ("Something there is that doesn't love a wall"; "Mending Wall" 1) and Stevens ("The only emperor is the emperor of ice cream"; "The Emperor of Ice Cream" 8, 16) use various forms of "universal" declamatory statements. Making declarations of a "public" kind is, as Altieri intimates, a possibility inherent in Modern poetics. What is unusual and eventually led to critical dismissal of Jeffers is the straightforward, non-ironic way in which he intends the statements to be taken and the philosophical content of the statements themselves. As with his unflinching acceptance of science, Jeffers's misanthropy can be seen as an extreme consequence of his isolation as a nature writer, at odds, as Thoreau was before him, with a society that did not value what he valued and that, increasingly, did not share in what he experienced as important. That his misanthropy should appear so often, and so blatantly, in the poems is consistent with the poetics of the time in which he wrote and, in particular, with the ideas that he sought to communicate through poetry. His development and codification of Inhumanism in an effort to shift emphasis from the human to the nonhuman was his attempt to remove the "self" from the interaction between the human and the natural—to, as he says in "Flight of Swans," "learn to touch the diamond within to the diamond outside, / Thinning your humanity a little between the invulnerable diamonds" (17–18). R. W. Butterfield discusses the critical neglect of Jeffers as a consequence of his didactic poetics, his unambiguous stances, and his position as a writer whose devotion to the natural world puts him at odds with his culture, concluding that "His neglect is by no means surprising, for the self-assured insouciance of his manner does not suit contemporary critical preferences, and the self-styled Inhumanism of his matter can appeal neither to people of benign, secular will nor to quotidian materialists of left or right; whilst 'Jeffers country,' the actual world he recreated as his poetic world, can only be imaginatively rather than immediately available to dwellers in city, suburb, or agribusiness countryside" (94).

Jeffers's straightforwardness is a key to his unusual status in the literary canon. Gioia finds his qualities more typical of "a distinguished jurist than a great poet" and goes on to liken Jeffers to a "judge—particularly the Old

Testament variety" (51). Vendler accuses Jeffers of practicing "oratory—a rhythmic, emotional, sensual, and imaginative public prose he had absorbed from the Greek political tradition" rather than true "lyric" (58). Though they differ in their ultimate evaluation of Jeffers's work, both Gioia and Vendler agree that it is the way in which he intends his pronouncements to be taken that sets him apart from other writers of his time. In the web of ambiguous and ironic qualification that characterizes the Modern poetry ethos, Jeffers is an anomaly. Despite the capacity for public poetry inherent in Modern poetics and noted by Altieri and others, the Great Moderns—Eliot, Pound, H. D., Williams, Moore, Stevens, Frost, Crane—generally recognized their own role in the creation of meaning and the subjectivity of their own ideas. Stevens, for example, never really claims that "a mind of winter" ("The Snow Man" 1) is possible or even desirable. Jeffers's naive faith in his own scientific objectivity sometimes masks rather thinly the considerable role his own inclinations have in shaping his panoramic, stoical, and violent interpretations of the natural world. Still, Butterfield is correct when he points to Jeffers's philosophical "insouciance" and his subject matter as two factors that have distanced Jeffers from much of the literary establishment; they are also, however, the two factors most responsible for his popularity among readers of environmental literature. For readers who come to the work more interested in content than in technique, Vendler's assertion that "A ceaselessly curious investigation of a chosen medium is the quality that above all distinguishes artists from the mass of other people (preachers, teachers, journalists) who spend time communicating thoughts, messages, and personal responses in prose and verse" (56) is basically irrelevant to their experience of the poetry. But Vendler's impatience with political statement in Jeffers's (and Snyder's) poetry is understandable in such a prominent reader of contemporary poetry, in which political expression has often seemed self-indulgent and inappropriate.

Natural Imagery in Jeffers and Roethke

Although the lifetimes and publication dates of Jeffers and Theodore Roethke overlap, they represent different moments in literary history. Jeffers, like Eliot, Stevens, H. D., Williams, Moore, and Pound, was approximately twenty years older than Roethke, who, along with such poets as

John Berryman, Elizabeth Bishop, and Charles Olson, falls into what James Breslin characterizes as the "middle generation" (3), poets who began writing between the heyday of the Great Moderns and the emergence of the later contemporary poets, such as Bly, Snyder, and Berry. As noted previously, Roethke was one of the pioneers of the post-Modern or contemporary poetics that followed Modernism in what was seen, at least by its proponents, as an aesthetic revolution. It is not surprising, therefore, to see the two poets treated by critics and anthologizers as noncontemporaries. Roethke is often included in anthologies of contemporary poetry; indeed, he is frequently among the earliest figures included.[4] In Bly's *News of the Universe,* for example, Jeffers's "Science," "Animals," and "Oh Lovely Rock" are included in the chapter designated "Poems of Twofold Consciousness: Early Twentieth Century."[5] Roethke, represented by "Her Longing," appears in the next chapter, along with Bly, Snyder, and Berry, among others. Furthermore, Bly's border between the two chapters is 1945, between the publication of Roethke's *Open House* and his *"The Lost Son" and Other Poems,* which, as Peter Balakian points out, is the first book employing recognizable contemporary poetics (3). It is in this second book that Roethke begins to display the open "organic" form and intense self-awareness that characterize the contemporary period.

In chapter 1, I discussed Roethke's "Death Piece" as representative of preshift writing, specifically of poetry by young poets who would later move into the contemporary idiom. For Roethke, the shift plainly took place sometime between the first and second books. The "Greenhouse Poems" that begin *"The Lost Son" and Other Poems* can be seen as initiating his contemporary period and indeed as ushering in the contemporary period itself. It is revealing to contrast the intimate, close greenhouse imagery with the expansive landscapes of Jeffers. In addition to its scientific bent, Jeffers's imagery bears the stamp of precontemporary poetics. Although the "Jeffers country" of California is clearly a real region, complete with place-names and references to specific landmarks, his imagery is sweeping rather than quotidian. This is so even when his own experiences are addressed, as in "Oh Lovely Rock," with its geological perspective. The frequently recurring images of ocean, coastal headlands, and wild birds form a kind of symbol system easily accessible to the reader because of the evocative nature of the images and the rather conventional interpretations they invite in the poetry. The slowly weathering cliffs are symbolic of the noble stoicism of nature, in which everything, eventually, must be swept away. The sea, enclosing as it does even the net in "The Purse-Seine," is the ultimate dissolution of form into formlessness. The vulture in the poem entitled "Vulture" appears as a kind of death angel. Raptors, for Jeffers, often symbolize nature's potential for complete and elegant expression, or even, as Elder notes, the spirit of nature itself (13), so that the poet-speaker sees the possible transformation into vulture flesh as a kind of evolution away from the comparatively heavy and awkward human form into a "higher" form and gladly consents. Perhaps Jeffers is attracted to raptors not only for their fierce wildness but also for their isolation in the sky, as in "Vulture," or on the windy headland he portrays in "Rock and Hawk."

The conclusions Jeffers invites readers to draw from his imagery may be idiosyncratic, but the images are both symbolic and readily accessible; John Elder uses "emblem" as an accurate term for a Jeffers image (13). Jeffers's emblematic imagery provides him with a link between the symbol-oriented imagination and the nature writer's desire to communicate plainly.

As in Jeffers's poetry, imagery with strong symbolic overtones appears in Roethke's poems. For example, Louis Martz has characterized Roethke's greenhouse as an Edenic symbol (32–33). Certainly, the greenhouse, a kind of enclosed garden, is a logical choice for such a symbol, much as Jeffers's emblematic images seem appropriate to their apparent symbolic meanings. However, though Jeffers's choice of landscape and natural images clearly depends on his own surroundings, the images themselves tend toward the impersonal or even the conventional. Roethke's greenhouse, on the other hand, derives its meaning not primarily from its appropriateness as a symbol, or even its nearness at hand, but from its particular ties to the poet's personal life history. The greenhouses are invariably shown in ways that emphasize the particularity of the place being described. "Weed Puller," for example, begins by describing the greenhouse as seen from an obscure and unique perspective:

> Under the concrete benches,
> Hacking at black hairy roots,—
> Those lewd monkey-tails hanging from drainholes.   (1–3)

Here the symbolic quality of the greenhouse is unmistakable. The "lewd monkey tails" suggest not only the sexuality of procreation but also the evolutionary context of creation itself. But the viewpoint, down below the benches, marks the idiosyncratic perspective of the particular person working there, later identified as an individual "Me down in that fetor of weeds" (14). Whereas Jeffers seeks a perspective beyond the scope of humanity, Roethke's intimate imagery locates the poem's perspective precisely and autobiographically. He approaches his subject through his own personal anxieties, so that the borderline between observation and affect becomes blurred if not obliterated, as in "Root Cellar," one of the "Greenhouse Poems," in which:

> Shoots dangled and drooped,
> Lolling obscenely from mildewed crates,
> Hung down long yellow evil necks, like tropical snakes.   (3–5)

The shoots are seen in close focus, but the presence of "obscenely" and "evil" adds to the description the element of psychological horror that Roethke also uncovers in the dark places of "The Lost Son," the intimate feelings of the poet confronted by a natural image loaded with personal as well as philosophical intimations. Eventually, in the "North American Sequence," the symbol of the rose becomes perhaps the most complete expression of Roethke's tendency to make the resonant quality of his imagery dependent on the particulars of his own experience.

In contrasting Roethke's use of symbols with that of T. S. Eliot in *Theodore Roethke: An American Romantic*, Jay Parini concludes that "Whereas Eliot's symbols remain emblematic, Roethke's continually refer back to the literal level; his rose is a *rose for real*. Also, he does not share Eliot's concern for history, his personal history remains primary" (170) Roethke "personalizes" Eliot's symbols by making them reflect the quotidian reality of Roethke's personal experience.

The contemporary character of "The Lost Son" sequence itself is evident in form as well as imagery. Here, the relatively self-contained lyrics of the "Greenhouse Poems" give way to the expansive journey format that characterizes the sequence. Rhythms become unpredictable, ranging from Roethke's characteristic nursery rhyme jingle:

> The shape of a rat?
> It's bigger than that.
> It's less than a leg

And more than a nose,
Just under the water
it usually goes.   (1.44–49)

or:

At the wood's mouth,
By the cave's door,
I listened to something
I had heard before.   (3.1–4)

to chanting phrases reminiscent of those he would later employ in "North American Sequence":

Hunting along the river,
Down among the rubbish, the bug-riddled foliage,
By the muddy pond-edge, by the bog-holes,
By the shrunken lake, hunting, in the heat of summer.   (1.40–43)

In "The Lost Son," the "nursery rhyme" passages are particularly revealing. The inward quality of the Lost Son's journey deeper into his own childhood puts the poet in a vulnerable position that Jeffers never approached. In Jeffers's longer poems such as "Tamar," characters are swept by uncontrollable passions and instincts, but he never allows such a close approach to his own individual self. The dramatic form and sensationalism of the poetry keeps the poet aloof from both content and reader. By developing the form from the content organically, Roethke invites the reader into the tight root-cellar corners of the life that "germinates" the poetry.

As is typical of contemporary poetry, the lineation also becomes irregular, often, as in "The Gibber," alternating a series of short-lined stanzas with strophes consisting of longer, more proselike lines. Despite his lifelong preference for end-stopped lines, his dropping of the last word in the following example, from "The Return," shows that he sees the line as a conceptual, as well as a rhythmical, unit:

The light in the morning came slowly over the white
Snow.
There were many kinds of cool
Air.   ("The Lost Son" 4.14–17)

One of the hallmarks of contemporary poetry is the use of lineation to provide a conceptual counterpoint to the rhythm of the poem, a technique derived primarily from Williams. One effect of this kind of lineation is that a visual, "private" reading is necessary for a complete understanding of the poem. It is interesting to note that other middle-generation poets, such as Charles Olson and John Berryman, develop their own, often unintentional, ways of "privatizing" the way a poem is read, Olson through his notion of lineation and composition "by field" and Berryman through his cubist point of view shifts. In the developing contemporary poetry, reading itself tended toward the introspective or meditative, sacrificing the possibility of an "outward-directed" didactic and declamatory poetry like that of Jeffers.

To match its idiosyncratic form, the content of the "Lost Son Sequence" is dramatically interiorized. The journey described is, in its essence, an interior voyage. Although the journey motif was employed by Modern poets, particularly Eliot, and although Eliot's journeys, such as "The Waste Land" and "The Love Song Of J. Alfred Prufrock" ("Let us go then, you and I"; 1), are plainly psychologized, still, in Eliot's poems, the journey takes the poet into a landscape that is at least as much culturally as individually determined. Eliot's frame of reference is wide-ranging, his overall effect as monumental as a Jeffers seascape. By contrast, even when echoing Eliot, the speaker in Roethke's "The Lost Son" journeys through a characteristically claustrophobic interior world of natural margins ("Down along the rubbish, the bug-riddled foliage, / By the muddy pond-edge . . ."; "The Lost Son" 1.41–42) and decaying vegetation ("Where do the roots go? Look down under the leaves"; 2.1) and also lapses into the apparent nonsense or nursery rhyme so diagnostic of Roethke's idiosyncratic style.

Despite the personal nature of his style and subject matter, Roethke's poems draw on a variety of literary influences. In *The Echoing Wood of Theodore Roethke*, Jenijoy La Belle traces Roethke's ties to the English literary tradition, especially the Romantic poets, and concludes that "The soil in which he transplants these flowers comes as much from Blake's 'Vales of Har' as it does from the Saginaw Valley" (6). Ironically, considering Roethke's rebellion against the formal expectations of late Modernism, one of his most pervasive influences is the most influential poet in midcentury American letters, T. S. Eliot. Roethke frequently echoes Eliot in structure, imagery, rhythm, and general technique. Eliot's influence can clearly be seen by comparing the passages of "The Lost Son" quoted above to the following lines from "The Waste Land":

> A rat crept softly through the vegetation
> Dragging its slimy belly on the bank
> While I was fishing in the dull canal.   (3.15–17)

Even such apparently idiosyncratic Roethke features as his use of horticultural imagery and his question-response technique have analogs in Eliot, such as these lines from "The Waste Land":

> What are the roots that clutch, what branches grow
> Out of this stony rubbish? Son of man,
> you cannot say, or guess . . ."   (1.19–21)

Typically, in "The Lost Son" and elsewhere, Roethke recasts Eliot's language in a more personal context and with a more internalized effect. This reflects both Eliot's dominance of the literary generations that succeed him and the conflicting desires of middle-generation and contemporary poets to escape from the shadow of the Great Moderns while at the same time recapturing the inventiveness and significance of these predecessors. Roethke's poems "break through" to his own life, but that life includes his exposure to literary influences, especially to the towering figures of the early twentieth century. What is contemporary about Roethke's adaptation of Eliot is his application of the earlier poet's work to the specific situation of Roethke's own life.

If Jeffers and Roethke adopt or develop poetic styles compatible with their respective eras, it is also revealing to compare the natural worlds that their poems encompass. Jeffers seems always to be involved in the sweep of nature, the elemental forces in which humanity is but a minor element. His poetry, as James Dickey says, offers a "gorgeous panorama of *big* imagery, his galaxies, suns, seas, cliffs, continents, mountains, rivers, flocks of birds, gigantic schools of fish, and so on" (qtd. in Smith 170). This, of course, is directly related to Jeffers's manifest desire to deflate the human ego. If the poet would "sooner . . . kill a man than a hawk" ("Hurt Hawks" 2.1), it is because he sees the hawk as a fuller, more complete, more perfect expression of the power of nature. That power ultimately overwhelms the characters in his longer poems, who, according to Tim Hunt, editor of a long-overdue multivolume collected poems, "are largely unable to recognize or accept themselves as elements of nature, and . . . suffer nature's power without experiencing the compensating vision of its beauty" (xxiv). In the lyrics, Jeffers consistently rebuffs the human tendency toward self-inflation. In "Boats in a Fog," for example, the arts are reduced to "antics" (1) that "have charm for children" (3) but pale before the "earnest elements of nature" (23). It is only in humanity's ability to share the day-to-day reality of "lesser" creatures that Jeffers sees humans achieving a measure of dignity. Similarly, in "Vulture," the human concept of immortality is replaced by a physical participation in life processes, including the reduction of the body to carrion and its subsequent transformation and apotheosis as animal flesh.

Natural imagery, in Jeffers's poems, is characteristically panoramic. In general, even the rare intimate descriptions of natural scenes reach outward ultimately, such as in the portrayal of coyotes in "October Evening":

Their little wolf-pads in the dead grass by the stream
Wet with the young season's first rain,
Their jagged wail trespassing among the steep stars.   (4–6)

Similarly, in "Oh Lovely Rock," a close portrait apparently of the poet and his family in a natural setting vaults outward and upward:

. . . . The revived flame
Lighted my sleeping son's face and his companion's, and the vertical face
    of the great gorge wall
Across the stream. . . .   (7–9)

For Roethke, nature is equally overwhelming, but it is the lone indi vidual, the poem's speaker, who is overwhelmed. It is the single human self who is assaulted by the "steady stream of correspondences" (13) in "In a Dark Time." While Jeffers's descriptive passages have an expansive, outward thrust, Roethke's attention to nature is generally directed inward and down-ward to a closely observed world, often a childhood world, of damp roots and invertebrates that he experiences intimately, sometimes through direct physical contact, as in "Moss Gathering":

To loosen with all ten fingers held wide and limber
And lift up a patch, dark-green, the kind for lining cemetery baskets,

Thick and cushiony, like an old-fashioned doormat,
The crumbling small hollow sticks on the underside mixed with
    roots,
And wintergreen berries and leaves still stuck to the top,—
That was moss-gathering.   (1–6)[6]

Even in Roethke's most expansive poetry, the "North American Sequence,"[7] his journey is described as a series of closely observed places rendered on a minute scale, as in "Meditation at Oyster River," in the same
general region, perhaps, as Jeffers country but observed close-up, from a
low and intimate vantage point:

Over the low, barnacled, elephant-colored rocks,
Come the first tide-ripples, moving, almost without sound, toward
    me,
Running along the narrow furrows of the shore, the rows of dead clam
    shells;
Then a runnel behind me, creeping closer,
Alive with tiny striped fish, and young crabs climbing in and out of
    the water.   (1.1–5)[8]

Indeed, spaces that are likely to facilitate escaping from the ego in Roethke's
poems often do so through excessive constriction, as in "The Far Field":

I dream of journeys repeatedly:
Of flying like a bat deep into a narrowing tunnel,
Of driving alone, without luggage, out a long peninsula.   (1.1–3)

Because of the internal, psychological quality of the journey, the "escape"
here is much less complete than Jeffers's apparent dissociation in poems
such as "The Purse-Seine." As in Roethke's earlier "Night Crow," the only
direction the poem offers is inward, the only escape into a powerless but
inescapable unconsciousness,

Where the car stalls,
Churning in a snowdrift
Until the headlights darken.   ("The Far Field" 1.10–12)

In "The Far Field," as in other Roethke poems, the poet finds himself in
forgotten corners of the natural world:

At the field's end, in the corner missed by the mower,
Where the turf drops off into a grass-hidden culvert,
Haunt of the cat-bird, nesting place of the field-mouse.   (2.1–3)

Roethke's interest in "The Minimal," as he titles a poem, reflects not only his own personal preoccupations but also the developing contemporary desire for a "breakthrough back into life," that is, to center the poetry in the world perceived by a specific individual in the normal course of quotidian experience. In "The Far Field," for example, it is the childhood discovery of a dead rat "lying among the rubble of an old coal bin" (2.8) that sparks the poet's empathetic and imaginative response and that transforms the ordinary neglected edge into "the windy cliffs of forever" (2.39) by the end of the section.

Like Jeffers, Roethke sees the natural world as a source of authenticity in which he grounds his poems. While the "North American Sequence" can rightly be considered a mystic's voyage "out of the self," the space in which the journey occurs is clearly the North American continent. His scenes demonstrate the poet's close familiarity and deep sympathy with nature, as well as his manifest concern with the human psyche. The field's overgrown edge really is a likely place to find catbirds and field mice, and the estuarine environment of "Meditation at Oyster River," even though intensely personalized as the root cellar was in the "Greenhouse Poems," is meticulously delineated, including the closely observed process by which the tide gradually seeps over the sandy edges. Furthermore, like Snyder, Roethke characterizes "The Longing" that sets him on his quest as a desire to get closer to the continent, to become a native ("Old men should be explorers? / I'll be an Indian"; 3.19–20).[9] In "The Rose," he contrasts his own relationship to his surroundings with that of others and in doing so presages Wendell Berry's assertion of the defining importance of a place in the life of an individual:

There are those to whom place is unimportant,
But this place, where sea and fresh water meet
Is important.   (1.1–3)

The confluence of fresh and salt water here has a symbolic resonance, perhaps recalling the Romantics' conjunction between the "fresh" individual and the "otherness" of the world beyond individual consciousness. But

Roethke continues to locate the rose "in its true place" (2.11), anchored in the natural setting as surely as in Roethke's personal history, as the "single wild rose" lifts:

> . . . out of the white embrace of the morning-glory,
> Out of the briary hedge, the tangle of matted underbrush,
> Beyond the clover, the ragged hay,
> Beyond the sea pine, the oak, the white tipped madrona.　　(2.14–17)

In the next stanza, the single wild rose merges with the poet's memory of the roses, "White and red, in the wide six-hundred-foot greenhouses" (2.22), so that personal family history is added to natural history to form a resonance both individualized and symbolic. In the poem's final stanzas, the rose links the poet with the surrounding cosmos, so that, by standing "outside myself" (4.13), the poet can see himself in the rose, which is described as:

> Rooted in stone, keeping the whole of light,
> Gathering to itself sound and silence—
> Mine and the sea-wind's.　　(4.24–26)[10]

By contrast, Jeffers, despite his desire to transcend the human viewpoint, does not approach transcendence as a personal process. Instead, he assumes the distanced perspective from "outside the poem" as a narrative shift, adopting a position isolated even from his own symbols, which he characteristically views from across a gorge or from a coastal headland or, in the case of raptors, from across the gap between the species.

Both Jeffers's and Roethke's portrayals of nature reflect the surroundings in which they found their "subject matter and inspiration." Jeffers's sweeping panoramas suit the open headlands of Big Sur just as Roethke's fascination with "minimal life" is a product of the miniature wilderness of his father's and uncle's "wildlife preserve" and the even smaller wild corners of the greenhouse. But Roethke describes the seacoast intimately in "Meditation at Oyster River," and Jeffers's sweeping style is apparent in "inland" poems like "Oh Lovely Rock." These portrayals reflect a crucial difference between Modern and contemporary poetry. Jeffers is more inclined to, and more able to, direct his poems outward and consequently toward public themes and concerns. Jeffers's natural world, Molesworth's "indisputable 'signified,'" encloses whole civilizations like the fishing net in "The Purse-Seine."

Roethke's approach to nature, on the other hand, reflects the contemporary desire to begin with individual experience. Roethke's natural world is quotidian, full of particular creatures encountered as if by a walking observer. The poet-speaker's response to nature is also cast in individual terms, sometimes as a catalog of "field guide" observations, as in "The Long Waters":

> The lily's piercing white,
> The mottled tiger, best in the corner of a damp place,
> The heliotrope, veined like a fish, the persistent
>   morning-glory.   (3.7–9)

Sometimes, natural descriptions are accompanied by more abstract reactions. In "I'm Here" from the "Meditations of an Old Woman" sequence, for example, the bickering sparrows spur the speaker to say, "I'm tired of tiny noises" (1.7). But even such a suggestive response is triggered by the act of encountering the sparrows at a particular moment and is dependent on the current mood of the observer. Roethke tends to approach the verifying presence of nature cautiously, on a case-by-case basis, avoiding or qualifying statements that for Jeffers would require only demonstration. When he asserts the importance of place in "The Rose," for example, it is specifically "*this* place, where sea and water meet" (emphasis added) that "is important."

Roethke's approach, in emphasizing the quotidian and the individual, reflects contemporary poetry's movement away from communicating generalized verities toward following the poet's sensations, dreams, thoughts, and observations developing in the normal course of living. Contemporary poetics in essence makes the poem a firsthand and perhaps fleeting experience, inexorably linked to a particular perceiver, rather than a timeless and public artifact. Contemporary poets, in breaking away from the restraints of late Modern poetics, have placed themselves, as Altieri suggests in *Enlarging the Temple,* in a rather private place, from which it has been difficult for them to address public issues and concerns. Later poets such as Bly,

Snyder, and Berry find themselves, aesthetically speaking, in Roethke's "far field" but compelled by a need to speak, as Jeffers felt he could, to the culture as a whole. Like prose nature writers, they have sought to come close enough to the settlements to interpret what they've found, while asserting the legitimacy of their own wild experience as the basis for their interpretation.

3 · Robert Bly

Robert Bly, the Body, and the Natural World

AT FIRST GLANCE, Robert Bly, whose concern has lately been directed primarily toward the dynamics of interpersonal relationships, may seem an unlikely choice for this study. Certainly, however, his work, particularly the lyrics of *Silence in the Snowy Fields, This Tree Will Be Here for a Thousand Years,* and the Unicorn Press chapbook, *The Moon on a Fencepost,* and also the prose poems of *The Morning Glory,* shows an acute awareness of nature. Moreover, his editing of *News of the Universe* demonstrates that his environmental concern is significant in the eyes of the Sierra Club publishers. In "News from Robert Bly's Universe: *The Man in the Black Coat Turns,*" Robert Peters links Bly to Thoreau (305) and goes on to say that, in "Visiting the Farallones," "Bly touches concerns that have occupied his energies for years—the pollution of the environment and the callous destruction of life on the planet" (307). Even Christopher Clausen notes, albeit snidely, Bly's "nature-mysticism" (132).

Like Snyder and Berry, Bly is a product of rural America, and he identifies with the natural surroundings into which he was born. But this has not been an easy process of identification, and perhaps even more so than in the case of Snyder or Berry, the road to his position as poet of place has been a long one. In his essay "Being a Lutheran Boy-God in Minnesota," Bly discusses the influence of his upbringing as something to be overcome (Anderson 206), and his often-discussed "wound," identified with his father and "maleness," also involves the basic provinciality of his upbringing.

In "Making a Farm," her "Literary Biography" of Bly, Deborah Baker notes that Bly was "bothered by this superficial cheeriness of his early life and would try to come to terms with the darker, more melancholy intuitions of his wound" (36). In fact, Bly's early career is strikingly similar to the model proposed, and later rejected, by Berry in "Writer and Region," in which the typical "hinterland writer" abandons his home for "some metropolis or 'center of culture'" (*What Are* 80). The cultural centers in which the young Bly found himself included Harvard University, New York, the Iowa Writers' Workshop, and, eventually, Europe, far removed from his native soil.

Bly was awarded a Fulbright grant in 1956, ostensibly to travel to Norway and translate Scandinavian poetry. But Baker quotes Bly as admitting that "I went there because I'm of Norwegian ancestry and I wanted to look up my relatives" (47). Baker emphasizes Bly's experience with his relatives, suggesting that, although the trip is best known for Bly's discovery of the poets Pablo Neruda and Georg Trakl, it also "provides another association between his own life and his Norwegian-American ancestry" (48). Bly's European experience taught him the value of rootedness, so that, although he still did not become an active farmer, he became aware of the rich traditions and possibilities offered by rural living. Baker notes that "The pace of life on the Bleie farm suggests the timelessness of farms that have been in the family for a thousand years" and that "This relaxed way of life was strikingly different from the fast pace of American farming with which Bly had grown up" (48). Upon returning to America, Bly went back to Madison, Minnesota, where "he chose not to work the land. His ambition in 1958 was to encourage a new imagination in American poetry" (49).

Of course, moving away from home does not necessarily lessen Bly's capacity to know and value the natural world. In fact, prose natural history writers, to whom poets like Bly were earlier compared, are as often explorers of new territories as rooted admirers of old ones. And, like Berry and Snyder, Bly eventually returned to his place of birth and has, for the most part, remained there. Furthermore, like Berry, he first returned to the exact spot that he had left—in Bly's case, Madison, Minnesota. Still, there is a sense in which Bly differs greatly from Snyder and Berry in his apprehension of and general relationship with nature, specifically with the nature of his immediate surroundings. One does not often find in Bly's poems the sense of direct "objective" observation or the awareness of or interest in the particulars of natural history "lore" that one finds in those of the other two poets. Even his attempts at writing descriptive "object poems" in prose have included a measure of "fantasy," as he admits in his preface to *What Have I Ever Lost by Dying?* his collected prose poems (xv). Moreover, Bly's approach to natural history, and to natural science in general, is less analytical. He tends to draw on empirical research and scientific theories primarily to verify aesthetic principles, as he does when he applies the "three brains theory" to the works of various poets in "Poetry and the Three Brains." He returns to MacLean's theory in his 1996 work, *The Sibling Society.* In another example, he applies the notion of natural "intricate harmonies . . . which have already lasted for millions of years" (*News* 17) in an attempt to establish a fundamental wrongheadedness in Matthew Arnold's "Dover Beach." Still, despite his respect for natural science as a source of verification, it is hard to imagine Bly "know[ing] the plants" (*Practice* 39), to use Snyder's phrase for a close working knowledge of the natural history of a particular area. At any rate, he does not generally exhibit such knowledge, or interest, in his poems. In his foreword to Bly's *Point Reyes Poems,* birdwatcher Michael Whitt comments on Bly's failings as a naturalist, remarking that "I was always trying to persuade Robert to be more scientifically accurate in the use of animal and bird images in his poems" (8).

Plants and animals are sometimes specifically identified in Bly's poems, as in "Poem in Three Parts," for example, in which appears the box elder tree, a Bly favorite. Typically, however, the tree seems chosen more for the sound and associative possibilities of its name than for any particular aspect of its natural history. Though Bly's poems often involve close scrutiny of natural objects and scenes, as in the prose poems of *The Morning Glory,* for example, Bly's concern with firsthand observation is directed more toward exploring relationships between the natural scene and his own personal reference point than toward developing an overall sense of the natural history of a particular process or place. "The Ant Mansion," for example, though evincing a degree of familiarity with ant life in general, is more involved with the ant dwelling as inspiration, as a trigger for metaphorical comparisons, including both physical resemblances ("The top four or five inches is also solid, a sort of forehead"; *Selected* 110), and less obvious, more idiosyncratic connections, such as the link between the ants' lives and those of Bly's ancestors (111–12). Furthermore, Bly rarely appears in his poems working outdoors, participating in the natural order. He is an observer of the farming life, not an active member of a farm community. As Baker points out, he decided early on that he was not, in the practical sense, a farmer. "Bly had chosen not to become a farmer," she says, "before he chose not to become an academic" (42). "Dawn in Threshing Time," a prose poem from *This Tree Will Be Here for a Thousand Years,* is typical of Bly's perspective on the farming life.[1] The poem includes enough details, like the "three-bottom plow" and "the wet pigeon grass" to show that Bly is intimately familiar with rural life, and even with the psychological state of the farmer, who "puts on besides his jacket the knowledge that he is not strong enough to die"; however, he does not identify with the farmer or partake in the scene. Instead the poem is narrated as if by a silent presence in the farmer's home, perhaps most aligned with the farmer as a child, "deep in his wooden cradle" (22). But even if this speculative autobiographical connection is plausible, then Bly's speaker represents a path that the farmer did not take, leading away from the farm.

Although Bly shows an easy familiarity with country and farming life, and although he occasionally refers directly to his own relatives or acquaintances, as in "The Ant Mansion," more typically his farmers are presented generically, as in "Cornpicker Poem" from *This Tree Will Be Here for a Thousand Years.* In poems like "Cornpicker Poem" and "Dawn in Threshing Time," his primary interest is in probing the psychology of the farm family. Although the poems have a general autobiographical resonance, and the social situation itself reflects Bly's own upbringing, he does not write about the natural environment of his own particular place with the passion and commitment of Berry or Snyder. Even in *Silence in the Snowy Fields,* Minnesota landscapes are evoked through broad strokes, with a preponderance of rather generic words and phrases such as "grass," "water," or "snowy fields." Moreover, many Bly poems depict places passed through (*Silence in the Snowy Fields,* for example, has three poems whose titles begin with "Driving." *The Moon on a Fencepost,* which includes only eight poems, has two "Driving" titles and a third whose title begins with "Arriving"), with the countryside providing a numinous setting in which the poet's mental state is formed or altered, as in "Three Kinds of Pleasures" and "Driving through Ohio" from *Silence in the Snowy Fields.* The former poem is particularly indicative, as is "Driving toward the Lac Qui Parle River," of the poet's relationship to the natural world. In both poems, the poet, encased presumably in a car, plummets through a changing landscape, but in each poem the poet's psychic life is propelled outward. The world of the car is essentially empty, the only reference to it being the statement that the poet is "driving." However, the natural landscape outside the car is richly subjective, rendered in evocative descriptive language punctuated with deep images. In other poems, Bly simply states outright that his own impressions have sources in the surrounding landscape. In "Driving to Town Late to Mail a Letter," for example, Bly asserts that "There is a privacy I love in this snowy night" (4). Similarly, in "Driving through Ohio," the poet finds that "North of Columbus there is a sort of torpid joy" (2.1).

Clearly less of an outdoorsman than Snyder and Berry, Bly is also less inclined to let nature have, in his poems, its own life. There's even a kind of dilettantism in Bly's easy commandeering of landscapes with which he is basically unfamiliar. In "Written from Mule Hollow, Utah" (*Of Solitude* 5), for example, he attests to his "love" for a "granite steep" (2) he probably had never seen before, and might very well not see again, as the poem is plainly set at some sort of conference ("After three days of talk, I long for silence and come here"; 1), very likely in nearby Salt Lake City.

Even so, Bly's sense of nature is vital to his work. His entire vision, in fact, rests on his belief in an underlying realm whose authenticity is unquestionable. Bly sees this realm as shaping and reflecting psychological states. His attraction to surrealism and his central role in deep image poetry attest to his interest in Jungian psychology, which has also been obvious in his prose, most notably in *A Little Book on the Human Shadow*'s discussion of psychic projections and how they affect perceptions. The influence of Jung, in fact, and of Jungian psychologists like Marie-Louise von Franz and James Hillman, is evident throughout Bly's writing, not only in such particulars as Bly's awareness of the archetypal possibilities in poetic imagery, but also in his evident acceptance of Jung's contention that "The poet's work is an interpretation and illumination of the contents of consciousness, of the ineluctable experiences of human life with its eternally recurrent sorrow and joy" (155–56).

Though Jung's influence on Bly is pervasive, it would be incorrect to categorize Bly as a doctrinaire disciple of Jung. In an interview with Joseph Shakarchi, for example, Bly criticizes Jung's fundamental belief that the "goal" of human development could with any degree of certainty be determined (330). Still, the Jungian conception of archetypes and Jung's belief in the psyche's ability to create "projections" of inner states are fundamental to Bly's understanding of poetry.

The deep image is sometimes referred to as the subjective image. The final stanza of "Driving toward the Lac Qui Parle River" illustrates the subjective nature of deep images. The imagery is clearly dependent for its literal meaning on the psychological state of the observer. How otherwise can water be apprehended as "kneeling in the moonlight" (3.2) or light as "on all fours in the grass" (3.4)? Moreover, nature responds in a decidedly Romantic way to the observing individual ("When I reach the river, the moon covers it"; 3.5). The Romantic nature of the connection between the human observer and the natural "observed" recalls Snyder's criticism of the Romantics as poets who did not really see nature but saw themselves instead.[2] Bly has acknowledged a similar human tendency toward self-reflexiveness. Howard Nelson notes that Bly cautions against reading human ideas into animal life. Nelson credits Bly's awareness that human intuition, essential as it is, also has the tendency to turn animals into symbols, thus replacing their intrinsic nature with human projections (*Robert* 134–35). In the Shakarchi interview, Bly warns that surrealists, because of their preoccupation with human consciousness, tend to neglect the consciousness inherent in nature, and he responds positively to Shakarchi's suggestion that "two-fold consciousness" therefore goes "beyond surrealism" (326). Still, Bly's own portrayals of animals sometimes seem to be more truly descriptions of aspects of his own consciousness, as in "Opening the Door of a Barn I Thought Was Empty on New Year's Eve" from *The Morning Glory,* which is reminiscent of Whitman's "I think I could turn and live with animals" section of "Song of Myself." Bly, however, goes on to say that each steer "has the wonder and bewilderment of the large animal, a body with a lamp inside fluttering on a windy night." The steers are "Bodies with no St. Teresas" and "large shoulders" capable of sight (*What Have* 69). The animals are described not so much as what they are but as incomplete beings, as if human consciousness consists of both the physical aspect, shared with the cows, and the spiritual part that acknowledges "St. Teresas." Unlike in Whitman's poem, or in Berry's "The Peace of Wild Things," the animals are not approached through a deliberate act of attention, but rather they are discovered by surprise in, as the title says, "a Barn I Thought Was Empty" or, as it seems irresistible to assume, in a part of Bly's own consciousness that he had neglected.

Excessive subjectivity, in fact, has been one of the two horns of the poetic dilemma that Bly has attempted to transcend throughout his career. On the one hand, the cold "picturism" of imagistic poetry has seemed to him to be dissatisfyingly dispassionate and superficial; on the other hand, the controlled, subjective orders composed by practitioners of late Modern autotelic poetics struck him as being arbitrary and stunting impositions on reality. Bly's antidote has been to assert that the mental world underlying the conscious "personality" and the natural world are in fact connected, even inseparable. He finds this idea in the continental European poetry by which he has been so influenced, and that he, in turn, has brought to many American readers for the first time through his translations and editing. The first of the aphorisms of the late-eighteenth-century German poet Novalis (Friedrich von Hardenberg) chosen by Bly for *News of the Universe* asserts that "The seat of the soul is where the inner world and the outer world meet. Where they overlap, it is in every point of the overlap" (48). According to Novalis, the human brain or "soul" has a direct line not only to a "collective unconscious" but also to nature itself. In Bly's interpretation, "Novalis says in effect that to break the Old Position we will have to study the outer world, study plants and animals and insects. The human soul he implies is not 'inside' the human being; it is not an immortal part given by God at birth, far inside; rather the seat is where the inner world and the outer world meet" (32).

For Bly, the way to reach this "seat of the soul" is through the physical body, "what we share with animals" (32). Movement into awareness through the body is typical of many of Bly's poems. He has, at various times, developed or incorporated different models to explain how consciousness "rises." Bly's application of brain researcher Paul MacLean's "three brains theory" is an early and particularly well-known example of the poet's tendency to use borrowed materials to create models of consciousness that explain, illuminate, or verify his aesthetic assumptions.[3] According to the theory, the reptile brain, located at the base of the skull, is a central source from which energy is transmuted upward through the mammal brain and eventually to the neocortex, or "new brain." Although this "new brain" is the seat of "higher consciousness," the failure to recognize and acknowledge the other layers of consciousness can result in what Bly sees, especially in his Vietnam-era political poetry, as a puritanical but superficial order overlying a dangerous and chaotic combination of "reptile" survivalism and "mammal" intensity.

Bly generally figures the physical nature of the "seat of the soul" through references to the body, nonhuman creatures, or the earth itself. As Charles Molesworth points out, Bly believes that "All artistic intuition is body-centered" (*Fierce* 112). So it is not surprising that, in the initial stanza of "Poem in Three Parts" from *Silence in the Snowy Fields,* Bly's speaker is "wrapped in my joyful flesh" (1.2). The poem ends with an assertion of the link between the spiritual and the physical, as eternal life is equated with becoming "like the dust" (3.5). Bly begins "The Origin of the Praise of God," which appears in *This Body Is Made of Camphor and Gopherwood* and in *News of the Universe,* and which is dedicated to physician-biologist Lewis Thomas, with an image that asserts the basic links between the body, animal life, and Novalis's "soul": "My friend, this body is made of bone and excited protozoa! And it is with my body that I love the fields. How do I know what I feel but what the body tells me?"[4]

Howard Nelson notes the importance of animals in Bly's poems. In "Robert Bly and the Ants," Nelson points out that "Animals are plentiful and of great importance in Bly's poetry" (192). In his study *Robert Bly: An Introduction to the Poetry,* Nelson says that Bly is drawn to animals as "masters of being at home in the senses and the present" (122). Nelson also notes Bly's mindful, if inconsistent, insistence on the independence of animal life. In *The Winged Life,* his edition of Thoreau's poetry, Bly explains how humans can assume the ability to identify with animals without compromising or suppressing the perceived independence of other creatures: "As we read Thoreau's work, especially his prose, we slowly become aware of a light in and around the squirrel, the ant, the woodchuck, the hawk, that belongs to *them* and not to the eyes observing or the brain producing words. The human mind, when it is in its own deeps, shares that light, so that it is not always improper to bring in human feelings when describing an animal or object. When people insist on keeping all human feelings out, they mean to retain single vision" (109–10; emphasis in original).

Therefore, Bly sees no essential "imperialism" in allowing his own mind to reach into the perceptions of animals and even plants, both of which are involved in the point of view of the final stanza of "Hunting Pheasants in a Cornfield" from *Silence in the Snowy Fields:*

> The mind has shed leaves alone for years.
> It stands apart with small creatures near its roots.
> I am happy in this ancient place,
> A spot easily caught sight of above the corn,
> If I were a young animal ready to turn home at dusk.   (4.1–5)

But Bly's egalitarian attitude toward the nonhuman is not without its own form of "speciesism." Although Bly rejects the human-centered "Old Position," his own position is not altogether free of hierarchy. In "Opening the Door of a Barn I Thought Was Empty on New Year's Eve," for example, the cattle are satisfied, and have to be, "to eat the crushed corn and the hay, coarse as rivers, and sometimes feel an affection run down along the heavy nerves" (*What Have* 69). The "three brains theory" is clearly hierarchical. Humans and animals share the reptile and mammal brains, but the "new brain" is exclusively human, having developed in "late mammal times," and is "incredibly complicated, more so than the other brains, having millions of neurons per square inch" (*American* 54). Even Richard Sugg's contention that, to Bly, animal and human consciousness are "different in degree rather than kind" (108) indicates, in effect, a hierarchical arrangement. The cumulative layering of "brains" in the three brains model allows humans to reach the animal in their own consciousness, but the "higher" regions of human consciousness remain exclusively human. Still, Bly's model does point out essential connections between animal and human and allows for a kind of internalized relationship that a model like Pope's Chain of Being, for example, would tend to prevent.

During the 1990s, Robert Bly has been somewhat of a celebrity, mostly for his role as leader and publicizer of the "men's movement." It is not surprising, therefore, that his writing has become increasingly concerned with matters of human social interaction. The "social Bly," always evident in his criticism and emerging into his poetry with the formation of American Writers against the Vietnam War in 1966 and the publication of *The Light around the Body* in 1968, is considerably different from the poet of *Silence in the Snowy Fields*. The change is apparent to publisher Harper and

Row, which, on the back cover of Bly's 1979 collection *This Tree Will Be Here for a Thousand Years,* bills the book as a "sequel" to *Silence,* in which "Bly returns to his early subject matter—land, nature, landscape." Deborah Baker says that "The tenor of Bly's poetry changed drastically" (58) between *Silence in the Snowy Fields* and *The Light around the Body.* As with Gary Snyder, however, Bly sometimes holds poems back in the process of constructing his books, so it is an oversimplification to say that Bly became a political poet in 1966 or 1968. In a 1971 interview with Peter Martin, Bly asserts that many of the poems in *The Light around the Body* were actually written before some of the poems in *Silence in the Snowy Fields,* and that he continues to "write what you call 'snowy fields' poems without pause, maybe eight or nine a year" (*Talking* 122). Even so, he focused on the "snowy fields poems" in his first book. In effect, *Silence in the Snowy Fields* established the base in nature upon which Bly could build both the political poetry of *The Light around the Body* and the subsequent books that focus more on human interrelationships.

Throughout his later work, Bly continues to maintain a basis in the deep unconscious channels that connect human individuals not only to each other but also to their origins in nature. Bly's popular version of the "Iron John" tale, for example, emphasizes the wildness of the hairy man living deep at the bottom of a lake, who offers the young boy essential knowledge of himself and his identity. The "initiation" process, in addition to recalling a rich complex of human social traditions, is seen as a way in which adolescent boys are provided with keys to the mystery of their own physical and psychological identity.[5] Bly casts Iron John as a composite being, consisting of both enchanted prince and wild man. For Bly, the Wild Man is not simply disguised; his "naturalness" is more than a literary device used to establish his enchantment. "We need to understand," he asserts, "the Wild Man is not 'inside' us. The story suggests that the Wild Man is actually a being who can exist and thrive for centuries outside the human psyche" (*Iron* 36). Bly enlarges on this point some pages later, claiming that "The story implies that we, as human beings, are not the only source of ordered intelligence and conscious awareness. 'The eyes in the water' can be regarded as an emblem of the consciousness in nature, the intelligence 'out there.' We know that neither consciousness nor 'intelligence' is quite the right word. Human beings invented the word 'consciousness' to describe their own particular sentience, but nature's awareness is not exactly intelligence nor sentience, nor consciousness, nor awareness. It falls between all the words" (52).[6]

Yet Bly also believes that the apprehension of the true nature of humanity requires an understanding that individual human consciousnesses are linked to each other, and to the environment as well, and that a failure to recognize those links is not only psychically stunting but also dangerous. Bly sees that danger expressed in American actions toward other peoples, perhaps most explicitly in his figuring of the Vietnam War as a reenactment of the genocidal campaigns directed against Native Americans. Bly connects the U.S. wars against American Indians with the war in Vietnam in various writings, among them *A Little Book on the Human Shadow* (12–14). In "Hatred of Men with Black Hair," also, Bly writes that "Underneath all the cement of the Pentagon / There is a drop of Indian blood preserved in snow" (17–18). Though he questions the validity of the connection, James F. Mersmann concedes that Bly's associating the two does constitute an incisive critique of American values (66).[7]

In *The Sibling Society,* Bly sees the abandonment of traditional initiation rites as a source of generational isolation, which is likely to be expressed in the violent disaffection of young people. Bly has also recognized the peril in adhering to the "Old Position" that "nature is defective because it lacks reason" (*News* 3). *News of the Universe* is his most fully developed statement that Descartes's limitation of consciousness to humanity leads logically to "'scientific' reductionism, which longs to flood the Grand Canyon behind a concrete dam."[8] Such "ideas act so as to withdraw consciousness from the non-human area, isolating the human being in his house, until, seen from the window, rocks, sky, trees, crows seem empty of energy, but especially empty of divine energy" (4). A dissociation dangerous to the land itself is apparent in "Cornpicker Poem" (in *This Tree Will Be Here for a Thousand Years*), in which unremedied separation within an individual consciousness is expressed in a violently aggressive agriculture. It is significant that, although the "stiff-haired son" (1.4) emerges from the dream of "fighting with a many-armed woman" (2.4) with "a victory" (2.8), he emerges into his waking hours tensely, "with jaws set" (2.7). The third stanza's "sullen chilled machine" (3.4), with its "empty gas cans" spread "around it" (3.5) like the arms of the woman in the dream, translates the anxiety of the dream into the daily activity of the farm. It is no wonder that the "stiff-haired son" approaches what to Berry would be a sacred ceremony, the harvest, by "hurtling / his old Pontiac down the road" (3.2–3).

Bly's ability to probe psychological reasons behind social problems provides him with an insightful approach to what Gary Snyder calls "the secret heart of this Growth Monster" (*Practice* 5), the underlying forces motivating what both Bly and Snyder see as a destructive and violent social order. But "Cornpicker Poem" also serves as an implied warning to poets, such as Berry and Snyder, who assert that a harmonious, ecologically sound alternative lifeway can be created or fostered in rural America. In general, Bly's farmers are far from the enlightened San Juan Ridge dwellers of Snyder's or Berry's idealized Jeffersonian husbandmen. A significant contribution Bly has made to environmentally concerned poetry is his recognition that the people who would "reinhabit" the American countryside in the visions of Berry and Snyder would very likely bring with them all of the philosophical and psychological dissociation inherent in the tendency to regard nature as virtually inert, neutral with respect to morality and values. In "The Dead World and the Live World," Bly connects a "dead" sense of nature with the tendency toward social aggression: "Suppose also that the human being is not studied in relation to nonhuman lives, or lives in other countries, but simply in relation to itself? One can predict first of all that such a nation will bomb foreign populations very easily, because it has no sense of anything beyond its own ego" (*American* 236). Bly contends that the same sense of inert nature is shared by the confessional poets, who "tend to believe that the human being is something extremely important *in itself*," and who "will accept calmly the extinction of the passenger pigeon or the blue whale" (238).

Bly also warns, however, against naive, superficial reliance on the verities to be found in nature, insisting instead that he is "not urging a nature poetry either, but rather a poetry that goes deep into the human being, much deeper than the ego, and at the same time is aware of trees and angels" (238). Like Berry, Bly is more involved with "wildness" in the human psyche than with physical wilderness, but Bly also acknowledges that, as Snyder says in *Earth House Hold,* the human unconscious and the physical wilderness are closely related, even equivalent (*Earth* 122). In *The Winged*

Life, for example, Bly admires the way Thoreau follows Emerson's suggestion by joining the study of himself and the exploration of nature (112). In
fact, Bly does call for a revival of a sacred sense of nature and credits Berry
and Snyder for incorporating "a sense of Gott-natur . . . at the very center
of ecological work" (*American* 239). Especially insightful, in relation to Snyder's notion of reinhabitation, is Bly's comparison of American artists to
American Indians at the beginning of the essay titled "Intense States of
Consciousness" (240). He has, like Berry and Snyder, been attempting
to build a sense of community in which this "Gott-natur" is recognized
and cherished. In "Making a Farm: A Literary Biography," Deborah Baker
notes that the search for community has grown as a concern for Bly since
his iconoclastic early days, citing his increased involvement in the 1970s
with those poets with whom he could ally himself in a "community with
integrity that was not defined by righteousness and moral indignation but
by personal affections and commitment" (70). Perhaps it is this impulse
that has led to his association with various "men's movement" workshops
and activities. His destination has been less geographically located than
Berry's Kentucky River or Snyder's San Juan Ridge and less "natural" in
the sense that it is primarily concerned with the human psyche; however,
Bly has also avoided the utopianism that tends to attach itself to Berry's and
Snyder's isolated, idealized communities.

Bly and the Prose Poem

In *News of the Universe,* Bly quotes and endorses an essay by the French
prose poem (and, according to Bly, "thing poem") writer Francis Ponge.
According to Ponge, "the function of poetry" is "to nourish the spirit of
man by giving him the cosmos to suckle. We have only to lower our standard of dominating nature and to raise our standard of participating in it
in order to make the reconciliation take place" (214).[9] About the prose
poem form itself, Bly says that "Something surprising happens often during
the writing. It is as if the object itself, a stump or an orange, has links with
the human psyche, and the unconscious provides material it would not
give if asked directly. The unconscious passes into the object and returns"
(212–13).

Interestingly, Bly sees the prose poem as a way to solve the nature writer's dilemma postulated by Fritzell. The prose poem, in which "great detail is possible when the object is being described" (212), links not only two genres but also two modes of perception, the "objective" observation associated with natural science and the ostensibly more "poetic" attempt to establish a personal connection with the natural object being described.

Bly's example of the stump, subject of "A Hollow Tree," one of his own prose poems, suggests that he is talking not just of Ponge's work but of his own work in this form, and in his *Selected Poems,* he specifically identifies Ponge, along with Juan Ramón Jiminez, as his "predecessors in the object poem" (199). Bly has been writing and publishing prose poems since the 1970s; his collection *The Morning Glory* appeared in 1975. In the preface to the "Morning Glory" section of his *Selected Poems* he considers his own prose poems as "object poems," noting that his prose poems have dealt with "a hollow tree, a bouquet of roses, a starfish, a dried sturgeon, and many other objects" (88–89). Like the deep image poem, the "object" or "thing" poem attempts to bridge worlds, "to journey, to cross the border, either to the other world, or to that place where the animal lives" (88). Rather than rely on the encapsulating or reaching capacity of the image, however, the prose poem relies on its "urgent, alert rhythm" (88) to create the contact. Also, the connection takes place not in the neutral space created by the image but in the larger space of the poem itself, within which both the mind of the poet and the object being described coexist in a kind of parallel movement, similar to a dance, rather than in the mingled form normally created through the image. In his essay "The Prose Poem as an Evolving Form," Bly compares the relationship of observer and observed with the tension between thought and meter in a metrical poem, observing that "The metered poem, as Yeats remarked, finishes with a click as when a box closes, and the metered poem has two subjects: the thought of the poet and the meter itself. One is personal, the other impersonal. The thing poem written in prose has two subjects but quite different ones; the movement of the writer's mind and the thing itself. One is personal, the other impersonal. While the poet concentrates on the object, the movement of his mind cannot be hidden" (*Selected* 200). Thus, instead of creating a zone of "overlap," the object poem in prose allows both mind and object to preserve their separate identities. The intelligence of the poet is able to "come close to the object and participate in its complication" (199). In return, as Bly says in the preface to the "Morning Glory" section of his *Selected Poems,* the poet functions as "the giver of attention" (89), with "attention" defined as Wendell Berry does in "Writer and Region": "To pay attention is to come into the presence of a subject. In one of its root senses, it is to 'stretch toward' a subject, in a kind of aspiration. We speak of 'paying attention' because of a correct perception that attention is *owed* that without our attention our subjects, including ourselves, are endangered" (*What Are* 83). Bly, too, notes that humanity has a stake in the paying of attention, as "The old people say that each object in the universe—seashell, bat's wing, pine cone, patch of lichen—contains some fragment of our missing soul" (*Selected* 89).

In "A Hollow Tree," one of the *Morning Glory* poems, the poet-speaker considers a cottonwood stump. True to the poet's contention, in this poem the movement of the observing mind is "not hidden." The mind characterizes the stump, considers the number of feathers present inside it, compares the stump to a "temple," and surmises that "some creature has died here." The metaphorical comparisons are consciously composed and reflect the image vocabulary and interests of the poet himself. "Inside the hollow walls there is privacy and secrecy" (*What Have* 68), for example, recalls the subjective landscapes of *Silence in the Snowy Fields.* But the purpose of this poem is not so much to plumb the depths of the human psyche. The "privacy and secrecy" are discovered by close observation rather than through psychological openness to a numinous presence. The poet's observations here seem to be the consequence of a close and deserved attention to the stump itself to what Berry calls "the proper discharge of an obligation" (*What Are* 83).

The writing of poems like those in *The Morning Glory* can be discussed in terms of Fritzell's self-conscious nature writing. Charles Molesworth identifies the connection between the prose poem and natural history in Bly's writing, noting that he turns to the prose poem to move from pastoral to natural history poetry (*Fierce* 120). In "The Ant Mansion," for example, Bly describes the tendency of the earth to "bury," by noting that "The earth never lies flat, but is always thinking" (*Selected* 110). In this poem, Bly explores Fritzell's "antipodes" of "fact and metaphor" (34). On the one hand, the observing mind seeks to accurately describe an observable fact, that the earth "finds a new feeling and curves over it, rising to bury a toad or a great man; it accounts for a fallen meteor" (*Selected* 110). Yet, on the other hand, the mind also concerns itself with the act of thinking, the composition of ways in which thought itself can be understood and described. The assertion that the earth is "always thinking" is directed at earth processes, but it also illustrates the poet's thinking about those processes. Ultimately, in the preface to *What Have I Ever Lost by Dying?*, his collected prose poems, Bly acknowledges the self-reflexive character of human thought, admitting that when he wrote the *Morning Glory* poems he had "hoped that a writer could describe an object or a creature without claiming it," but that "I no longer think that is possible" (xv).

Bly's "natural history" prose poems, those that are "concerned with observing precisely and labeling tentatively" (Molesworth, *Fierce* 120), include those in *The Morning Glory*. About these poems, Bly observes that "When one gives attention to objects, as in the *Morning Glory* poems, one remains in the eyes and looks out through the eyes at another body, perhaps at a starfish, and the mind is focused on the starfish when it writes" (*Selected* 130).

In what Bly calls the "object poem" or "thing poem," poetry approaches Fritzell's self-conscious nonfiction nature writing, a connection that Bly himself recognizes when he lists "Thoreau in his journals" among the "masters of the 'thing' poem" (*Selected* 200). In observing that a complete identification with an object is impossible, Bly himself may be mildly disappointed by what he perceives as a limitation to his art, and his later prose poems, such as those of *Old Man Rubbing His Eyes*, do tend toward the "fantasy" he now believes is inevitable, as well as toward more social subject matter, but the tension between the poet as scientific observer of the independent natural object and the human "soul," which is "as much nature as the rice grain or the pine cone" (*What Have* xv), is intrinsic in the nature writer's situation.

It is interesting to note that recent prose poem writers sometimes characterize their art in terms of generosity. Bly quotes Ponge's assertion that poetry's function is to "nourish the spirit of man" (*News* 214). Bly himself speaks of one of Ponge's prose poems in reader-directed terms, saying that it "offers language" (*Selected* 199). Bly's own initial use of the form is traced

to a response to a gift, "when Mary at three brought me an English cater-
pillar" (88). Perhaps the reader-directed way in which these poets characterize the prose poem is a result of the form itself, which can be seen as a
logical development of the Wordsworthian trend toward the language of
common speech. As Russell Edson points out, "Natural speech is prose"
(322). Donald Hall links the prose poem's appeal to its ability to include
narrative and informative elements normally excluded or limited by the
poetics of the contemporary lyric: "Prose poems can carry information too.
Prose poems can tell stories. Stories are information. Prose poems can do
this because they are associated with prose" (103).

Prose poems, therefore, constitute an effective antidote to the "private"
sense of the contemporary free verse lyric by characteristically including
such accessible language functions as storytelling and the communication
of information.[10] They realize a communicative stance without sacrificing the experiential quality so important in contemporary poetics. In *The
Morning Glory,* Bly communicates, as information, the experience of observing and interacting with the natural world.

Bly and the Public Voice

In an early (1961) essay, "Voyages of the Body and Soul," Bly asserts that
"We know that the latent intelligence, or the biological reservoir of experiences, touches our instinctive life, and through that the life of all animals"
(*American* 40). The conviction that nature and the deep unconscious of the
human "soul" are intricately connected has been discussed earlier as the
cornerstone of Bly's nature poetry. However, it can also be viewed as the
basis for his poetics and for his attempt to blend the private perception of
the individual with a more public voice. At the levels of consciousness underlying or encompassing what might be called the "outward" personality,
Bly maintains, the private and public become, in a sense, interchangeable.
This has been a constant of his thinking since *Leaping Poetry,* in which, in
the "Looking for Dragon Smoke" section, he announces that "The associative paths are not private to the poet, but are somehow inherent in the
universe" (*American* 47). This belief in the "objectivity" of the unconscious
has led to his later peopling the collective human psyche, and even the

physical world as it appears in his writing, with archetypal "beings" such as the "Wild Man." It has also provided him with a way to avoid Molesworth's "trap of autotelism and excessive self-consciousness" (*Fierce* 131).

The focal point of Bly's poetry, the place where the conscious and unconscious meet and where subjective becomes objective, has been the image, which, as he says in "A Wrong Turning in American Poetry," "is made by both the conscious and the unconscious mind" (*American* 21). This is the root belief behind Bly's working with the deep image, a kind of imagery that attempts to penetrate shared layers of consciousness. Thus, in theory, the deep image is "public," in the sense that it is not held within the confines of a single brain or a single life.

In practice, Bly's conception of the deep image has been different from, say, Roethke's, and the difference can be seen as a function of Bly's devotion to the collective nature of the unconscious. Whereas Roethke's imagery, as in "The Lost Son," tends to continue penetrating inward or downward into the poet's own psyche and to become notably less communicative in the process, Bly's imagery, despite the value he puts on "inwardness," tends to expand outward, with each perception serving as a guidepost to reach the next. Alan Williamson's observation that the later deep image poets, such as Bly and James Wright, employ straightforward syntactical relationships (68) attests to the methodical process by which their imagery advances. Bly's "leaps" are surprisingly orderly; they cover some distance, but ladders are provided. Consider, for example, this stanza from "Poem against the British" from *Silence in the Snowy Fields:*

> The wind through the box-elder trees
> Is like rides at dusk on a white horse,
> Wars for your country, and fighting the British.   (1.1–3)

The movement of the imagery is difficult, but not disjunctive. The motion of the wind leads to the similar motion of riding a horse. In the stanza's most difficult connection, its longest leap, the reader must vault from riding the white horse to "wars for your country." However, the dusk ride on the majestic "white horse" has just enough martial sense to allow the leap, though perhaps not predictable, to be accomplished without hesitation. The progression to "fighting the British" is imagistically nothing more than a further modification of the beginning of the line.

Even in his more sweeping political poems, Bly maintains the accessibility of images and connections between images. The "equations" that characterize "The Teeth Mother Naked at Last," for example, are essentially logical in nature, counterpointing the content against the logic of the syntax:

> It's because the aluminum window-shade business is
>   doing so well in the United States
> that we spread fire over entire villages.
> It's because the trains coming into New Jersey hit the
>   right switches every day
> that Vietnamese men are cut in two by bullets that
>   follow each other like freight trains.   (3.26–29)

Charles Molesworth contrasts Bly with symbolist poets, contending that "Bly's hidden order differs from, say, Mallarmé's, because we can trace it from the dailiness of the world" (*Fierce* 118). One reason why Bly's imagery is accessible is its typal quality. As in Jeffers, the interpretations invited by the imagery are more or less conventional. In "Poem against the British," for example, the darkening ride on the white horse suggests both the danger of nightmare and the pretense of martial glory associated with the call to war.

Bly's imagery tends to move from individualized experience toward the archetypal, a movement that, in effect, is similar to Jeffers's expanding perspective. Roethke, by contrast, tends to interiorize or privatize archetypal imagery. Thus, for Roethke, the archetypal garden is transformed into the idiosyncratic greenhouse. Bly, though his imagery may move from the literally descriptive toward the surrealistic or "deep," employs as a kind of counterstrategy a broadening of scope from a particular landscape or scene into a generalized territory that is by its very nature shared or communal. Nowhere is this more apparent than in Bly's persistent use of the metaphor that links the American Midwestern plains to the ocean. Of course, this comparison is in itself a kind of cultural convention; images of the prairie as a "sea of grass" are an American commonplace. In his poems, therefore, Bly frequently uses a comparison derived from what Snyder might term the "common knowledge of the tribe" to transform his own private experience into the archetypal language of the shared unconscious. An example is the poem that closes *Silence in the Snowy Fields,* "Snowfall in the Afternoon." The poem is typical of Bly's early "deep image" poems, with characteristic images like the "little houses of the grass" (1.3) and "handfuls of darkness" (2.2) gathered from the ground. It also demonstrates the movement from private to shared or public imagery. The first step in the sequence is the substitution of "we" for "I" that occurs in the last line of the second stanza.[11] Shortly after, in the third stanza, the barn is cast adrift, moving "all alone in the growing storm" (3.3), transforming the solid ground into sea, a movement that echoes on a more archetypal level the discovery of the destabilizing layer of darkness in the second stanza. Finally, in the fourth stanza, the land completes its metamorphosis, and the final image is an unexpected but certainly archetypal image of a ghost ship. Furthermore, the plural blind "sailors" (4.3) now are seen to populate the ship, which has previously, in the third stanza, been "all alone."

That Bly's descent into the deep image coexists with or even constitutes a passage from the private to the archetypal public is not really as paradoxical as it sounds. Theoretically, the deep image uses poetic figures as portals linking the individual consciousness to a collective realm beneath or around it. In his essay "What the Image Can Do," Bly says that "the image merges worlds" (*American* 278). Clearly, one set of worlds that the image can link is the consciousness of the individual person and that of a shared "collective unconscious," so that, as Breslin points out, the shared unconscious is seen as the "basis for community" (179). This is why it seems to Bly, as he says in "Leaping Up into Political Poetry," that "the political poem comes from out of the deepest privacy" (*American* 247). "Out of" suggests an expansive movement, starting from within the individual and developing or perhaps "leaping" outward into "The life of the nation," which "can be imagined also as a psyche larger than the psyche of anyone living, a larger sphere, floating above everyone" (249).

Another set of "worlds" that the image can link or "fuse" consists of the human consciousness and "something else not entirely human" (279). In "What the Image Can Do," Bly compares this function of imagery to that of a "bridge" or "arm" that can "carry us to conscious or superconscious matter" (280), concluding that "The bridge or arm images work against the notion that human intelligence is alone in the universe, isolated, and unchangeably remote from the natural world" (280). That the natural world constitutes a kind of consciousness that envelopes and originated our own, and which our own contains enough of to make contact with, is the central theme of *News of the Universe,* Bly's most obviously "ecological" work. For Bly, the poetic image, if the poet is open to its psychological possibilities, is the doorway through which an individual can contact both the public voice and the natural world. In "Kneeling Down to Peer into a Culvert" from *The Man in the Black Coat Turns,* for example, Bly begins his observation as "I," but by the end of the first stanza he is already able to use the plural pronoun "our" because he has already reached, by delving into the processes of light and water, an area of shared experience:

> I kneel down to peer into a culvert.
> The other end seems far away.
> One cone of light floats in the shadowed water.
> This is how our children will look when we are dead.   (1–4)

Thus, Bly's blending of "nature mysticism and new-left politics" (132) is not as eccentric as it appears to Christopher Clausen, if one holds, as Bly does, that human societies, as well as individuals, are contained concentrically in the encompassing circle of the natural, and that the experience of writing, or reading, poetry involves a movement back and forth between these spheres.[12] That the concentrated power of poetry, which makes unconscious linkages visible, can have a communal, even moral, purpose, is noted by Altieri, who claims that, by revealing the deep "force" that connects the individual, the society, and nature, poetry "has a moral function; it makes man aware of what he shares with all life, and thus it can help combat the egocentric violence of American culture" (*Enlarging* 85). The moral and ethical effectiveness of Bly's poetry depends, in practice, on the validity of his application of a Jungian model of consciousness and on the ability of readers to experience and, albeit unconsciously, understand the connections that the deep image reveals. But Bly also provides prose keys to understanding the poetry, and the popularity of his prose books, as with Snyder and Berry, has provided him with a forum in which to discuss poetry in general and his own poetry in particular, bringing poems to an audience that extends beyond the world of poetry and its aficionados.

During the 1990s, Bly's popularity has unexpectedly reached a peak rivaling, even surpassing, his popularity in the 1960s. This is primarily due to his rise as spokesman for the "men's movement." In fact, his prose works *Iron John* and *The Sibling Society* have become best-sellers, and Bly is now a reasonably familiar public person (he was even selected as one of the "twenty-five most intriguing people for 1991" by *People* magazine). Still, he maintains a poet's identity; he is generally introduced as a poet first; in a conversation with Deborah Tannen in *New Age Journal,* for example, Bly is hailed as "the muse of the men's movement" ("Where" 28). Actually, the men's movement is a natural outgrowth of Bly's versatility and breadth of interest. He has never confined his interests to poetry alone. It is arguable, in fact, that "No poet has ranged more widely in his interests or had a greater reciprocal relationship with writers and thinkers in other disciplines than has Bly," as William V. Davis claims (6). Bly has used both his prose writing and his "extra-poetic" activities to become perhaps the most visible American poet since Ginsberg in the 1950s and 1960s. One could say that Bly has bounded into the public eye in the same way that one of his images breaks from the private world of individual experience into the "national psyche." Although he consistently maintains that poetry is by its very nature limited to a relatively small audience, the poet himself can function as an effective and compelling public figure, as Bly demonstrated during the Vietnam war, and as he currently is demonstrating again.[13]

One consequence of Bly's involvement with the men's movement is his apparent forsaking of his devotion to the "Great Mother," a multiform and mythically personified feminine principle that appears in his early work and that has connections to Gaia and other manifestations of the Earth Goddess of some ecofeminist and New Age thought. Though having dangerous aspects, as Bly demonstrates in "Cornpicker Poem" and, more obviously, in "The Teeth Mother Naked at Last," the return of what Bly characterized as "Great Mother energy" was generally welcomed by the poet as an antidote to the overly rational and puritanical masculine principle that, according to him, had dominated Western civilization since Descartes. In early poems such as "In a Train" and "Driving to Town Late to Mail a Letter," Bly cultivated what he saw as a "feminine" receptivity to nature and to his own empathetic responses, much as Roethke had done in poems such as "The Meadow Mouse." He nurtured a corresponding wariness toward "male" egoism that finds expression in Vietnam-era poems such as "Asian Peace Offers Rejected without Publication" and "Hatred of Men with Black

Hair." In *Iron John,* however, though he still admits in the preface that "The dark side of men is clear," and that "Their mad exploitation of earth resources, devaluation and humiliation of women, and obsession with tribal warfare are undeniable" (x), he fears that men have been psychologically emasculated by social and personal concessions to women. As feminist Susan Faludi observes, Bly has come to believe that "the Great Mother's authority has become too great" (308). Far from the ostensibly hyper-rational but at heart darkly chaotic patriarchy he envisioned in poems such as "Asian Peace Offers Rejected without Publication" ("Men like [Secretary of State Dean] Rusk are not men only—/ They are bombs waiting to be loaded in a darkened hangar"; 3–4), the "masculine" aspect of American society has been reduced, by the time of *Iron John,* to the bumbling, ineffectual fathers of television sitcoms (23). Bly's response to this perception is to attempt to renew what he calls the male "Zeus energy" (22). In terms of Bly's mythological representations, the men's movement seeks to rehabilitate the traditional male role of "protector" by placing nonhuman nature and human society under the guardianship of the "Wild Man." In *Iron John,* he asserts that "It is the Wild Man who is protecting the Spotted Owl. The Wild Man is the male protector of the earth." He continues, "I think we are remembering the Wild Man now—and women are remembering the Wild Woman and other Invigorators—because men and women need now, more than ever in history, to protect the earth, its creatures, the waters, the air, the mountains, the trees, the wilderness" (223).

In *Iron John,* Bly de-emphasizes the more martial aspects of the folk tale, favoring instead a notion of a "male protector" resembling, in effect, Berry's idea of the husbandman who protects the farm and thus preserves the family inheritance. The similarity between the Bly of *Iron John* and Berry is unexpected but unmistakable. For example, Bly says that "In the garden the soul and nature marry. When we love cultivation more than excitement we are ready to start a garden. In the garden we cultivate yearning and longing—those strangely un-American feelings, and notice tiny desires. Paying attention to tiny, hardly noticeable feelings is the garden way. That's the way lovers behave" (132). This passage recalls Berry's claims for the subversive nature of careful farming, his frequent linking of marriage with cultivation, and his belief in the value of "paying attention."

But Bly's new position has troubling aspects. In her classic study *The Lay of the Land,* Annette Kolodny convincingly discusses the psychic and physical dangers inherent in the traditional mythic and psychological establishment of an active male principle over a passive and dependent "female" nature. The psychological tension resulting from the conflicting myths of earth as revered mother and earth as desired lover can and often does, in Kolodny's post-Freudian analysis, result in the violent exploitation of both human women and nonhuman nature. Furthermore, though he pauses, rather self-consciously, to note that there is also a "Wild Woman," Bly comes perilously close to advocating what amounts to psychological gender warfare, with the Wild Man seeking to free men from the domination of the Great Mother or, in the case of the fairy tale around which he builds *Iron John,* from their own mothers. As Kolodny recognizes, mythic representations translate, in complex and indirect ways, into human actions.

It is not surprising, then, that the men's movement has sometimes been seen by feminists as threatening, and that Bly himself has been characterized as adopting a reactionary position in response to the perceived increase in the power of women in American society. Susan Faludi, for example, says that "Bly may be an advocate of world peace, but as the general of the men's movement, he is overseeing a battle on the domestic front" (310). Faludi devotes several pages of her book *Backlash* to Bly, claiming that, in addition to personal aggrandizement, Bly is motivated by a desire to reassert male dominance in response to perceived increases in the influence of women, resulting from feminism. Faludi concludes that "The true subject of Bly's [male conference] weekends, after all, is not love and sex, but power—how to wrest it from women and how to mobilize it for men" (310).

Bly himself has usually been conciliatory, although Faludi discusses his propensity to get carried away at times with his own male warrior image. For his part, he offers a bit of "countercriticism" against Faludi, who "could stand as a representative of the kind of writer who knows only adversarial thinking" (*Sibling* 204–5). Still, he insists that he is sympathetic with women's attempts to gain a more equal social footing, and he distances himself from antifeminist groups like Promise Keepers (179). In his conversation with linguist Deborah Tannen, recorded in *New Age Journal,* Bly reiterates his opposition to the patriarchal power structure, saying that "the patriarchy is disappearing—and I think that it is quite rightly and properly going down and isn't going to come up again for a while" (33). His 1985 collection, *Loving a Woman in Two Worlds,* includes depictions of gentle and noncompetitive relationships between men and women.[14] Still, Bly's new advocacy of what might be called male consciousness seems to have affected, to some extent, his attitude toward both women and nonhuman nature, placing both in a more dependent position in relation to the resurgent male and emphasizing the hierarchical sense from which Bly has never been able to completely escape. As noted earlier, in "Poetry and the Three Brains," Bly interprets neurological research in an attempt to establish that human intelligence is linked to and includes "reptile" and "mammal" intelligence but is accorded an additional level, not shared with other creatures, in the "new brain." Similarly, the Wild Man is first discovered in a natural setting, but his truest, most complete form is as a human being, the prince. Even in *News of the Universe,* it is up to the human to acknowledge or "grant" consciousness to the nonhuman.

Bly's involvement with the men's movement has brought him to the attention of feminist critics, but there are troubling aspects to his ideas about art, nature, and gender that predate the men's movement, and that perhaps are a result of his tendency to describe the world in mythic or archetypal terms. In a 1966 interview with Cynthia Lofsness, Kathy Otto, and Fred Manfred, Bly acknowledges that there are significant female writers but claims that art is basically a male pursuit, since women's reproductive power gives them a natural "connection with the universe" and makes it therefore unnecessary for them to forge such a connection through art (*Talking* 65–66). Despite his criticism of America's "brutal masculinity" (66) in the same interview, Bly's linking women and nature on one side as opposed to a male principle of intentional creation on the other reflects a traditional order critiqued by Kolodny and Andrée Collard, among others.

Even in "Ferns" from *Loving a Woman in Two Worlds* ("Through you I learned to love the ferns on that bank"; 3), Bly's linking of the feminine and the natural is problematical. Bly may not invoke gender conflict here, but the poem does offer an animate, apparently male, force learning from and about a passive, objectified female, the teaching occurring primarily as a function of the male's explorations, without any active participation on the part of the female.

The Sibling Society shows Bly continuing to walk a line between the liberal positions he has traditionally favored and the more conservative tack

the men's movement has led him to adopt. In this book, Bly tries to rehabilitate the notion of hierarchy itself, or "vertical thought" as he calls it. He
is clearly concerned that his old left-leaning readers understand that his
sympathies are still with them. The patriarchy, materialism, multinational
corporations, and Ronald Reagan are roundly criticized. But in the face
of the disintegration of links between the generations, Bly adopts a position favoring a kind of self-generated traditional authority, necessary to reestablish relationships between men and women, parents and children, and,
by extension, between rich and poor, strong and weak, human and nonhuman. At one point, he even tries to salvage the reputation of Andrew
Carnegie and the robber barons, who, unlike today's transnational capital-
ists, "felt a loyalty to the nation, and, as we know, provided thousands of
libraries across the United States to large towns and small" (157). As he does
with gender issues, Bly finds himself in dangerously contradictory terrain
in his views of nature also. His environmental advocacy is present in *The
Sibling Society,* and he continues to recognize and demonstrate the connections between social justice and environmental issues. But there is a subtle
difference in his portrayal of the "three brains." Bly first discussed Paul
MacLean's theory in *Leaping Poetry.* As stated earlier, Bly's interpretation of
MacLean's model is hierarchical, with human consciousness containing animal consciousness in addition to a species-specific neocortex. In his earlier
application of the theory, the transfer of energy to the "new brain" from
the other levels was seen as a source of power in poetry, the poetic image
deriving a kind of evolutionary validity from the more primitive animal
levels. Full consciousness also allowed for more self-knowledge, so that the
potential for paranoia associated with the protective reptile brain, for example, can be understood and kept in harmony with the rest of the brain.
In *The Sibling Society,* the emphasis is on the chaotic and self-serving aspects of the reptile and mammal brains, and the ways of nonhuman nature
seem closer to Matthew Arnold's "ignorant armies" than to the "intricate
harmonies" Bly cites in *News of the Universe.* In *The Sibling Society,* the
reptile brain is reduced to an "Alarm System," and the old mammal brain,
despite being the source of "artistic madness," is labeled the "Feeding,
Sexuality, and Ferocity System" (18). And both are in need of "executive
control" (171). Bly's willingness to "grant consciousness" to animals seems
subtly compromised also, as he feels obliged, in discussing the maturation

process of apes and baboons, to follow "Animal adolescents" with "if we can use such a phrase" (45). While it would be wrong to make too much of this example, Bly has, throughout his career, employed much more extravagant diction without offering a disclaimer.

It is tempting to see the Bly of *Iron John* and *The Sibling Society* as an older writer turning conservative like T. S. Eliot or John dos Passos. But this would not be quite accurate. In fact, his self-conscious insistence that he still believes in most of his old liberal positions gives *The Sibling Society* the sense of a book arguing with itself. Perhaps the inconsistencies are simply a measure of the complexity of the problems with which he is grappling and the complexity of consciousness itself. There is a sense that Bly is being drawn from one idea to another in his explorations of gender and intergenerational relationships, and that he is not totally comfortable with the directions taken by his own thought. Perhaps, as with the people depicted in Bly's Vietnam poems, it has not always been possible for Bly to tell to what extent his own perceptions are determined by his society, and how much they reflect the larger, "objective" level inherent in both nature and human "deep mind." He acknowledges the role of social factors in the human psyche, but in the case of his fluctuating and sometimes combative attitude toward women especially, he may be unable to clearly identify and overcome such factors in his own life. Even this is consistent with poems such as "Cornpicker Poem," in which an unconscious violence permeates everyday activities. Jungian psychology offers methods of detecting such "projections," but their ramifications concerning the poet's ability to reach an "objective" deep consciousness remain troubling. Even if it is granted that an "indisputable signified" can be apprehended in the natural world, how can that apprehension be separated from the personal and societal levels of consciousness that Bly acknowledges as coexisting with the "deep mind"? Put another way, when is a Wild Man telling, in an absolute sense, the truth?

Bly's long-term interest in psychology indicates considerable struggling on his part to come to grips with his own psychological complexities, as does his poetic depiction of individuals whose perceptions have been distorted by societal factors. Perhaps his penchant for adopting new models of consciousness and new descriptions of what poetry does constitutes a tacit admission that, in the final analysis, consciousness refuses to be pinned down from within. In "The Poet," Emerson proposes that poetry is a series of tentative intuitions, one leading to the next but none containing more than a fleeting and provisional hold on essential truth:

> But the quality of the imagination is to flow, and not to freeze. The poet did not stop at the color or the form, but read their meaning; neither may he rest in this meaning, but he makes the same objects exponents of his new thought. Here is the difference betwixt the poet and the mystic, that the last nails a symbol to one sense, which was a true sense for a moment, but soon becomes old and false. For all symbols are fluxional; all language is vehicular and transitive, and is good, as ferries and horses are, for conveyance, not as farms and houses are, for homestead.   (136)

Likewise for Bly, writing is an exploratory process. Bly's scientific borrowings, such as the "three brains theory," as well as the myths he has fostered and popularized, whether of the Great Mother or the Wild Man, seem basically intended as agents of psychic readjustment and may best be understood as provisional alignments and "entities." The "fluxional" character of Bly's explorations may leave him open at times to his own and his society's prejudices, but it also allows, or even requires, him to periodically revise his ideas, as he has done in both poetry and prose throughout his career.

Like Emerson, Bly is convinced that poetry, and the poetic image in particular, which can function as a bridge between worlds, at least potentially can provide access to a kind of unquestioned reality underlying or enveloping both natural and social realms. Although his increasing interest in myth and psychology has led him away from the more ostensibly nature-oriented subject matter of his early work, he still maintains, at the center, that poetry's authenticity and its "wildness" derive from the same source, which is both individual and communal, private and public. In "Fifty Males Sitting Together," for example, what Bly typically calls a "wound" occurs in a dysfunctional family, in which "the woman stays in the kitchen" (27), and when her husband comes home drunk, "Then she serves him / food in silence" (31–32).[15] However, the "wound" can also be found in "the woods clear cut for lumber" (1), where the "few young pines" that "lit up" (2) the scene, and the reeds, which

. . . stand about in groups
unevenly as if they might
finally ascend
to the sky all together!"   (17–20),

parallel the son's incandescent but isolated ascent, in which he

goes outdoors to feed with wild
things, lives among dens
and huts, eats distance and silence;
he grows long wings, enters the spiral, ascends.   (36–39)

Significantly, the son's retreat into the wilderness and his "feed[ing] with wild / things" leave him isolated, "far . . . from working men" (40), unable to join the "males" because he has not earned, or been initiated into, their company. In his discussion of prose nature writers, Fritzell distinguishes between a fundamentally naive and escapist reliance on nature as a realm free of human concerns and responsibilities and a more complex, self-conscious awareness of the nonhuman as intertwined with the human, even with the personal. In "Fifty Males Sitting Together," the individual son's inability to advance beyond the initial escape, to reach the "males," who are both natural shadows and cultural emanations, is an inevitable consequence of his personal and familial isolation. As in "Cornpicker Poem," the quality of the human relationship with the nonhuman is inevitably tied to the everyday relationships within the family.

Referring to Bly's article "Five Decades of Modern American Poetry," Harry Williams concludes that "Bly would require the poet's imagination to operate in three realms: 'the dark figures of politics, the world of street-cars, and the ocean world'" (164).[16] In "Fifty Males Sitting Together," Bly addresses environmental politics, family sociology, and the possibilities and limitations inherent in the solitude of wilderness.

According to Deborah Baker, Bly has been evolving a sense of community ever since he journeyed to Norway and saw his relatives living in a supportive and enduring social and natural matrix. Like the Bleies' farm, Bly's poetry depends on nature as its foundation. To Bly, poetic language rises from the earth to blend individual experience with social vision. At least twice, in the 1960s and currently, Bly has brought his poetry to the attention of a large and varied audience of his contemporaries. Bly has been accused, by Susan Faludi and Dana Gioia, for example, of repackaging himself as a way of courting celebrity.[17] There is some justice in this criticism, but it should also be noted that, unlike many who have achieved contemporary celebrity status, Bly has done so through a lifelong dedication to serious art and difficult issues. He has built a position from which a contemporary poet can address a varied audience on public concerns, among them the crucial, threatened viability of the environment, the connection between social and environmental issues, and the essential role the nonhuman plays in the continued ability of the human mind to understand itself.

4 · Gary Snyder

Gary Snyder, Nature, and Science

IN CONTRAST TO Bly, no poet seems more obviously appropriate for this study than Gary Snyder. Snyder is an advocate for wild nature who grapples with the attempt to carefully study while at the same time experience membership in that vast system. Snyder's selected poems is entitled *No Nature*. As he indicates in the preface, the title is meant to suggest "*know* nature," while admitting that nature cannot be held at a distance and understood. "The greatest respect we can pay to nature," he concludes, "is not to trap it, but to acknowledge that it eludes us and that our own nature is also fluid, open, and conditional" (v).

Like Bly and Berry, Snyder acknowledges the formative role of place in shaping his work and his experience. Snyder's sensibility owes as much to the Cascade Mountains and Sierra Nevada as it does to his immersion in Asian culture and his associations with the Beat movement and San Francisco Renaissance. Snyder recognizes this in the preface to *No Nature*, in which his acknowledgments include "the old growth forests of the far west" and "the snowy peaks of the Pacific crest" (v).

Following Thoreau, who went to Walden Pond "to front only the essential facts of life, and see if I could not learn what it had to teach" (*Walden* 90), Snyder has sought in his early wilderness experiences and in his current life in the Sierra forest a solid base from which to explore his own existence and his connections with other creatures, along with the myth systems of various human cultures. Max Oelschlaeger follows George Sessions and Bill

Devall in applying the term "spiritual ecology" (261) to describe Snyder's exploration of the natural world, which enlists approaches ranging from the science of ecology to the religious and spiritual teachings of Native Americans and, of course, his own Buddhist beliefs. Devall himself notes Snyder's charge to "those who write poetry to experience their place deeply before writing" (75). If Gioia hails Jeffers as the "unchallenged laureate of environmentalists" (49), then Snyder is, according to Oelschlaeger, the "Poet Laureate of Deep Ecology" (261).

For Snyder, poetry can function as a way of probing the natural world that surrounds and incorporates any society or national organization that humans might attempt to build. Thus, Snyder's poetry, although as individual as any contemporary poetry in the sense that its usual subject is Snyder himself in his various activities, jobs, beliefs, and surroundings, is more expansively outward-directed than that of most of his contemporaries, embracing what Molesworth calls the "indisputable signified," the natural world encompassing and sustaining all human experience. Even with the richness of natural history detail and scientific theory, though, the human presence, the individual presence of the poet himself, is characteristically seen as a part of the net of associations. For example, "Pine Tree Tops" from *Turtle Island* consists mostly of observations of a natural landscape. As in many of the *Turtle Island* poems, "Pine Tree Tops" features unorthodox punctuation. There is only one "human" detail in the poem, the boots creaking, isolated between two periods as if to separate the human from the natural surroundings:

> . . . sky, frost, starlight.
> the creak of boots.
> rabbit tracks, deer tracks.   (6–8)

But the division is artificial, perhaps illusory, as the lack of a capital at the beginning of the line suggests. Syntactically, "the creak of boots" is no more a separate unit than "starlight," and the content of the line itself seems to link naturally to the following "rabbit tracks, deer tracks." Finally, a period replaces the expected question mark at the end of the final line, "what do we know" (9), perhaps implying that, although there may be many things that we do not know, the things in the poem, the physical, natural details, provide a solid base from which to ask the question, a ground against which to test potential answers.

Snyder's placing the human presence in the natural scene may seem Wordsworthian, and Snyder has, at times, acknowledged the English Romantics as an influence on him. Steuding considers Snyder's focus to be the key difference between Snyder and traditional Romantic poets (37–38). While the focus of the Romantics, and of the self-absorbed contemporary poets criticized by Alan Williamson, is phenomenological, concerned with the imagining self in its encounter with the world, Snyder seems equally interested in the surrounding environment encountering the self or, on a larger scale, the society. The human presence is not needed to complete or ennoble the scene but rather provides the necessary perspective from which the human experience derives its meaning. As with Jeffers, the natural world provides the real context for Snyder's own experience as well as for human mythic and philosophical systems. Like nature in Jeffers's poetry, Snyder's nature puts the human in perspective. As a contemporary poet, Snyder remains aware that "what is 'real' is only the poet's own variation of it" (40), but he is also convinced that "poets *could* get closer to a realistic depiction or a re-creation of nature" (40). Certainly, a poem like "Pine Tree Tops" illustrates Snyder's practice of close observation of the nonhuman, as well as his grappling with the notion of an underlying reality, with the final line of the poem serving both as an unanswerable question and a statement of faith.

The contemporary individual perspective allows Snyder, like Roethke and Berry, to demonstrate that "Our relation to the natural world takes place in a *place,* and it must be grounded in information and experience" (*Practice* 39). Nordström links the regional awareness he finds in Snyder, as well as in Roethke and William Stafford, to the shift from Modernist to contemporary poetics, viewing it "as a rejection of some of the tenets of the Modernist movement in poetry, especially perhaps those of T. S. Eliot and Ezra Pound emphasizing the subordination of the poet to the general flow of the Occidental literary tradition" (148). Accordingly, Snyder's poetry, though often set geographically near that of Jeffers, replaces Jeffers's sweeping impersonal panoramas with close descriptions of both the natural surroundings and the poet's own everyday activities, as in "Mid-August at

Sourdough Mountain Lookout" from *Riprap*. Like Jeffers, Snyder speaks from an elevated vantage point, "Looking down for miles / Through high still air" (9–10), and also like Jeffers, he rejects human society. But for Snyder the dismissal is more personal, involving "a few friends" (7) left stranded behind one of the poem's rare periods. And despite the elevated setting, the poem occupies itself with ordinary, common subjects, like the weather, and activities ("Drinking cold snow-water from a tin cup"; 8), and the poem's imagery seems near at hand, with closely observed details such as glistening pitch and newly emerged insects.

As is the case with Jeffers, Snyder's perspective is influenced and informed by the natural sciences. Earlier, I noted Snyder's linking of intelligence with the biological concept of biomass. Physics is important in Snyder's *Regarding Wave* (36). Patrick Murphy notes that Snyder uses the natural sciences to provide a literal level of meaning corresponding to a symbolic or metaphorical level; Snyder's wave imagery "accurately depicts the wave/particle relationship of matter, as well as images a Buddhist conception of human life as a particular turbulence in the energy flow" (*Understanding* 98). Like Jeffers, Snyder sees empirical observation, with the resulting awareness of what Elder calls "the energy of the nonhuman" (35), as an antidote for the isolated self-involvement of human consciousness. Thus, in "What You Should Know to Be a Poet" from *Regarding Wave*, Snyder advises readers to discover

> all you can about animals as persons.
> the names of trees and flowers and weeds.
> names of stars, and the movements of the planets
> and the moon.   (1–4)

Elder finds a Jeffers-like use of natural science in the poem "Toward Climax" from *Turtle Island*, although Snyder's placing himself among the poem's "we" differs from Jeffers's tendency to remove himself from the evolutionary process being described. Snyder's tone is also different from that of Jeffers. According to Elder, "Snyder offers to our perplexed present the augmenting perspective of science, in an effort to set human history in a larger, and more hopeful, perspective than modern culture has usually achieved" (187). In fact, the poem's first section reports in considerable detail the evolution of the human species, from its beginnings in the "cell mandala holding water" (1.2) to the "brain size blossoming / on the balance of the neck" (1.15–16). The evolution of culture eventually leads, in the poem, to a stage in which people

forget wild plants, their virtues
lose dream-time
lose largest size of brain.   (1.49–51)

Still, the overall evolutionary direction continues, as the title suggests, "Toward Climax." The poem ends with "Two Logging Songs" illustrating two ways of considering old-growth forests.[1] The first of these songs makes a Bly-like comparison between the clear-cutting of a forest and the "harvesting" of people in the Vietnam War, but the second song, the poem's conclusion, leaves the forest "Stable; at / Climax" (4 "Virgin" 5–6). That this, too, is called a "logging song" suggests that the "clear-cutting phase" can be seen as an unstable, temporary stage not only in the forest's evolution but in human evolution as well.

Similarly, in "Bubbs Creek Haircut" from *Mountains and Rivers without End,* Snyder, like Jeffers, finds in his distanced perspective a means to understanding, as "the crazy web of wavelets makes sense / seen from high above" (76–77). Thomas Lyon links Snyder and Jeffers as poets of "ecological vision" ("Ecological" 36), as does Steuding, who adds that "Snyder's conception of life is nonhumanistic; for man is not seen as the center of the universe" (89). Nordström concludes that, for Snyder, "The dedication to pursuing an awareness and understanding of the natural order sometimes leads to a radical questioning, much in the spirit of Robinson Jeffers, of the actual importance of man within the ecological system" (132). Still, the act of questioning, for Snyder as for Jeffers, reveals the essential harmony of natural processes viewed on a large scale. Thus, in "Toward Climax," into which Snyder compresses an entire evolutionary history of humanity, the poet discovers that, in a line echoing the Navajo "beautyway" ceremony, "science walks in beauty" (3.1).[2]

As Elder notes, this line "sums up much in Gary Snyder's poetry" (192), particularly regarding the tendency of the poet to focus on the "edge" where culture and nature meet. In "Toward Climax," for example, biological evolution shades into the evolution of culture so that the two are not easily separated ("tough skin—good eyes—sharp ears— / move in bands";

1.17–18). Snyder's evolutionary linking of nature and culture approaches sociobiology, but his interrogation of the scientific method itself shows that he sees science as one of many interacting means of understanding; his view of the relationship between nature and culture is synergistic and ecological, rather than deterministic. In the "Points for a New Nature Poetics" listed in "Unnatural Writing," Snyder urges nature poets to "fear not science," but also to "go further with science—into awareness of the problematic and contingent aspects of so-called objectivity" (*Place* 172).

The merging of objective and subjective elements recalls nonfiction nature writing. Snyder acknowledges his early exposure to natural history writers. Bert Almon notes that Ernest Thompson Seton was an early influence on Snyder (6), and Snyder himself, in David Kherdian's *Six Poets of the San Francisco Renaissance,* calls Seton "the biggest probable childhood influence on me" (47). *Myths and Texts* includes a lineated quotation from John Muir (Steuding 87). Snyder's many borrowings from Thoreau include the title of an essay, "Tawny Grammar," Thoreau's translation of the Spanish *gramatica parda.* In "Ancient Forests of the Far West," Snyder refers to Aldo Leopold's maxim, "think like a mountain" (*Practice* 118).

But Snyder's similarity to prose nature writers extends beyond influences and echoes. Like Fritzell's self-conscious natural history writers, Snyder takes his scientifically informed perspective into the field of day-to-day individual experience. In doing so, Snyder's route parallels that of the other poets in this study. Like Bly, Snyder associates the wilderness with the human unconscious, "the other—both the inner and the outer" (*Practice* 179), and sees the Romantic movement's discovery of wild nature as "a reaction against formalistic rationalism and enlightened despotism" (80).[3] As Roethke did, Snyder claims an innate "immediate, intuitive, deep sympathy with the natural world which was not taught me by anyone" (*Real* 92). Snyder sees individual experience as a legitimate source of knowledge about nature because, like Bly, he believes that a person's relationship to the natural world goes beyond the level of the subjective personality to an underlying objective level. On that level, "Our nature is no particular nature; look out across the beach at the gulls. For an empty moment while their soar and cry enters your heart like sunshaft through water, you are that, totally. We do this every day. So this is the aspect of mind that gives art, style, and self-transcendence to the inescapable human plantedness in a social and ecological nexus" (*He* x). As it does for Aldo Leopold, this sense of experience in the natural world as common foundation provides Snyder with a shared basis for meaning and a ground for communication. Charles Altieri says that "One might even claim that Snyder is preeminent among the literary figures concerned with ecology because he has developed a lyric style which itself embodies a mode of consciousness leading to a state of balance and symbiotic interrelationship between man and his environment" ("Gary" 48).

This ecological grounding is reflected in both the subject matter and style of Snyder's poems. His attempt to uncover meaning in nature and to develop a poetic style that reflects that meaning is informed by his knowledge of science and by the work of nature writers such as Thoreau and Muir. But his exploration remains largely individual, based on the particulars of his own experience. In the preface to *Myths & Texts,* Snyder says that he "set out, like everyone else, to make sense, and to find somehow a way to actually 'belong to the land'" (viii).

Snyder's style of communicating the meaning he finds can be seen as "ecological" in that it locates the experiencing human being as one element in a web of interdependent organisms and relationships. Unlike other poets who have developed a similar view of poetry, the Black Mountain poets, for example, Snyder has kept enough distance from his own net of associations to preserve something of Jeffers's sense of distanced perspective.[4] Marta Sienicka discusses the projectivist, or Black Mountain, poets as, like Snyder, nonhumanistic and ecological, asserting that, to a projectivist poet, "human consciousness is merely an aspect of the over-all life-energy and participates in the universal processes by essentially instantaneous, fleeting but continuous experience of the outside phenomenal world" (22). This experience is to Charles Olson, by its very nature, "unselected" (22). The emphasis on the participatory nature of human consciousness to the exclusion of the observing, separate aspect of it does, Sienicka says, result in a solipsistic poetry (95), although she asserts that, ultimately, "the projectivist vision of man and world is carried on both individual and communal levels" (99). Snyder, in developing what both Thomas Lyon and Charles Altieri describe as an ecological style, never commits himself completely to Olson's "unselected" experience, as this would be inconsistent with his idea of poetry's purpose. In poems such as "Toward Climax," Snyder turns toward a more or less objective view of human evolutionary history. And in "Foxtail Pine," he does not allow his struggle to come to grips with his own categorizing ("—what am I doing saying 'foxtail pine'?"; 23) to prevent him from observing, in a detached "objective" way, the various features of the tree's physical makeup.

As with Jeffers, the detached perspective of natural science gives Snyder a place from which he can formulate and communicate ideas based on field observations, as in "Foxtail Pine," and more theoretical concepts, as in "Toward Climax." In an interview included in *The Real Work,* Snyder tells Gene Fowler that the poet can "call the society's attention to its ecological relationships in nature," which is especially necessary in a society that "doesn't see its position in nature" (4). In another interview in the same collection, one with *Road Apple* editor Doug Flaherty, Snyder says that a poem can remind a person that "My God, I'm living in the world!" (19). Seen in this light, the details in "Foxtail Pine" provide this kind of reminder of the physical qualities of "the world."

The erotic sensuality of poems such as "The Bath" is one way in which the poet locates the reader within the real, physical world. In "Song of the Taste," Snyder combines sensuality with the language of science. The relationship of the materials of the poetry to Snyder's actual experience and the fact that Snyder, even more than Bly, is a recognizable presence in his poems constitute other methods of locating the reader within a recognizable physical world.

By including himself as an active participant in his poems' content and process, Snyder reflects more skepticism than Jeffers about the ability to assume an objective viewpoint and is more in line with Fritzell's concept of the self-conscious nature writer. Thomas Lyon finds Snyder's poetry "fundamentally nondualistic" ("Twenty" 46). Snyder himself differentiates between what might be termed essential and practical senses of nature. Near the beginning of *The Practice of the Wild,* he says that "The physical universe and all its properties—I would prefer to use the word *nature* in this sense. But it will come up meaning 'the outdoors' or 'other-than-human' sometimes even here" (9).

Like Jeffers and Bly, Snyder recognizes the human tendency toward self-absorption, which he says, in an interview with Julia Martin, "you don't have to encourage" (167). Considering nature as "other," as a "thou" to contrast with "I," in Martin Buber's terminology, offers Snyder an antidote for excessive self-awareness. On the other hand, Snyder also criticizes the tendency of American society to divide things into "just a 'self' and the 'world,'" a division that fails to recognize "that grandparents, grammar, pets, friends, lovers, children, tools, the poems and songs we remember, are what we *think with*" (*Practice* 60). Snyder therefore finds himself, like Fritzell's self-conscious nature writers, seeking a position at once objective and subjective, experiential as well as cultural or public.

Snyder and the Purpose of Poetry

Along with Robert Bly and, particularly, Wendell Berry, Gary Snyder has long been concerned with the purpose of poetry. In *Turtle Island,* which won the Pulitzer Prize for 1975, he finishes the poem "I Went into the Maverick Bar" by leaving the Farmington, New Mexico, saloon where he has been swept into the "stupidity" (20) of unexamined American life, at which point

> I came back to myself,
>   To the real work, to
>   "What is to be done."   (25–27)

That "What is to be done" is directly related to his work as a poet is borne out later, in the prose "Plain Talk" section of the book, in which he asserts that as a poet he is someone who, devoted to the Muse, "the voice of nature herself" (107), can "be a spokesman for a realm that is not usually represented either in intellectual chambers or in the chambers of government" (106). Snyder's belief in the centrality of this role is shown by his claim that "At the root of the problem where our civilization goes wrong is the mistaken notion that nature is something less than authentic, that nature is not as alive as man is, or as intelligent, that in a sense it is dead, and that animals are of so low an order of intelligence and feeling, we need not take their feelings into account" (107).

Snyder's view of poetry as having an important (if neglected) cultural purpose recalls the major projects of Modern poets Ezra Pound and William Carlos Williams. Pound's sense of public purpose is evidenced by the epic quality of his major work, *The Cantos,* by his singular presence in advancing and defining his entire generation of poets, and by his tragic role as a political figure. Williams, whose *Paterson* also has epic characteristics, strikes a particularly resonant note in relation to Snyder when he claims in "Caviar and Bread Again: A Warning to the New Writer" that "On the poet devolves the most vital function of society: to recreate it—the collective world—in times of stress, in a new mode" (*Selected* 103). This sense of high, collective purpose is understandably rare in contemporary poetry. Preordained notions of a poem's content and purpose are inconsistent with "a poetics of immediacy" (Breslin 70) based on the individual's exploration of unfolding experience, which is why William Stafford finds "intention" dangerous to art (qtd. in Nordström 115). Although much of Snyder's poetry, in accordance with Breslin's definition of contemporary poetry, may be grounded "in a sharply observed physical present" (60), it is more difficult to consider as "contemporary" Snyder's idea of the poet in service to the Muse, since, according to Breslin, contemporary "Poetic authority was located not in the cultural tradition but in the literal reality of a physical moment" (60).

Snyder believes that poets and other artists, having access to traditions dating back to French cave paintings and Pueblo dances (*Turtle* 108–9), must be instrumental in developing a way to "incorporate the other people— what the Sioux Indians called the creeping people, and the standing people, and the flying people, and the swimming people—into the councils of government" (108). Snyder believes that this ability of ancient artists to take "it on themselves to interpret, through their humanity, what these other life-forms were" (109) is both spiritual and political, individual and public. In his 1990 *TriQuarterly* interview with Martin, Snyder discusses the function of art in regulating the relationship between human beings and their environment. "Don't imagine that we're doing ecological politics to save the world," he concludes. "We're doing ecological politics to save ourselves, to save our souls" (161–62).

Snyder seeks to describe the natural world not only as he experiences it but as others might experience it also. In fact, Snyder recognizes the theoretical possibility that the arts in general and poetry in particular can be useful in maintaining or altering the way in which nature is experienced. Coupled with his concern for the environment, this sense leads Snyder to an anthropological and instrumental view of poetry's purpose, anthropological in that it recognizes that purpose from an etic, or distanced, perspective.

Anthropologists distinguish between the *etic* perspective of the objective observer and the *emic* perspective of the group member. It should be noted, though, that among anthropologists, neither perspective is considered complete in and of itself, and there is considerable debate about whether a truly etic perspective is even possible. Snyder, however, finds that the study of other cultures provides alternative models—sometimes directly applicable, other times useful for analogy—particularly of different ways in which people can react to the natural environments in which they live. Bioregionalism drawing on these models, if deeply incorporated into everyday life, could provide modern Americans with a "depth ecology" system for regulating and correcting attitudes and actions. Similarly, for Snyder, involvement in Zen Buddhism has provided an alternative to the Judeo-Christian tradition in which "The kings of Israel began to cut down the sacred groves and the Christians finished the job" (*Practice* 80): in other words, in which wild nature and the idea of the sacred became not only divergent but antithetical. This, for Snyder as well as for Bly, creates a dangerous and wrong-headed notion that nature is deficient or "fallen." Questions remain, however, as to whether a culture as a whole can intentionally adopt information gathered from an etic perspective to alter its own emic sense of reality, and to what extent this information itself is dependent on its cultural context.

Snyder's interest in what he calls "depth ecology," defined as the use of "myth or folklore or shamanic constructions" to fine-tune "the way you treat creatures" (Martin 162), dates back at least to the "Hunting" section of *Myths & Texts*, in which he considers the perceived rupture that occurs when a hunter kills prey. Several of the "Hunting" poems are titled as dedications, and those dedicated to deer ("this poem is for deer") and bear ("this poem is for bear") acknowledge the sacrifice made when one life-form serves as food for another. In depicting a response to the animal as a "person," Snyder illustrates an imaginative atonement for or healing of the perceived transgression by recasting it as a gesture on the part of the eaten animal, in a manner based on Native American traditions:

Deer don't want to die for me.
    I'll drink sea-water
Sleep on beach pebbles in the rain
Until the deer come down to die
        in pity for my pain.   ("this poem is for deer" 47–51)

Snyder believes that literature can, or at least should, as Wendell Berry says, "affect, even in practical ways, the life of a place" (*What Are* 84). Accordingly, taken as a whole, his poems are a compendium of instructive, sometimes practical, information. His early book *Riprap* begins with a definition of "riprap" as "a cobble of stone laid on steep slick rock to make a trail for horses in the mountains." Typical of Snyder is his valuing of physical work, not only for the effort involved but for the practical result as well. And if the poems themselves are considered as riprap, as the title and accompanying definition invite and as the poem "Riprap" makes explicit, then they have an implied pragmatism, not only for the writer but also for anyone who may come across them. In "Riprap," the reader, as well as the composing poet, is asked to "Lay down these words / Before your mind like rocks" (1–2).

In the *"Road Apple* Interview," Snyder considers the poems of *Riprap*, along with those of *The Back Country,* as having "at least one level that people can get into right away" (*Real* 20). Molesworth, in *Gary Snyder's Vision,* links the deceptively simple form of many of Snyder's poems with the contemporary rejection of "the autotelic, formalist solution which said that only strictly structural and technical criteria should determine the worth of a poem" (105–6). The rejection of the primary or exclusive value of a poem's technical mastery constitutes a questioning of the New Critical assumption of the strictly aesthetic nature of poetry's purpose. By contrast, Molesworth quotes Michael Oakeschott's claim in *The Voice of Poetry in the Conversation of Mankind* that poetry freed from practical ends is a "comparatively new and still unassimilated experience" and notes Snyder's assertion in *The Real Work* that a practical end for poetry has traditionally been the transmission of cultural lore (*Gary* 10).

In Snyder's poetry, this "lore" takes two forms, corresponding to the two types of poems discussed in the *"Road Apple* Interview": the first type being the "objectivist," easily accessible poems such as those in *Riprap* and *The*

Back Country; the second being the more encompassing poems, such as those in *Myths & Texts* and *Mountains and Rivers without End,* in which his goal is "working with myths and symbols and ideas. Working with old traditions and insights" (*Real* 20). In his introduction to *The Real Work,* William Scott McLean also divides Snyder's poems into two general categories. The first type is the object or objective poem, typically a "short lyric that pushes up against an edge of silence" (xii). Typical of this type of poem, which Steuding also considers to be objective (42), are the lyrics in *Riprap* and *The Back Country.* McLean characterizes Snyder's other mode as "the long poem that begins in the everyday world but then spirals up from that area, working on more mythological and archetypal levels" (xii–xiii). Though this classification system becomes problematical when applied to a work like *Turtle Island,* Snyder has at least in spirit endorsed the division himself.

Snyder, however, sees his more mythic poetry as less direct, but no less practical, than the *Riprap*-style lyrics. Poetry dealing with archetypes, says Snyder, is a way of "getting at people's dreams about a century before it actually effects historical change" (qtd. in Nordström 156). As Molesworth indicates, "To the extent poetry transmits value it has practical ends, however deferred or remote" (*Gary* 10).

Earlier, I noted Nordström's observation that an increasingly didactic strain has developed over time in Snyder's poetry, which he attributes to Snyder's growing awareness of his position as what William Stafford calls a "leader-spokesman poet" (qtd. in Nordström 115). Snyder's response is that he has always seen instruction as one of poetry's traditional options and duties and "as a continuance, as biological almost" (qtd. in Nordström 138).

If Snyder, like Jeffers, sees poetry's purpose as including the didactic, a necessarily public function, his contemporary individuality is reflected in the way in which he appears in his poems and in the kind of relationship he assumes with his readers. In poems like "I Went into the Maverick Bar," Snyder appears as the central "character," and it is understood that the reader will recognize him. Snyder's long hair serves as a kind of counterculture badge in the poem. But when Snyder leaves the Maverick Bar to return to "What is to be done" (27), the reader is able to identify the speaker not only as a "hippie" but as Snyder himself and therefore to have a reasonably specific idea of what is meant by "What is to be done." The reader is treated as a confidant of Snyder's, and a Whitmanesque camaraderie is expected to link reader and writer.

As with Whitman, however, the role of "Snyder as Snyder" in his poems is complicated by other dimensions that his "character" assumes. For example, Murphy demonstrates that the haircut in "Bubbs Creek Haircut" from *Mountains and Rivers without End* also suggests the traditional ritual of head shaving practiced by Buddhist acolytes, and that even the presence in the poem of the first-person autobiographical narrator reflects the Japanese Noh tradition, which Snyder had thought of as a structuring model for *Mountains and Rivers without End* (*Understanding* 67). That Snyder's Whitmanesque camaraderie is linked to his sense of the essentially social function of poetry as well as to the individualistic "real life" focus of contemporary poets is attested to in "The Landscape of Consciousness" interview in *The Real Work,* in which Snyder asserts "the importance of a sense of community, a need for the poet to identify with *real* people, not a faceless audience" (5). Snyder has long been convinced that "poetry is a communal, social, human thing," and that poems are not really to be read "all by yourself with a dictionary in hand, but are something to be excitedly enjoyed in a group, and be turned on by," as he states in a panel discussion with Lew Welch and Philip Whalen (*On Bread* 13).

The specific audience Snyder has in mind is a kind of primitivist subculture that he sees as underlying and undercutting the current social order, a "tribe" that shares his dissatisfaction with the current "backwards" (*Practice* 37) and ultimately self-destructive society, and for which Snyder's blending of Buddhist philosophy and Native American attitudes toward nature seems logical and appropriate. Like Bly, Snyder connects Western civilization's estrangement from its natural environment with "The line of thought that is signified by the names of Descartes, Newton and Hobbes," featuring "a profound rejection of the organic world" (18–19). According to Snyder, "We need a civilization that can live fully and creatively together with wildness. We must start growing it right here, in the New World" (6).

For Snyder, poets and poetry are potential instruments toward that end. As noted earlier, Snyder has been criticized for his assumption that poetry is instrumental, or at least for the poetry that results from that assumption. Steuding defends Snyder from critics who object to his "'use' of poetry and the function of the poet to attain social ends" (160). As Alan Williamson observes, Snyder sees himself as a potential leader in a radical revision of his society: "In the face of the disasters likely to ensue from growing populations increasingly dependent on fossil fuel or nuclear technology, Snyder has presented himself as spokesman for a 'great Subculture' which, throughout history, has periodically reinvented the small community, based on directly affectionate bonds between the members and a sense of affectionate interdependence with the environment, as an alternative to the efficient order of the State" (73–74).

Snyder himself goes even further. Like Berry in *The Unsettling of America*, he finds the "efficiency" of large abstract social orders to be illusory, neglecting as they do the particular natural and social exigencies of specific localities. In his essay "The Place, the Region, and the Commons" from *The Practice of the Wild*, Snyder notes that "The world of culture and nature, which is actual, is almost a shadow world now, and the insubstantial world of political jurisdictions and rarefied economies is what passes for reality. We live in a backwards time" (37). As Williamson observes, Snyder's own attempt to foster this "small community" is inherent in the way in which he "mingles a somewhat Thoreauvian poetic treatment of the psychic value of simplification . . . with direct social advocacy in prose" (74). Probably the most obvious example of this strategy is *Turtle Island*, which combines poems with brief but detailed instructional essays, designed to foster philosophical and political change.

In Snyder's view, poetry can speak not just for neglected human constituencies but even for nature itself. In *Turtle Island*, he calls the wilderness "my constituency" (106). And in "Knots in the Grain," he asserts that "My political position is to be a spokesman for wild nature. I take that as a primary constituency. And for the people who live in dependence on that, the people for whom the loss of that would mean the loss of their livelihood" (*Real* 49). In "Civilization" from *Regarding Wave*, Snyder intends to speak for both wild nature and the human livelihoods dependent on it. This poem, though, illustrates a potentially significant problem with Snyder's concept of his constituency. When speaking for indigenous people, Snyder himself is not a member of the group he represents—rather, he belongs to the group that he implicitly condemns, "those . . . people who do complicated things" (1). Snyder's attitude toward his own culture is therefore at least reminiscent of, if not directly analogous to, Jeffers's attitude toward artists in particular and humanity in general. From an anthropological standpoint, Snyder is assuming an emic perspective in a culture of which he is not a member and is neglecting his own emic perspective, or how his own culture has formed his attitude toward the people he seeks to represent. Snyder addresses this problem by keeping the indigenous people here general, so that he represents not a particular group but a "class" of people, who in turn form part of the cross-cultural primitivist "tribe" in which Snyder and the world's indigenous peoples share a kind of membership.

Snyder's interest and background in anthropology is an important source of his belief in poetry's purposiveness. Anthropologists are trained to view cultural artifacts and customs from an objective perspective, theoretically allowing them to examine other cultures as functioning systems. Snyder studied anthropology at Reed College and Indiana University and has published his Reed College thesis, an analysis of a Haida myth, as *He Who Hunted Birds in His Father's Village*. His experience with anthropology reflects and has heightened his interest in other cultures, particularly Native American cultures. Snyder's formal and informal anthropological studies have been instrumental in his honing his sense of poetry as myth, which in turn is defined as "functionally, the verbal equivalent of ritual" (107), and which "provides a symbolic representation of projected values and empirical knowledge within a framework of belief which relates individual, group, and physical environment, to the end of integration and survival" (111).[5]

The anthropological approach has also opened Snyder to charges of cultural imperialism, since anthropology attempts to extract the "truth" behind a people's beliefs and lifeways by applying an "objective" Western method of understanding. Snyder himself acknowledges that "Anthropological curiosity only occurs if you are a member of an expanding civilization" (*Place* 132). The appropriative potential of anthropology has perhaps actually been heightened by Snyder's belief in the practical application of information gathered from other cultures. But Snyder's sense of practicality extends to anthropology itself. In "The Politics of Ethnopoetics," Snyder acknowledges that as an anthropology student he was taught to passively accept the destruction of "traditional cultures" as a consequence of "an almost automatic melting-pot process of assimilation" (134–35). He has since come to believe, however, that anthropology can serve to augment a studied people's sense of identity. Moreover, he echoes Jack Stauder's claim that anthropologists "should be able to teach members of an oppressed culture the dynamics of imperialism and useful economic understanding, insofar as they want to learn it" (133). Finally, Snyder argues the "positive side" of "going into other people's cultures and bringing back their poems and publishing them," as "simply this. . . . An expansionist imperialist culture feels most comfortable when it is able to believe that the people it is exploiting are somehow less than human. When it begins to get some kind of feedback that these people might be human beings like themselves, exploitation becomes increasingly difficult" (138–39).

In keeping with his populist sentiments and his concept of poetry's essential practicality, Snyder believes that "academic" contemporary poetry has failed to make itself available and important to its audience. In "Poetry, Community, Climax," he criticizes the idea that "poetry cannot have an audience" (*Real* 163). In *He Who Hunted Birds in His Father's Village,* Snyder links contemporary poetry's perceived irrelevance with the loss of its mythic function, quoting Philip Wheelwright's assertion that "The poetry of our time doesn't matter much, it is a last echo of something important that was alive long ago" (111). In short, to be valued as a vehicle for myth, poetry must address itself to the entire culture. It must be experienced as "magic" (111) and not be exclusively for the detached, professional perusal of specialists. In acting on such a judgment, Snyder must sacrifice his etic "objectivity." He must internalize what he learns from other peoples and provide some way for his readers to do likewise. By indicating that poetry can cause, or at least prepare people for, "historical change," but only in the distant future, Snyder, in effect, recognizes this problem by applying his findings not to the society in which he lives but rather to the one that he hopes is in the process of developing. In doing so, he necessarily relies on speculation and projections. In "The Place, the Region, and the Commons" from *The Practice of the Wild,* for example, Snyder agrees with a Crow elder whom he quotes as saying, "You know, I think if people stay somewhere long enough—even white people—the spirits will begin to speak to them. It's the power of the spirits coming up from the land. The spirits and the old powers aren't lost, they just need people to be around long enough and the spirits will begin to influence them" (39). Clearly, this requires a leap of faith for most contemporary Americans. It does, however, illustrate Snyder's own belief that Western civilization inevitably must move away from the condition of "a culture that alienates itself from the very ground of its own being" (*Turtle* 106) toward a more located bioregionally defined society or group of societies.

Although Snyder did not become, strictly speaking, an anthropologist, his interest in ethnopoetics and in primal and Asian cultures is pervasive and obvious. Moreover, that anthropology has affected his view of the purpose of poetry is unquestionable, most noticeably in the "mythic" type of Snyder poem, a category in which Snyder himself includes *Myths & Texts* and *Mountains and Rivers without End* and that he characterizes as "working with myths and symbols and ideas. Working with old traditions" (*Real* 20). These poems rely heavily on Native American materials, particularly *Myths & Texts,* in which, according to Nathaniel Tarn, there are "Indians everywhere" (xv). Native American influence is also apparent in *Turtle Island,* which takes its name, as Snyder says in the "Introductory Note," from "the old/new name for the continent, based on many creation myths of the people who have been living here for millennia." *Turtle Island* begins with "Anasazi," which, as Molesworth points out, reads "More like an ethnographic field report than an art-lyric" (*Gary* 94), as it attempts to re-create the lives of people who lived "tucked up in clefts in the cliffs / growing strict fields of corn and beans" (3–4).

Snyder's use of Native American materials has been controversial. He is always careful to apply Indian materials accurately and respectfully. Most observers grant that he is not to be classed with outright exploiters of Indian cultures. He does not, for example, claim membership in a tribe or "Indian blood." And his acknowledgment that he turned to Buddhism because Native American religions were not accessible to non-Indians is well known. Snyder has many supporters, such as Simon Ortiz, among American Indian writers, but questions remain. Some find white use of Indian spirituality to be the ultimate in colonial appropriation. Indian critics have pointed to the irony of Snyder's Indian-influenced *Turtle Island* winning literary prizes while books by real Native Americans are bypassed. More fundamentally, indigenist activists question the validity of any appropriation of Native

American religious materials. One of his harshest critics, Ward Churchill, argues that Snyder is guilty of "proprietary interest in Native spiritual tradition" (319). Churchill notes that Snyder "has won literary awards for the penning of verse in which he pretends to see the world through the eyes of an American Indian 'shaman'" (319), and he applies to such practices Russell Means's assertion that "What's at issue here is the same old question that Europeans have always posed with regard to American Indians, whether what's ours isn't somehow theirs," a question that is "always answered . . . in the affirmative" (qtd. in Churchill 320). In "The Bioregional Ethic," however, Snyder rejects suggestions of this kind from Leslie Silko and Gerald Hobson by asserting that shamanism, the religious tradition on which he has frequently drawn, is universal in its origins and is therefore not the property of any one people (*Real* 154–55). He advances a similar argument in "The Politics of Ethnopoetics," utilizing his familiar expansion of time to suggest that, in its origins, "All poetry is 'our' poetry. Diné poetry, people poetry, Maydy poetry, human being poetry. In the forty-thousand-year timescale, we're one people" (*Place* 141–42).

As egalitarian as it sounds, this response is only partially satisfying. One might well ask to whom the "our" he includes in the quotations above really refers, human beings in general or the members of the exploitative "biosphere cultures" (186), who, as Snyder himself establishes, are the people most likely to exercise this kind of appropriation.[6] Moreover, as William Jungels has demonstrated, Snyder derived the concept of shamanism he employed in *Myths & Texts* primarily from the practices of the Northwest tribes, with whom he shares a geographical affiliation and whom he studied at Reed College (Murphy, *Understanding* 31), and not from a generalized past.

Ultimately, Snyder's belief that bioregional cultural identification is essential leaves him little choice but to turn to Native American history and lifeways, since the inability to identify with a particular place as home is the source of the environmental destruction caused by the United States and other "biosphere cultures." Snyder has occasionally appeared somewhat impatient with his Native American critics. Churchill, for example, quotes Snyder as calling such criticism "absurd in the extreme" (319). Perhaps his reaction reflects resentment based on his sense that his intention has been to honor cultures he genuinely admires, rather than to exploit them. But more fundamentally, if the cultural wisdom of indigenous peoples is off-limits, the practicability of bioregionalism, which holds that healthy life-ways must develop in place through long association with the conditions of a particular environment, is called into question, at least for a white American in North America. And if a bioregional tradition cannot embrace the majority of the continent's current population, the result could be tragic for Native and Euro-American alike and for the continent itself. To his credit, Snyder has always been humble before his Indian sources and has credited contemporary Native American figures as well. He asserts that re-lying on indigenous people creates an obligation to them, so that "The way to express gratitude and respect for these teachings of poetry, music, and song is to join in the work of helping your nearest endangered subsistence society in its struggle against the rape of land and culture" (*Place* 147).

Still, it is not unreasonable to question the ability of a contemporary American poet to speak for indigenous peoples, especially since, like Bly, Snyder sees the arts in the West as suffering from corrupting or co-opting so-cial forces. Under these conditions, there is a certain presumption involved in the poet "speaking for" anyone or anything, including the nonhuman elements of Snyder's "constituency." When Snyder "grants consciousness" to animals, to use Bly's phrase, the gesture implies that consciousness is his to grant, and that he can somehow speak for that consciousness. For ex-ample, in "Jackrabbit" from *Mountains and Rivers without End,* Snyder's assertion that the rabbit knows more about him than he does about it is a little like the case of the person who says that it is the truth that he always lies, since the poem's speaker presumes to know what, or at least how much, the rabbit knows. But such arguments are perhaps necessary absurdities inherent in the power of poetry to make connections between humans and other life forms. Snyder believes that, for historical reasons, poetry retains more of its original essence than other art forms and so is the most readily available and powerful artistic vehicle he can employ in accomplishing the necessary task of speaking for his chosen constituency. In "Poetry and the Primitive" from *Earth House Hold,* he claims that of those human endeav-ors whose "archaic roots" give them "a shared origin with poetry," includ-ing "Music, dance, religion, and philosophy," poetry retains more of this original power than the others, since "the poet can make it on his own voice and mother tongue, while steering a course between crystal clouds of utterly incommunicable non-verbal states—and the gleaming daggers and glittering nets of language" (118).

In addition to expressing the tension between the incommunicable individual, "private" vision and the public voice, and the complexities involved in communicating meaning, Snyder's reference to "the glittering nets of language" reflects his concern that language must be grounded in actual experience and his rejection of artistic autotelism. In general, it is fair to say that, for Snyder, the idea of "language for its own sake" is incompatible with the basic purpose of poetry. After offering and critiquing a deconstructionist analysis of Snyder's idea of the tribe, Molesworth concludes that "Part of Snyder's value as a political visionary rests, I would argue, on his recalling of inescapable realities" (*Gary* 121–22).

Snyder, then, regards the poet as an important, even necessary, figure, in the tradition of Romantic thinkers for whom poets were, according to Shelley, "the unacknowledged legislators of the world" (1087), and recalling, as Williamson says, "our old vision of the poet as world-historical figure" (78). Emerson and Whitman are obvious earlier American exponents of a similar notion of poetry's significance. Snyder's vision of poetry, however, as Williamson goes on to say, is less involved with individual ego than those of his predecessors, since, to Snyder, who envisions a world in which "future poets will write, with less premeditation, for an immediate communal context," the idea of the "major poet" is "a myth fostered by bourgeois competitiveness" (78). Certainly, poems such as "Hay for the Horses" from *Riprap* have an "unpremeditated" flavor, as if the poet were simply recalling an event, unaware that he was writing a poem until it had been completed, just as the subject of the poem realizes that his life story has been completed without his conscious direction. But it is uncertain how, in the present, and especially when working in the individualistic framework of contemporary poetry, a poet can be a "world-historical figure" without developing an "egoistic" persona such as Bly's.

Snyder believes that the kind of awareness that poetry fosters is particularly badly needed as an antidote to the fundamental wrongheadedness of the present society. But Snyder also accepts basic assumptions common to most contemporary poets. Although he sees poetry as communal and collective, embodying the sum experience of the tribe, he shares with other contemporary poets the practice of making the poem's center the specific perspective of the individual. Snyder's individual presence in his poems is complex, leading to Helen Vendler's claim that "he has . . . changed what we consider the lyric self to be" (117). Vendler comments on how Snyder's "riprap" method of composition tends to present a "montage of noun phrases" building a world around an "I" who "prefers to obscure himself" (121). This obscuring is often accomplished by borrowing the Chinese convention of avoiding direct reference to the speaker of the poem, opening up the possibility of multiple points of view, as Murphy shows in his reading of "Mother Earth: Her Whales" (*Understanding* 121). Still, the autobiographical element is always prominent in Snyder's work. Snyder's poems are, in fact, quite personal, though not confessional. His wives, children, and friends are named, and intimate details of their lives are described in poems like "The Bath." Not only are major events in his life (a marriage, for example, or his decision to return to the United States after years of primary residency in Japan) traceable in his books, but the poems in a given book may be arranged to parallel his movements in his life, as Murphy demonstrates in *Understanding Gary Snyder*. Even the stylized landscape of *Mountains and Rivers without End* follows the contours of Snyder's own experience.

In order to fulfill his idea of poetry's purpose, Snyder requires an audience broad enough to be thought of as the "tribe" for which "the poet articulates the semi-known" (*Real* 5). Like other contemporaries, Snyder has found that addressing such a community from an isolated individual perspective is complicated by the poet's resulting lack of a consensually defined public role. Moreover, the peculiarities of Snyder's own experience—his devotion to Buddhism and the primary position of wild nature in his own belief system and lifeways—have made his life anything but typical. It should be noted, however, that, even if his religion may isolate him from usual American life, Snyder himself sees Buddhism as an open alternative or complement to Native American religious traditions. As he says in the "*Road Apple* Interview," although Native American traditions are more community oriented and less monastic, they are mostly designed for the "closed" societies that develop them (*Real* 16–17). Buddhism offers a world religion "in many ways ecological in outlook and orientation" (Steuding 56) and having a "strong nonhumanistic bias" (55). It should also be noted that Asian cultural influences are, in general, more pronounced and familiar in Snyder's West Coast surroundings than elsewhere in the United States. Still, Snyder's way of life is significantly different from that of large segments of his audience, as David Perkins's response to his "strange and wonderful" settings indicates (564).

Snyder has developed various strategies for overcoming the "nontransferable" quality of individual experience in general and of his own experience in particular. In addition to poetry, Snyder has a considerable body of prose publications. In the prose, the eclectic nature of his sources is countered by the simple, direct accessibility of his style. His prose has in fact grown more conventional over the course of his career and more accessible to a wider audience. This stylistic adaptation corresponds, perhaps, to Snyder's developing awareness that the "tribe" or "subculture" for which he intends to speak is no longer recognizable by its outward appearances and manners, as it seemed in 1969, when, in *Earth House Hold*, he addressed himself to the "ab/originals" of "the celebrated human Be-In in San Francisco, January of 1967, [which] was called A Gathering of the Tribes" (103). At that time, Snyder noted that "The number of committed total tribesmen is not so great, but there is a large population of crypto-members who move through many walks of life undetected," and he somewhat naively concluded that the "impact . . . on the cultural and imaginative life of the nation" of the tribes and their activities "is enormous" (104). By 1974, when *Turtle Island* appeared, the "crypto-members" had dispersed so that their recognition as a group had become difficult if not impossible. Snyder responded by listing various enclaves of society that, although not forming any unified whole, were to be "encouraged" as working "through history toward an ecologically and culturally enlightened state of affairs" (100).[7] By 1990, in *The Practice of the Wild*, Snyder focuses on bioregionalism, replacing the notion of a single tribe or subculture with that of various small-scale societies working toward similar ends.

Snyder's changing prose style is evidence of a gradual evolution in his concept of his audience. *Earth House Hold* is a free-form combination of notes, journal entries, and essays, while *The Practice of the Wild* is a recognizable, even conventional, essay collection. Though as a gathering of occasional pieces *A Place in Space* shares something of the structural fluidity of *Earth House Hold*, Snyder himself considers it as "a further exploration of what the 'practice of the wild' would be" (vii). And while both *A Place in Space* and *The Practice of the Wild* may still strike some readers as arcane and idiosyncratic, Snyder reaches out in pieces such as "Ancient Forests of the Far West," in which he couches his bioregionalist message in an account of his life as a lumberjack, giving the essay a strong populist flavor: "Our conservationist-environmentalist moral outrage is often (in its frustration) aimed at the logger or the rancher, when the real power is in the hands of people who make unimaginably larger sums of money, people impeccably groomed, excellently educated at the best universities—male and female alike—eating fine foods and reading classy literature, while orchestrating the investment and legislation that ruin the world" (*Practice* 119).

Despite this stylistic evolution, it would be incorrect to say that Snyder retreated from the basic substance of his ideas in the twenty-three years between *Earth House Hold* and *The Practice of the Wild*. His themes and opinions have been generally consistent and have been reflected in both his prose and his poetry. *Riprap's* "The Late Snow & Lumber Strike of the Summer of Fifty-four" shows the same populist or proletarian strain as "Ancient Forests of the Far West," although the earlier poem does not carry the same openly didactic message as the later essay. In the poem, Snyder's manifest empathy with working people is combined with "utilitarian" pro-sodic technique. Molesworth's contention that Snyder's prosody is often more complex than it appears is evidenced by the poem's trochaic lines with medial caesuras.[8] Still, the straightforward simplicity of the language, em-ploying a bare minimum of poetic figures and no elevated diction or osten-sibly poetic description, gives the poem an overall sense of utility. Moles-worth notes the "use value" of the "economical language of a Snyder poem" (*Gary* 46).

While it is easy to see the language of a poem like "Riprap" or "The Late Snow & Lumber Strike of the Summer of Fifty-four" as both eco-nomical and utilitarian, the same could be said for the language of the more "mythic" poems of *Myths & Texts,* in which the "Logging" section also includes Snyder's "populist" theme:

> In 1934 they lived in shanties
> At Hooverville, Sullivan's Gulch.
> When the Portland-bound train came through
> The trainmen tossed off coal.   (5.16–19)

The language is equally transparent in "Journeys," a "mythic" poem from *Mountains and Rivers without End*. The language is economical in that it is simple and direct, with descriptive passages and imagistic renderings kept to a minimum; the setting is described only enough so that it is understood. In the ninth section, for example, the canyon is simply "rock-walled," (9.5), and the distant mountains are described only as "farther peaks stony and barren" with "a few alpine trees" (9.3). The passage serves transparently as a vehicle for narrative and idea together. The other side after death is straightforwardly portrayed in the poem as a place similar to the place the speaker currently inhabits, but farther off, remote, a "back country" (9.16). If, as Nordström notices, there is an increasing prosaic and "instructional" quality in Snyder's poetry, this development does not represent a change in philosophy or even a wholesale shift in style but is simply a matter of Snyder's emphasizing qualities that have always been found in his poetry as well as his prose, in response to a developing sense of the role of the poet and a changing conception of his own audience.

Over the course of his career, Snyder has been able to adapt his style, and the way in which he presents his information and instruction, to changes in his perceived audience. Since *Earth House Hold,* Snyder's concept of his readership has evolved from a rather vague "tribe" to a firmly located "primary audience," which he described in 1990 as both regionally and temporally located, consisting of "people born since 1925, living in California, Oregon, Washington, British Columbia and Alaska" (Martin 169). As Snyder's conception of his audience has become more geographically and less socially defined, both his poetry and his prose have relied less on the coded counterculture language of the 1960s and early 1970s (*Earth House Hold* is subtitled "Technical Notes & Queries to Fellow Dharma Revolutionaries"). Simultaneously, Snyder has also lessened the distance between poetry and prose in his verse, increasingly incorporating his more "objective" renderings into larger frameworks, perhaps most notably in the long-awaited *Mountains and Rivers without End*. As Nordström points out, Snyder has also increasingly tended toward the didactic in his poems. For example, the Pound-influenced "Axe Handles," from the collection with the same title, is a kind of treatise on the value of "right work" reminiscent of Thoreau's parable of the Artist of Khourou in *Walden* (326–27). Early anecdotal poems such as "Hay for the Horses" reflect Snyder's long-standing interest in narrative, also evident in the early mythic poems.

Although these elements have always been a part of Snyder's repertoire, they become increasingly evident after *Riprap* and *The Back Country*. Even the short poems in Snyder's later collections tend to be more inclined not only toward narrative but even toward what might be called fable, and consequently they tend to be less "objectivist." Consider, for example, "Shark Meat" from *Regarding Wave*. Like the early poems of *Riprap* and *The Back Country*, "Shark Meat" celebrates the world in its specifics, the tools of fishing, for example, or the "miso sauce" (15) eaten with the shark. And the rather short, clipped lines also are reminiscent of "Riprap." In this poem, however, an entire narrative is presented, from the accidental capture of the shark through the feast on the next day, and there is an implied "lesson" that nature's surprises, such as the unintentional capture of the shark, are better seen as gifts than unfortunate consequences of humanity's imperfect control over natural resources. By the last lines of the poem, the shark's capture appears both destined and voluntary, the act of "re-crossing his own paths" (20) aimed at becoming "part of / this loom" (22–23). In the space of a short lyric, "Shark Meat" comprises a conscious attempt to communicate elemental anthropological and mythic "lore."

In *Mountains and Rivers without End,* Snyder uses the unifying device of the Japanese scroll to incorporate short "fables" such as "Jackrabbit" into a larger, more narrative framework. The book also links East and West through portrayals of a series of "lived landscapes" placing Snyder's own life experience in the context that has produced and shaped Snyder himself as well as his poetry, the Pacific Rim. Moreover, because the individual pieces in the book are both independent poems and parts of an encompassing, evolving creation, this book, forty years in the making, represents the culmination of Snyder's attempt to achieve a kind of "stylistic ecology" in his poems.

The Naturalist-Poet:
Contemporary Poetry and the Shaman's Journey

For Snyder, the central problem of his time is how to remake Western civilization in such a way that its pointless and destructive conflict with the natural world is mitigated or, if possible, eliminated altogether. Understandably, Snyder is concerned with what the poet, and poetry, can do as part of this process, a concern made problematical by the individual-specific focus of contemporary poetics, which tends to isolate the poet from consensual, publicly held value structures. Snyder's knowledge of nature and natural science provides him with a sense of a solid and unquestionable underlying reality, and his exposure to anthropology makes him aware of the role that literature plays in other cultures in which it is more central than in contemporary America, but he is still faced with the question of how to apply that knowledge to his own situation.

In *Gary Snyder's Vision,* Molesworth considers Snyder as a kind of reverse Thoreau, citing Snyder's movement away from the "dense factuality" typical of the early poems in *Riprap,* which, though not altogether abandoned, gradually becomes less central to his work, and toward "a prizing of mental operations" (7). This distinction correlates roughly with the aforementioned division of Snyder's poems into the direct, "scientific" style evident in *Riprap* and the more "mythic" approach that characterizes such books as *Myths & Texts* and *Mountains and Rivers without End.* In any sort of chronological assessment of Snyder's poems, though, it is important to realize that the publication order does not necessarily indicate the order in which the poems were composed, as Snyder will hold some poems for a suitable book. There are also the exigencies of publication itself. For example, *Myths & Texts* was written before *Riprap* but was published after it. Even so, Nordström finds an increase of what Molesworth calls "impure" (*Gary* 5) political material in Snyder's work since his early books. For example, the poems in *Axe Handles,* as Nordström points out, tend to transform Snyder's Northwestern regionalism into a didactic bioregionalism, the apparent purpose of the transformation being to encourage his readers to advance the cause of reinhabitation (136). The poem "Axe Handles" itself is elegantly practical on a literal level, the tool used to make the handle serving as model also: "When making an axe handle, / the pattern is not far off" (16–17).

In "Axe Handles," Snyder transmits an ancient lesson, "First learned from Ezra Pound" (14), who translated Confucius's adaptation of a Chinese folk tale, in contemporary and individual terms by adopting the context of a conversation between Snyder and Kai, his son. "Axe Handles," then, not only provides potential "reinhabitants" with a practical lesson in how things are made but also comments on the way information is passed on from parent to child and from sources of ancient wisdom through mentors such as Pound (and Snyder) to current readers of Snyder's poem. Despite the layered quality of the instruction, the didactic element is one way in which Snyder makes his poems accessible to a wide audience. By its nature, didacticism leads to unambiguous statement and an accessible relationship between images and ideas.

Snyder's didacticism is typically directed toward living in compliance with natural laws and conditions. Snyder shares with Berry a deep conviction in the value of "living right" (Martin 162). Didacticism applied to this task constitutes a logical synthesis of several of Snyder's long-standing concerns and influences: the oral, communal quality of the Beats,[9] the proletarian voice of his work poems, his anthropological belief in the instrumentality of art, and his reverence for the natural world. This reverence itself brings together several key strands of Snyder's experience, originating in an innate sense and augmented by his exposure to prose nature writers like Seton and Thoreau and by his long-term commitment to the "ecological" discipline of Zen.[10] Despite these deep personal resonances, direct advocacy for a cause has put Snyder at odds with the individual, private character inherent in contemporary poetics. Charles Molesworth discusses this situation at length, focusing on the unusual nature of Snyder's sense of his own role as both contemporary poet and, as he claims to be in *Turtle Island,* "spokesman" for "the wilderness, my constituency" (106). Molesworth points out that Snyder's essay collection, *Earth House Hold,* which he links to the American poetic-prose tradition of Thoreau's *Walden* and Williams's *In the American Grain,* is "remarkable . . . because it was written by a post-war American poet" (*Gary* 69), and yet it incorporates recognizable political views. Molesworth observes that the sweeping changes that Snyder proposes further isolate him from the community he is trying to change, concluding that Snyder "wants more than most to overcome the alienation and isolation of the poet in the modern world, but the terms of his vision have, by their very extravagance, made him often seem a party of one" (126).

The "extravagance" of Snyder's vision includes its shifting of emphasis from European cultural forms and sources to Asian and Native American sources. But although seriously identifying with the American Indian may isolate Snyder from the mainstream of his culture, he is convinced that an Indian-inspired model of the fundamental relationship between the human and the nonhuman is bound to replace the European idea that humanity is set apart from, and essentially superior to, the rest of nature. Snyder prophesies that "We won't be white men a thousand years from now . . . [or even] *fifty* years from now" because "our whole culture is going someplace else" (qtd. in Steuding 102). In 1995, Snyder offered a "Three Hundred Year Kitkitdizze Plan" (*Place* 261) for his home and the surrounding "Inimim Forest, from the Nisenan word for *pine*, in recognition of the first people here" (260), a plan that concludes with the hope that in the future "There might even be a civilization with a culture of cultivating wilderness" (262). As noted earlier, Snyder sees the complex of Native American cultures as an essential model on which to base this evolving civilization, or group of civilizations. As for the role of poetry in this evolution, he believes that "The work of poetry is to capture those areas of consciousness which belong to the American continent, the non-white world" (qtd. in Steuding 102). (Of course, Snyder's use of the word "captures" again calls into question the ethics of appropriating American Indian spirituality. Ward Churchill might well ask from whom these "non-white" areas of consciousness are being captured.) [11]

Nordström traces Snyder's efforts to achieve this goal all the way back to *Myths & Texts,* which, he says, begins the "transformation of place into a metaphor" by changing the "frame of reference from white settler realism to a broader sense of realism with a foundation of Native American mythology" (113). Both of these frames of reference are juxtaposed in "this poem is for bear" from *Myths & Texts* and in "Journeys" from *Mountains and Rivers without End.* In the latter poem, Snyder sometimes adopts the point of view of the early Euro-American explorer who travels "Through deep forests to the coast" (2.1) to survey a landscape "where no one had ever been" (2.4). In other sections, however, the journey goes through dream into the realms of myth, as in the first section, which concludes with an allusion to the biblical creation story: "the woman transferred a piece of fresh-tasting apple / from her mouth to mine. Then I woke" (1.15–16). The poem's journeying ranges from the level of personal experience, as in the bus trip of the eighth section, to the mythic confrontation with the sun in the third section.

"Journeys" incorporates the tension between the suggestive but essentially private language of the contemporary poet and the more "archetypal" language through which Snyder attempts to pursue public themes. In the eighth section, "Lew" is introduced casually, as is the bus trip itself. The logical assumption is that Lew is a friend of Snyder's, probably the poet Lew Welch. Like the Beats, his early associates, Snyder relies on the reader's knowledge of his own life to give identities to the "characters" introduced, much as Ginsberg does in "Howl." [12] Although similarly abrupt introductions occur in other sections ("Ko-San" in the ninth section, for example), their context is primarily literary or mythic, and they assume the role of "spirit guides" more than or in addition to actual associates of Snyder's. The imagery also shifts back and forth from the suggestive series of glimpses in the eighth section to mythic narratives involving the sun in the third section and death in the ninth section.

In this and similar poems, Snyder takes part in mythopoeia, defined by Murphy as "the adaptive retelling and creating of myths that have guided or are needed to guide a culture" (*Understanding* 21). Shifting the frame of reference also involves a kind of transformation of Snyder himself, and one of the guises he assumes is that of a "poet-shaman," at least potentially empowered to speak for animals, plants, and perhaps landscapes and bioregions as well. It is important to understand that, on one level, this assumption of the shaman's mantle is metaphorical. Snyder is not really claiming to *be* a shaman any more than he is claiming to be Adam in "Journeys." The term "poet-shaman" can be seen as a condensed metaphor. But while the metaphor is in force, it provides Snyder with a new position from which to speak for the constituency of the wilderness and wild nature, and it in turn is one source of Snyder's increasing awareness of his own social role. It also helps account for the increasingly didactic strain in his poetry and prose. According to Nordström, "Snyder used the Shaman persona in his early poetry, but it is not until his later essays and interviews that he begins to talk extensively about the role and the function of the shaman as a poet. The new aspect of this shaman is not that he is seeking power, but that he is transmitting it" (130).

According to comparative religion scholars William Lessa and Evon Vogt, the shaman can be defined, and distinguished from the priest, as "a ceremonial practitioner whose powers come from direct contact with the supernatural, by divine stroke, rather than from inheritance or memorized ritual" (301). The shaman can achieve a direct and individual contact with the "spirits" either by "acting as their mouthpieces" or through "a less usual procedure in which the shaman's soul dissociates itself from his body and travels to the spirit world" (308). Snyder has attempted to "deepen" his travels through the natural world by casting them as a kind of shaman's journey.

In *Dreamtime and Inner Space,* Holger Kalweit discusses the motif or idea of the shaman's travels: "Reports about shamanistic practices frequently refer to the theme of the 'journey' in an attempt to describe how the soul leaves the body and travels through the landscape of the realm of the dead. This metaphor of a journey to the Beyond is a classical image of which practically all cultures make use to bring the travels of the consciousness of shamans or saints within the range of people's understanding" (15). In "Journeys," Snyder (as shaman) approaches the realm of the dead at the end of the poem. More typically, the motif of the shaman's journey serves to transform his own individual experience into mythic terms, a journey out of the quotidian reality of his own life and into the wilderness, as well as into its psychic analog, the unconscious.

Understandably, shamanism appeals to Snyder for its anthropological and religious significance and also for its practicality. Since the shaman is a socioreligious healer or practitioner, such a journey is, by nature, functional. The healing capacity of the shaman is achieved, according to Claude Lévi-Strauss, by combining the physical and the psychological in order "to bring to a conscious level conflicts and resistances which have remained unconscious" (193). This "is a matter of provoking an experience; as this experience becomes structured, regulatory mechanisms beyond the subject's [that is, the shaman's patient's] control are spontaneously set in motion and lead to an orderly functioning" (194). Through the figure of the shaman, Snyder applies a mythic overlay to his own experience. This mythic dimension, if it could be shared with or "provoked" in even a contemporary American reader, could, at least theoretically, alter or "correct" that reader's conception of nature and could help to heal the perceived split between the human and the nonhuman. In traditional American Indian societies, Catherine Albanese notes, the shamans were "leaders in communication with other-than-human persons who dwelled in nature" (24). David Abram observes that shamans regulate the relationship between human and nonhuman, acting "as an intermediary between the human community and the larger ecological field" and ensuring "that the relation between human society and the larger society of beings is balanced and reciprocal" (7) in spiritual as well as physical terms. Snyder typically applies the idea of the shaman as a way to work toward an American resacralization of nature. Snyder's revitalized shamanism is a potential way to influence his culture's relationship with the natural world while he continues to work within the experiential and individualistic limits of contemporary poetics.

Unfortunately for Snyder, the transformation of his already atypical experience into a shaman's journey tends to further increase his distance from what is familiar to a broad contemporary audience. Snyder's answer to the contention that his stance seems obscure or exotic to most contemporary readers—that he might, as Molesworth suggests, be "a party of one" (*Gary* 126)—is to assert that these are abnormal times, and the best, perhaps, that a poet can hope for is to act as a kind of cultural advance guard. In this way, Snyder responds to critics who find his vision anachronistic by asserting that the truly progressive stance is to recognize, as Jeffers did, the ephemeral quality of Western civilization, which "is very brief when measured against one time-transcending bison corpse, or the wandering calligraphy of a river down the Yukon flats, or the archaic circumpolar cosmopolitanism of the traditions that connect with the Kuuvangmiut people" (*Practice* 67–68). By aligning himself with a vast and ancient cultural heritage, Snyder attempts to rebuff charges that he desires to live in the past with the assertion that "I'm in line with the big flow" (*Real* 112). But in doing so, he also takes two risks. One is mentioned, and discounted, by Molesworth, as the result of an ultimately pointless deconstructionist exercise. In this analysis, the "tribe" that Snyder represents is said to derive its meaning from its opposition to and rejection of the values of the dominant tradition and is therefore subsidiary to the culture to which it seeks to provide an alternative. Molesworth points out, however, that "there is a limit to the extent to which even deconstructionists can treat political structures as no more than rhetorical systems" (*Gary* 121). The other risk may be potentially more serious. When Snyder adopts a didactic or morally superior tone, as he does, for example, in "I Went into the Maverick Bar," he assumes just the type of authoritarian position that the decentralized, democratic bioregionalist might logically be expected to resist. Furthermore, the shaman, as one with direct access to the supernatural, becomes particularly dangerous as a political figure, as is evidenced, for example, by the shaman-kings of the Mayans. Snyder counters this tendency with the offhand, almost irreverent tone of his poems and with the sort of self-deprecating humor that characterizes poems such as "this poem is for bear" and "Elk Trails." Of course, as long as Snyder remains a marginal figure, the question of the ramifications of his political role remains hypothetical. Ironically, though, the shaman's moral authority becomes more questionable as the shaman gains more success in exercising that authority. This is a problem characteristic of all social and political systems, but the shaman's claim to direct and individual contact with the supernatural has not, when politicized in Mesoamerica, for example, always been a reconciling force.[13]

Like Bly and Berry, Snyder sees himself as a representative of an alternative way of thinking that should and must resurface. Bly sees the "Great Mother consciousness" and the "Wild Man" as psychological "entities" that reappear, apparently spontaneously, in a kind of natural shifting of psychic balances. Berry questions the stability of a society featuring the Western notion of specialization and the oversimplified manipulation of the basic processes that support life and sees the Jeffersonian agrarian tradition as perhaps the only way to avert disaster. Similarly, Snyder sees the return to a "pagan" sense of the sacredness of nature, with Native American cultural traditions serving to "show us the next stage of this other culture" (qtd. in Steuding 101), as a cure for the destructive and anomalous Euro-American industrial society. Snyder's belief that a new order of society is inevitable and may be already in the process of developing leads him to a basic optimism that is surprising considering the depth of his alienation from his society in its present state. His faith in this process of societal evolution is evident in "Survival and Sacrament," the concluding essay in *The Practice of the Wild,* in which he asserts that the "movement toward creating a 'culture of the wilderness' from within contemporary civilization" is already underway,[14] and that "It is a cause for hope that so many people worldwide—from Czech intellectuals to rainforest-dwelling mothers in Sarawak—are awakening to their power" (180).

Because of its speculative optimism, Snyder's vision might be thought to risk, or even invite, criticism that he is naive, that the "power" of mothers in Sarawak is at best theoretical. In his own words, his hope appears "outrageously optimistic" (*Place* 262). On the other hand, there is a desperate character to Snyder's vision, resting as it does on the potential for a complete reversal in the manifest and well-established direction that Euro-American culture has taken. Indeed, Snyder's vision of virtually utopian bioregionalist communities living in harmony with their natural environments requires a far more comprehensive faith in social evolution than does Marxism, for example. Furthermore, Snyder must be able to maintain faith in "the real work," even when, as in "I Went into the Maverick Bar," he is the only one who has a sense of its value.

Molesworth captures both the naiveté and the desperation of Snyder's solution when he notes that "The religion of Paleolithic shamanism and the utopianism of postindustrial science can, and in Snyder's view must, be brought together if the current impasse is not to result in irreversible ecological disaster" (*Gary* 109). In light of Snyder's comprehensive synthesis of scientific observation of and personal connection with the natural world, the dilemma ascribed by Fritzell to American nature writers can be seen as a necessary process of cultural development. Snyder's concept of the poet as shaman provides an illustration, a working example, of how such a "hybrid" mode of thinking can function. The resulting poetry is Snyder's major contribution to what he sees as "the real work" of creating a sustainable, ecologically viable society.[15] In the context of contemporary poetics, "poetic shamanism" lends to individual experience the public resonance of myth.

In *The Shaman's Doorway,* Stephen Larsen notes that "The shaman is the archetypal technician of the sacred, and his profession is precisely the relationship between the mythic imagination and ordinary consciousness" (59). This relationship is manifested in Snyder's poems in various ways. In "Spel against Demons," for example, Snyder invokes the idea of magic in lines that combine a rhythmic, chanting quality with conventionally rhetorical, even at times colloquial, diction:

> The release of Demonic Energies in the name of
> the People
>   must cease

Messing with blood sacrifice in the name of
               Nature
        must cease.   (1–6)

"Elk Trails" is one of two introductory poems in *Left Out in the Rain,* a book of previously uncollected poems that, like *Mountains and Rivers without End,* encompasses some forty years of writing. Murphy describes the book as following a chronological order, so that "Elk Trails" would be a very early poem, perhaps even predating Snyder's stay at Reed College. Remarkably, the poem already shows Snyder's exploration of the shaman persona and his desire to combine contemporary poetry's basis in individual experience with the mythic sense of the shaman's journey. The opening stanza again features "chanting" rhythms, perhaps indicative of the special frame of mind required of the shaman at the onset of the journey:

Ancient, world-old Elk paths
Narrow, dusty Elk paths
Wide-trampled, muddy
Aimless . . . wandering . . .
Everchanging Elk paths.   (1–5)

As the poem progresses, the reader finds that the trails in this poem, in addition to representing the mythic "road" or lifeway of the elk as experienced by the poet-shaman, are encountered at a particular place, eventually labeled as Spirit Lake, on Mount St. Helens in Washington, and in contemporary times, which Snyder indicates by references to modern logging. The image of the ridges, "Sharp-topped and jagged as a broken crosscut saw" (17), suggests, in addition, Snyder's own personal experience as a logger. Finally, at the end of the poem, Snyder seems, in a parenthetical aside, to be returning to the perspective of ordinary consciousness:

(High above, the Elk walk in the evening
From one pasture to another
Scrambling on the rock and snow.   (49–51)

But the reader quickly realizes that the poet-shaman has "returned" not empty-handed but with significant information delivered from the point of view of the elk themselves, who, with:

. . . their ancient, coarse-haired
Thin-flanked God
Laugh in silent wind-like chuckles
At man, and all his trails.)   (54–57)

In "Birth of the Shaman," another early poem from *Left Out in the Rain,* Snyder asserts that shamanism is not anachronistic, that it is as valid in the contemporary world as in the distant past.[16] The poem presents the shaman's birth in a manner that emphasizes both the redemptive quality of the event and the contemporary setting in which it occurs. The "Apple blossoms at Hood River" (5) suggest rebirth, as does the timely emergence of the mountain through the clouds. But the honking of a truck appears late in the poem to shock the reader back into the contemporary world, earlier invoked by "six a.m." in the first line. Still, the poem chooses to emphasize the miraculous, closing with a reiteration that the shaman, at last, has arrived. This poem suggests Snyder's optimism that, even in irreverent and troubled contemporary times, renewal or redemption is possible, perhaps inevitable.

Snyder's mythopoeia is often quite comprehensive, as is illustrated by "this poem is for bear" from the "Hunting" section of *Myths & Texts.* At the center of the poem, which Bly says "hints continually of the interplay between humans and animals in their consciousness" (*News* 128), is a retelling of the "Woman Who Marries a Bear," the story that led Snyder to his concept of depth ecology (Martin 162).[17] In *The Sacred Paw,* a study of bears in literature, myth, and natural history, Paul Shepard and Barry Sanders note that "Snyder recounts the entire history of man's treatment of the bear in this poem—from the Bear Mother legend through our various perceptions of it and appellations bestowed on it, to its eventual destruction. Yet he insists, in his own perception of the animal kingdom, on referring to the pursuers of the bear as his own brothers. The bear remains, even in our adverse treatment of him, a distant cousin" (179).

Snyder's poem acknowledges the sources of the story in the ancient myths of Native Americans, even including a series of euphemistic names for the bear, despite his awareness that such techniques are foreign to modern Western peoples, as he confirms in "The Etiquette of Freedom" (*Practice* 21). But he alludes, also, to the mythic history of Euro-American culture ("Odysseus was a bear"; 38) and even to the classifying impulse of natural science ("twelve species north of Mexico"; 34). Encompassing all of this information is the perspective of the individual human observer, evident in the disjointed observations and halting grasp of lore at the beginning of the poem and in the acknowledgment of personal limitations at the end, which, echoing the similar structure of "Elk Trails," takes the form of an aside marking a return to the everyday voice of normal consciousness.

In poems such as "this poem is for bear," Snyder blends myth and natural history, public and individual perspectives. Questions remain as to how and to what end his poems affect a real, contemporary audience, but by their elevation of the individual experience to the level of myth, a myth clearly intended for public recitation and information, they explore one avenue by which the poet can link individual experience in the natural world and communication of a decidedly social nature, providing a basis for an experiential poetry that addresses the community and imbues individual experience with shared meaning. His effort has had some impact if one is to judge from the makeup of his audience. Murphy notes that, as of 1992, all of Snyder's major collections of prose and poetry were in print (*Understanding* 167), a remarkable accomplishment for any contemporary writer but virtually unheard of for a poet. Snyder's popularity extends beyond the current audience of poets and poetry aficionados to include something approaching Dana Gioia's "community of educated readers" (16), which, according to Gioia, is "the audience that poetry has lost" (18). Murphy observes that "There is probably no other serious American poet writing today who is read more widely outside of academia than Snyder" and goes on to say that his work is gradually making it "within the college classroom as well" (*Understanding* 167). Thus, Snyder's reputation has been built in precisely the opposite direction from the usual route that has proven so frustrating to many contemporary poets who have found that academic or peer acceptance does not translate into the interest of the general educated public. Perhaps Gioia's "cultural intelligentsia" (18) is not quite as sweeping as the "tribe" that Snyder once envisioned, but it is, as Gioia points out, the key to restoring poetry to a position that "matters" and, consequently, restoring the poet to a position where he or she can function as a kind of cultural prophet. Murphy points out that the final line of "I Went into the Maverick Bar" is the title of Lenin's call for a vanguard party to lead Russia's revolution (*Understanding* 112). At this point Snyder sees "What is to be done" as an incremental, painstaking process by which North America will become again "Turtle Island" and by which American culture will be transformed into something ultimately more joyful as well as more sustainable. In order for this process to have any hope of succeeding, it will have to renew every aspect of life in Western Civilization, with a "new society emerging from the shell of the old" just as a new notion of the poetic self emerges from contemporary poetics in Snyder's poems.

5 · Wendell Berry

The Farm and the Wilderness

IN *Remembering,* Wendell Berry tells the story of Andy Catlett, who leaves his family's farm to build a life for himself in the city, eventually returning as an advocate for the way of life into which he was born. A central scene has Catlett arguing with his employer, the editor of *Scientific Farming.* The argument revolves around the farming methods of Bill Meikelberger, a modern corporate agribusinessman, and Isaac Troyer, a traditional Amish family farmer. Knowing that he is taking the probable losing side, both in terms of his career and the course of events in general, Catlett favors Troyer's traditionalism in what becomes for him a question of honor and loyalty, since "He was arguing for the cattle coming to the spring in the cool of the day, for the man with his hand on his boy's shoulder, saying, 'Look. See what it is. Always remember'" (86).

Much of Berry's life has been spent making the same argument. Like Catlett, Berry himself left his ancestral farm for what he envisioned as a typical writer's life. He attended Stanford University, visited Europe on a Guggenheim fellowship, and eventually moved to New York City. But rather than remaining in New York, he found himself drawn back to his original place, against the advice of his peers and associates, among them his former teacher Wallace Stegner. In retrospect, Stegner finds Berry's return to Kentucky "as radical as Thoreau's retreat to Walden, and much more permanent" (51). Berry's choice is described in his essay "The

Long-Legged House" and constitutes a central moment in his life and in
his writing career. It marks his definition as a poet of place and his reversal
of the process he describes in his essay "Writer and Region," by which
"hinterland writers" have generally left their birthplaces for "some metropolis or 'center of culture'" (*What Are* 80). According to Berry, what
generally happens there is that the writer is exposed not only to the expected wealth of ideas and cultural influences but also to the tradition of
deprecating a rural or hinterland upbringing as provincial and embarrass-
ing. As Stegner says, young writers are told that they cannot "come into the
literary world with manure on your barn boots and expect to be welcomed"
(51). So writers are pressured to escape from their origins by denying the
significance and value of rural life and ultimately of heritage in general. The
escaping writers become ethereal cosmopolites, committed to increasingly
distant and abstract "territories" of escape.

Berry's identification with his native Kentucky is similar to Bly's home-
coming to Minnesota and, even more so, to Snyder's reinhabitation of California's San Juan Ridge.[1] But Berry's move is more literally a return than
either Bly's or Snyder's. Whereas Bly identifies with Minnesota in a general
way, mostly centered around the idea of "northernness" connecting not
only to the upper Midwest but to Bly's Scandinavian heritage as well,[2]
and Snyder's San Juan Ridge is a new kind of community entirely, at least
in the United States, Berry aligns himself frankly and happily with the
world as he believes his parents and grandparents experienced it. In Berry's
fiction, most notably *Remembering* but also the earlier novels *A Place on
Earth* and *The Memory of Old Jack,* characters are rendered not so much
as individuals but as avatars of basic types, most prominently the post-
Jeffersonian family farmer who attempts to maintain durable values and
practices in the face of economic and cultural disruption. Similarly, in the
poems of *The Wheel,* Berry "would have" ("The Dance" 1) each generation
sustaining, and sustained by, recurring processes they reenact:

> . . . woven
> in the circle of a dance,
> the song of long time flowing.   (4–6)[3]

Each of the three central poets in this study is a kind of spokesperson.
Bly speaks on behalf of Romantic traditions of poetry, psychology, and

philosophy that have taken various forms throughout his career but that generally entail commitment to the notion of full or twofold consciousness. Snyder more self-consciously identifies with a constituency of wild nature and indigenous peoples. Both Bly and Snyder have often contrasted their constituencies with those that dominate society. For Bly, the poets gathered in *News of the Universe* represent not only a general aesthetic agreement in principle but also a kind of alternative community based on a rejection of the Cartesian "Old Position" in, presumably, its practical and political as well as aesthetic manifestations. Snyder also clearly sees himself as a spokesperson for an alternative community. At first glance, Berry's constituency may seem more mainstream than those of Bly and Snyder. Like his character Andy Catlett, Berry sees himself "arguing his father's argument" (86), on behalf of Port Royal, Kentucky, and, by extension, other small rural communities. Berry is quick to point out, however, that despite the apparent mainstream ordinariness of small-town America, American rural communities have been subject to the profoundly disruptive effects of the homogenization of countless local cultures that characterizes post–World War II American life. In "The Work of Local Cultures," he attributes this disruption to "the prevailing assumption . . . that if the nation is all right, then all the localities within it will be all right also," an assumption of which he says, "I see little reason to believe that this is true." Instead, rural America has become "a colony of what the government and the corporations think of as the nation," resulting ultimately in "the departure of young people, of soil and other so-called natural resources, and of local memory" (*What Are* 167).[4]

"Local memory" is a key to Berry's idea of the link between the community and the land. As with Snyder's depth ecology, Berry's local memory provides a way in which the relationship between community and land can be regulated and kept healthy and harmonious. Even Berry's poems of natural description, such as the frequently anthologized "The Peace of Wild Things" from *Openings* and "The Lilies" from *Farming: A Hand Book* ("Amid the gray trunks of ancient trees we found / the gay woodland lilies nodding on their stems"; 1–2), generally describe cyclic events returned to many times and rediscovered.

The "we" in "The Lilies" is unspecified and serves to show that Berry is rarely alone in the woods and fields, even when he seems to be by himself.

As it does for Aldo Leopold, memory populates Berry's farm. Human history joins with natural history to create a continuous and encompassing "land community." It is not surprising, then, that in "The Old Elm Tree by the River" from *The Country of Marriage*, for example, Berry "grants consciousness" to the elm tree, making possible a kind of friendship held on an equal footing between poet and tree, described as "neighborly as two men" (11).[5]

Throughout his work, Berry shows the land physically retaining what amounts to a memory of its past. In "Damage," which opens *What Are People For?*, Berry recalls his failed attempt to build a pond on his farm. The resulting damage remains years later, as a gash in a hillside and also as a reminder to Berry that, as Bly and Snyder have also discovered, individuals must bear the mark of the culture in which they live, even if they attempt to represent an alternative society or lifeway.[6] Through leaving "a lasting flaw in the face of the earth, for no lasting good," Berry has "carried out, before my own eyes and against my intention, a part of the modern tragedy" (6, sec. 2). Berry suggests that local memory can play a role similar to that of Snyder's depth ecology. So long as the scar on the hillside exists, Berry will remember his error and proceed more carefully. But if the scar is lost, the error will likely be repeated. Like Snyder, Berry sees art as a way to preserve information or lore; he concludes that "An art that heals and protects its subject is a geography of scars" (7, sec. 3).

Given the key role that memory plays in his work, it is not surprising that Berry is, as he says in "Requiem" from *The Wheel*, a poet for whom "elegy is my fate" (1.7).[7] As in "Elegy," also from *The Wheel*, Berry often focuses on the transmission from one generation to the next of lifeways preserved in the memory of the poet and in the collective memory of the community. In "Elegy," the deceased Owen Flood appears to Berry as an embodiment of the sum of the experience that was shared between them. Like the scar of the failed pond in "Damage," Flood's presence remains visible on the land, "for his story lay upon it, a bloom, / a blessing" (6.7–8), requiring only the agency of the poet's memory to bring it to life. Here, through memory, the poet becomes "inheritor of what I mourned" (8.6), a kind of keeper of the life of Owen Flood. But the poet's life, through what he learns from Flood, also becomes a reenactment of Flood's life. Throughout *The Wheel*, the image of the square dance illustrates the continuity of the community through reenactment across generations. In "Elegy," for example, both past and future generations "encircled us, as in a dance" (7.17). This continuity provides Berry with an expanded perspective, and as with Jeffers and Snyder, it is only in light of the "big picture" that the value and meaning of human actions can truly be seen. But the poem's point of view remains within the present moment of the observed scene; the past and future are palpable through the reenactment of lives and the embodiment of ideas and lifeways in succeeding generations.

In his fiction, Berry's characters tend to recapitulate central character types over generations. The resulting flatness of characterization is perhaps an aesthetic flaw, which Berry himself takes steps to rectify in his more recent fiction with characters like the distinctive Ptolemy and "Miss Minnie" Proudfoot of *Watch with Me* and Uncle Andrew Catlett of *A World Lost*, although the latter can be seen as a complex version of Berry's familiar "wayward uncle" character. But the echoing of character types over generations stems from and illustrates Berry's belief in the importance of continuation. Memory is the mortar that binds the generations into a durable social structure. In *The Memory of Old Jack*, for example, Jack Beechum's collected experience is a mine of lore, seeking to be transferred before its failing vehicle, Jack himself, is gone. The transfer is completed with the passage of title to Jack's farm to Elton Penn. There is a ritual sense to this reenactment, a kind of mnemonic by which the culture and its relationship to its surroundings are preserved.[8] The ritual re-creation of lives in contact with the land, a recurrent theme in both Berry's poetry and his fiction, extends the collective memory far beyond the apprehension of any one person and, in fact, embraces the future as well as the past, as the square dance does in "Elegy" and again in "Our Children, Coming of Age," also from *The Wheel*, in which the dancers move "in / and out of time" (1–2).

Berry's use of the dance image in *The Wheel* is unusual for a contemporary poet. Far from being a "discovered" image welling up from deep in the unconscious or from the quotidian wanderings of the poet, the image is, despite its rusticity, overtly literary and consciously chosen to fulfill the poet's preordained purpose.[9] Its effectiveness rests squarely on its aptness as a vehicle for an idea. But Berry is typical of his generation in other ways. Perhaps most obvious is the central role of his own experience in all of his writing. Most of his poems are set, quite plainly, on his Kentucky farm, and they are peopled largely by himself, his family, and his neighbors, with the biographical content much more central and obvious than in the rural landscapes of perhaps the most superficially similar Modern poet, Robert Frost. And when, in the "Mad Farmer" poems, Berry assumes what Lionel Basney calls his "one extended experiment in the half-dramatized persona" (180), the persona appears, much as Roethke's "Old Woman" does, as a thinly disguised version of the poet himself, in Berry's case as a "mouthpiece" for his beliefs. As Michael Hamburger says, he "has resorted to the persona of the 'Mad Farmer' to render some of his more recondite insights" (86). "The Mad Farmer Manifesto: The First Amendment," for example, begins with a quote from Thomas Jefferson, one of Berry's principal cultural icons, and goes on to express ideas that obviously reflect the opinions of the poet himself. An earlier poem, "The Mad Farmer in the City," echoes Berry's own path into the city and out again. Despite the persona, the "Mad Farmer" poems are among Berry's most personal. They are charged with emotions Berry tends to moderate in his other poems—personal anger and frustration at the "mad time" in which he lives and pride in his own independence and ability to effect change. The "Mad Farmer" persona affords Berry the opportunity to reflect his alienation from a society unquestioningly committed to values opposite his own. These poems are almost confessional. For example, one of Hamburger's examples of a "recondite insight" from the Mad Farmer series, "For I too am perhaps a little mad," is more like a confessional personal revelation than a learned insight, as Hamburger himself indicates when he says, "one takes that as being a statement in his own person" (86–87).

Another reflection of Berry's contemporariness is his interest in and respect for the position of the lone individual, despite or along with his commitment to community. Besides Jefferson, the historical figure most commonly on his mind is Daniel Boone. Another persona poem, "Boone," from *The Broken Ground,* shows a sharp awareness of the tragic situation of the aging American pioneer, living with the diminished state that is the inevitable result of turning wilderness into settled country. Berry is moved by the pioneers' situation, perhaps even admiring of their accomplishments, but "Boone" carries a considerable load of irony. The settlers' dream is an "encroachment" (20) that "descended" on the wilderness, only partially mitigated by the gentle "like doves" (21) that follows. And there is irony in the situation—the arrival at the finish rather than the beginning of spring, the vision held in the coals of the dying fire, and finally the landscape itself, which "began to live" (41), but only after sacrificing, to time and the seasons but also to the settlers' dream, its "dying green" (40).

As seen by Berry, Boone feels the settled life as a loss of harmony and intimacy with the natural world, as John Muir did, and is not without regret as he nears the end of his life. The irony is inherent in the success of the pioneers' effort to impose "a country in our minds" (18) on the natural world. Boone is left wishing instead that he could be "submissive / to the weather" (96–97). The aged pioneer can trace his life history in the transformations that he has been instrumental in bringing about, but the perspective gained with age is double-edged, and he sees himself as both betrayed by and betrayer of nature. As he is no longer "innocent of ripeness" (91) and no longer living according to the natural order ("faithful to solstice"; 92), the poem implies, the natural world will no longer "recognize" Boone as it does the "faithful" flocks of migratory birds (92–94).

Berry's treatment of Boone is sympathetic, if ironic. Despite generally identifying with the settled world of the farm, Berry understands the impulse that drives the pioneers away from the community and into the wilds. Though less enamored of wilderness than Jeffers or Snyder, Berry admits, in "An Entrance to the Woods," that removal from human society leaves him feeling lighter, as if he has lost fifty pounds (*Recollected* 241). Like Bly and Snyder, Berry sees nature as a counterpart of culture in the formation of the individual life and consciousness. In "Getting Along with Nature" from *Home Economics,* he claims that "the survival of wilderness—of places that we do not change . . . is necessary. Our sanity probably requires it" (17). Berry concludes, like Aldo Leopold, that wilderness keeps the human economy conscious of its place within the natural order. "Only by preserving areas where nature's processes are undisturbed," he says in *The Unsettling of America,* "can we preserve an accurate sense of the impact of civilization upon its natural resources" (30). As it is for Jeffers, the study of the wild for Berry is a way to break beyond the limitations of a strictly anthropocentric perspective in order to place human life in the context of a larger order.

Despite acknowledging the value of wilderness, Berry is unlikely to seek refuge there. He often notes the frightening or indifferent aspect of country without people. His former teacher, Wallace Stegner, in advising that any comparison between Berry and Thoreau be qualified by acknowledgment of their differences in temperament and preferred surroundings, says that Berry's "province is not the wilderness where the individual makes contact with the universe, but the farm, the neighborhood, the community, the town, the memory of the past and the hope of the future" (49). In "The Native Grasses and What They Mean" from *The Gift of Good Land,* Berry describes a visit to the Tennessee Valley Authority's Land Between the Lakes, where the agency has attempted to reestablish wilderness character-istics in a formerly settled area. Berry concludes that "Pleased as I was to see the buffalo and the woods and the renewing meadows of tall grass, I would much have preferred to see the 2,738 [relocated] people back at home" (81). The first two principles of the "middle way" that he defines in "Preserving Wildness" identify wilderness with the physical universe itself, at times supportive but fundamentally dangerous and overwhelming, as human life is "absolutely dependent" on it (*Home* 138). In fact, one of the valuable insights gained from exposure to elemental nature is the realization that "The universe . . . is unimaginably large, and mostly empty, and mostly dark" (*Long-Legged* 131). Like Jeffers and Snyder, Berry adopts an expanded perspective, but the effect is to increase his sense of belonging to his own moment in time and his own human society.

Certainly, Berry is less at home in the wilderness than Snyder, much as the rural naturalist John Burroughs was less at home in the wilds than was his contemporary, John Muir.[10] Because Berry prefers his country "hu-manized," Fritzell categorizes him as a "rural or country" writer rather than a nature writer (76). However, such a distinction neglects the fact that, for the most part, the natural surroundings explored by Thoreau, univer-sally recognized as a central figure in the development of nature writing, were humanized also. And this distinction misses not only the importance granted to the nonhuman by Berry but also his personal attraction to it, evident in poems like "The Peace of Wild Things."[11] One of the most compelling characters in Berry's fiction is Burley Coulter, the night hunter, who, reminiscent of Faulkner's Isaac McCaslin, identifies as much with the woods as with the town of Port William (the fictionalized version of Berry's Port Royal); he is described in the short story "The Wild Birds" as "a man of two loves, not always compatible: of the dark woods, and of the daylit

membership of kin and friends and households" (*Wild* 127). Berry's own
"Long-Legged House" was originally the cabin of a similar "bachelor uncle
Berry admired in childhood," as Herman Nibbelink points out (141). The
impulse to "escape to the territories" that Berry criticizes in "Writer and
Region" finds expression in his own work in poems like "The Peace of Wild
Things" and "The Long Hunter" and is represented in *The Wheel* by "Set-
ting Out," which finds:

> the husbandman become again
> the Long Hunter, and set out
> not to the familiar woods of home
> but to the forest of the night.   (2–5)[12]

Berry's idea of community is complemented by his respect for the basically unfettered individual, the "Long Hunter." In "A Few Words in Defense of Edward Abbey" from *What Are People For?* Berry claims that a
writer's value to the community depends on his or her independence from
that community. Like Thoreau, Berry concludes, Abbey writes as an "au-
tobiographer" (40), his value stemming from the fact that "he speaks in-
sistently as himself" (41). Although perhaps inconsistent with his general
sense of the formative value of culture (some characters in his novels, for
example, seem almost like interchangeable products of their upbringing),
Berry's evaluation of Abbey does point to his belief in a community composed of individuals acting responsibly, according to their own lights. In
"Think Little," Berry criticizes environmentalists for lack of independence,
noting the tendency to dissent, not as individuals, but as a group (*Continuous* 76). In "Property, Patriotism, and National Defense," he favors looser,
grassroots associations formed within a particular community, with a local
goal, whose work constitutes, for Berry, a real effort at national defense
(*Home* 110).

The vision of the community composed of free individuals—a logical
extension of his favoring small and local social orders over large and abstract
ones—is potentially empowering, particularly for a poet such as Berry,
who finds himself at odds with the "official" or dominating thought of his
society. As an agreement between individuals, the community can potentially bypass altogether the institutionalized culture of nations and societies, which Berry recognizes as early as "To a Siberian Woodsman" from

Openings. As with Thoreau, what differentiates Berry's vision from simple anarchy is the unfailing belief that nature, as the indisputable signified, is an underlying source of moral values. Just as in Whitman's "Song of My-self" "the look of the bay mare" is enough "to shame silliness" (13.20) out of one, in "To a Siberian Woodsman" nature is the ultimate source and arbiter of truth and value. And nature as a source of underlying values is subversive, undercutting and superceding the authority of the state:

I do not see the national flag flying from the staff of the sycamore,
or any decree of the government written on the leaves of the walnut,
nor has the elm bowed before monuments or sworn the oath of allegiance.
They have not declared to whom they stand in welcome.   (5.3 – 6)

Berry is as aware as any contemporary poet of the importance of culture in forming the individual. He tends to see the "wild" as anything that exists outside of the domestic order tentatively, and often locally, established and maintained by culture. Culture can be seen as both a necessary protection from the unknown wilderness and a way to translate that wilderness into understandable terms. In either case, the possibility of a deep intuitive connection between wilderness and the human unconscious is at least sharply qualified by the inaccessibility or fundamental mysteriousness of that connection. But although he is reluctant to postulate a direct connec-tion between wild nature and the human unconscious, as Bly and Snyder do, Berry shares with them the natural history writer's belief in the truth-revealing quality of the natural world. And although his personal and pro-sodic conservatism is atypical of contemporary poets, he adheres to the central principle of contemporary poetics, that the poet's own life should be the central subject matter of the poem. Berry's deepest personal affilia-tion may be with the Jeffersonian farmer, but by adopting the Long Hunter as a counterpoint, he echoes Thoreau's stance with one foot planted in town and the other in the wild.

The "Use Value" of Berry's Poetry

Although I earlier contrasted Berry's attitude toward wilderness with that of Snyder, Berry and Snyder are unexpectedly similar in some ways. Like Bly, Berry and Snyder believe that the history of Western thought has created a serious perceived gap between human consciousness and nonhuman nature. This gap, resulting in a sense that humanity is superior to the rest of nature, is central to the basic problem of the current era, the increasing destruction of natural systems and the human cultures dependent on them. In "A Poem of Difficult Hope," an essay on Hayden Carruth, Berry states flatly that "We are living in the most destructive and, hence, the most stupid period of the history of our species" (*What Are* 61–62), echoing Snyder's contention that the current period in the development of human civilization is "backwards." Like Bly and Snyder, Berry sees the disconnection between human and nonhuman as requiring a spiritual solution, since "perhaps the great disaster of human history is one that happened to or within religion: that is the conceptual division between the holy and the world, the excerpting of the Creator from the creation" (*Continuous* 6). Moreover, Berry, like Snyder, also believes that literature is basically instrumental, insisting "That its real habitat is the household and the community—that it can and does affect, even in practical ways, the life of a place" (*What Are* 84).

Berry's statement presents a challenge to himself that has also been understood by Bly and Snyder: how can a writer, as an individual not representing an institution or organized group, achieve an authoritative position from which to address public issues and concerns? Like Bly and Snyder, Berry has emerged as a major prose writer and arguably has become more prominent as an essayist than as a poet.[13] In discussing prose poems, Donald Hall has noted the capacity of prose to carry information (103). In Berry's writing, this capacity works two ways: the ideas that inform the poems are explored in depth in the essays, and both the essays and novels serve to "flesh out" the autobiographical context of the world of the poetry. The prose provides a narrative and philosophical matrix in which the poems can reflect both quotidian experience and ethical positions, enabling Berry to maintain the individual focus of contemporary poetry while at the same time consciously speaking to and for his chosen constituency, the rural community.

Berry's work also extends the range of literary subject matter to include the natural sciences, particularly the soil and plant community studies of researchers like Wes Jackson, to whose efforts Berry has lent his now-considerable name recognition. However, like Fritzell's self-conscious nature writers, Berry is aware, as he points out in his "Letter to Wes Jackson," that natural science, in its assumption of objectivity, has secularized the "mystery" in nature into "randomness" (*Home* 3–4). According to Berry, because scientists are apt to discount those things that they cannot quantify or measure, scientific explanations of the basic character of the "unknown" are likely to be arbitrarily based on the premise that, taken as a whole, nature complies with no overall pattern, since none can be detected.

Berry's desire to reassert the importance of unrecognized or neglected connections has led him, perhaps more intentionally than Bly or Snyder, to compose his prose collections as gatherings of apparently disparate materials. His essay collections are both "cultural and agricultural," as three of them are subtitled. Berry is highly critical of specialization in writing, agriculture, and contemporary life in general. In his view, the current state of overspecialization results in a world where poets, as well as farmers, tend to become "industrialized," the writer's output marred by the demands of the profession. "A good poem," says Berry in "The Responsibilities of the Poet," "cannot be written or understood by anyone thinking of praise or publication or promotion," because the context of the poem is altered, narrowed to appeal to a select and specialized audience of, presumably, other writers, editors, critics, and university scholars. Berry advocates what he calls amateur standards, "the standards of love" as an alternative, the amateur's effort based on concentration and avocation. Such standards imply a poetry that must prove itself in a community setting, since "The context of love is the world" (*What Are* 90).

In "Writer and Region," Berry refers to Emerson's distinction between "total" and "partial" acts, noting that specialization, to Emerson, did not justify or require relinquishing the "total" act of living for the "partial" act of following one's profession (84–85). Bly makes a similar point in "Leaping Up into Political Poetry," when he says that "most critics," literary professionals in Berry's view, "believe that poetry on political subjects should not be attempted," because "national political events are beyond the reach of ordinary, or even extraordinary, literary sensitivity" (*American* 243). Snyder, too, rejects the notion of the isolation of literature and, in doing so, according to Molesworth, risks the possibility that readers might "judge the vision negatively as a literary displacement of concerns more properly addressed by other means" (*Gary* 10). Berry's merging of the "cultural and agricultural" is consistent with his belief, shared with Bly and Snyder, that literature's purpose extends beyond the universities and publishers into "the household and the community" (*What Are* 84).

Like Bly and Snyder, Berry sees the separation of humanity from the rest of nature in Western culture as a fundamental force behind current ecological and cultural problems. His formulation of how that connection can be maintained and how it was originally broken, however, is somewhat different from theirs, especially from Bly's. In "Poetry and Place," Berry even defends Alexander Pope from what Jeffery Alan Triggs calls "some rather ill-considered criticism by Robert Bly" (193–94), which, as Berry notes, is based on passages taken out of context (*Standing* 143). In other places, also, Berry defends Pope and the idea of the Great Chain of Being as a legitimate way of envisioning humanity as part of the natural world. In "Preserving Wildness" he says that "humans differ most from other creatures in the extent that they must be *made* what they are—that is, in the extent to which they are artifacts of their culture" (*Home* 141). Because humans are so dependent on culture, without which "people are monsters, not ordinary animals" (142), Berry concludes that "The only thing we have to preserve nature with is culture; the only thing we have to preserve wildness with is domesticity" (143). In "Two Economies," he sees the idea of the Great Chain of Being not as a way of devaluing nature but instead as a reminder that the "human economy" is surrounded by a "great economy" of which it is only a part. Berry points out that, in Pope's *An Essay on Man,* "Man, then, is *not* 'at the top,' but somewhere in the middle of an orderly hierarchy that *joins* (it is a 'chain,' not a set of discrete categories) all creatures from microbes to God. That this is a chain, that it describes a necessary kinship among all the creatures that it joins, Pope understands as clearly as any ecologist" (*Standing* 143).

Pope's statement that "the proper study of mankind is man," which for Bly encapsulates the arrogant "Old Position," is seen, in this light, not as evidence of hubris but as a statement of human limitations. Berry concludes that, rather than illustrating the perceived separation of humanity from nature, Pope's lines represent a last attempt to preserve awareness of that connection, lost "Sometime between, say, Pope's verses on the Chain of Being in *An Essay on Man* and Blake's 'London'" (*Home* 70). Still, Berry agrees with Bly that modern Western civilization is destructive because of the perceived separation between humanity and the rest of nature, even describing that split in terms that call Bly to mind. Humans have come to a point, "the level of consciousness," at which "they must become conscious of the creation . . . or else . . . the spirit of the creation will go out of them, and they will become destructive; the very earth will depart from them and go where they cannot follow" (*Long-Legged* 193).

Berry's differing version of literary history, though, does reflect and in part determine the direction he follows in attempting to devise solutions to the perceived rift separating culture and nature. Perhaps the most obvious result of Berry's version of literary history is his attitude toward form in poetry. In addition to reflecting his fundamental devotion to "inwardness," Bly's early de-emphasis of poetic form can be seen as a natural development of his philosophical distaste for Enlightenment notions of a "clockwork universe," most recently and immediately embodied for Bly in the autotelic late Modern poem. Because the "clockwork poem" was confined to its own internal energy circuitry, Bly quite naturally rejected it as turning its back on the energies of the universe, and he favored instead the notion of organic, self-generating form. Later in his career, when Bly has turned more of his attention to form as such, he tends to see it as he does imagery, that is, as a means involved in the poem's process of capturing or embodying natural energies apprehended by the unconscious mind.[14] Berry, on the other hand, sees poetic form not as a mechanistic contrivance or psychological power source but instead as evidence of and a means to clear thought. It is not surprising that even Berry's free verse poems have an elegance that seems "old-fashioned." What Berry means by "standing by words" is careful attention to rhetoric and syntax, to the formation of meaning, and this rhetorical precision is reflected in his poetry as well as his prose.[15]

For Berry, a poem's formal elements also provide a measure of continuity. "Open form" poetry, despite its "democratic" attempt to incorporate the language of common speech, has, as Pinsky and von Hallberg have established, its own conventions. Because twentieth-century open form poetry tends to adopt unfamiliar or nonce formal devices and structures, readers from other than the "literary world" must approach it as an uncertain and novel reading experience. Triggs finds that "Wendell Berry is part of this [contemporary] generation, and for most of his career he has followed its predilections as to form" (192), but characterizes his shift from "supple free verse" (195) to a more tightly controlled verse form in the Sabbaths poems as resolving "a latent contradiction in Berry's work between the formality of his philosophical positions . . . and the colloquial freedom of his chosen verse forms" (193). But Berry has not shifted completely into traditional formal verse since his first collection of Sabbaths verses was published in 1987. Instead he continues to work in both formal and free verse modes. Moreover, many of the later Sabbaths poems are close in both style and subject matter to Berry's other lyrics. Poems such as IV in the 1997 series are as personal and autobiographical as any of Berry's work, and the formal structure of many of the 1990s Sabbaths poems is very similar to that of Berry's earlier free verse poems. In his preface to *A Timbered Choir,* his 1998 collection of Sabbaths poems, Berry asserts both his belief that poetry "can be a way of saying something of public interest in public" and his continuing allegiance to contemporary poetics, since "poetry also has a private life that is more important to it and more necessary to us" (xvii). In Berry's work, the two modes—public and private, formal and contemporary—are not really at odds. Gregory McNamee's characterization of Berry's lyrics as "stunning georgics" (101) serves as a reminder that the idea of the "received" in poetry involves traditions of subject matter and diction as well as of rhyme and rhythm. Berry's "georgics" use plain, graceful language in a traditional if not strictly definable way.

Berry's approach to free verse has always been to blend his generation's chosen conventions with older traditions of diction and content. In the free verse poems, as well as in the Sabbaths poems, Berry uses rhetorical formality and sound to offset or "ennoble" his plain vocabulary. For example, "History" from *Clearing,* though it employs simple diction and colloquial phrases ("The crops were made"; 1), combines syntactical patterning with assonance to lend to its common language a formal grace that reflects its themes and subject matter. Plural nouns ("crops," "leaves," 1; "frosts," 2; "houses," 6; "smokes," 7; "women," "hearths," 8; all in the first eight lines) enfold the central "I" in the community and the natural order. As Michael Hamburger notes, Berry's poems, as well as his prose, make use of what Berry, in *Standing by Words,* calls "community speech." Hamburger observes that "this plain 'community speech' can convey straight narrative and dialogue, but also an almost mystical undercurrent that allows him to make connections between the concentric orders of human life, like that between love of the land and love between men and women" (86).[16] In an interview with Mindy Weinreb, Berry elaborates on his notion of concentric orders: "Human reality, as I understand it, can be diagramed as a series of concentric circles or spheres: nature, human economy and culture, community, household, marriage, and family. There is a complex interdependency among all of these spheres, and each one and its connections with the others must be preserved. They must be kept together in some kind of union—consciously understood (though understanding can never be complete), loved, honored, and cherished—for which marriage, I suppose, is as good a metaphor as any" (29). Berry frequently employs the metaphor of long-standing monogamous marriage to figure the relationship between farmer and farmland. Annette Kolodny's *The Lay of the Land* critiques this sort of gendering, incisively identifying implications and dangers inherent in the metaphor of the land as woman. Berry's marriage metaphor is in practice limited to a masculine "husbandman" and a feminized farm, in keeping with the strict sex role patterns in his novels. He is arguably more aware of the historical consequences of the particular application of this metaphor that leads to the agribusiness he condemns in *The Unsettling of America* than he is of the dangers that may be inherent in the metaphor itself. But Berry is attracted to the metaphor of marriage because of its apparent aptness and familiarity; it is in effect a "community image" made "as good as any" by virtue of long use.

An aesthetic danger inherent in Berry's "community speech" is that it sometimes lapses into cliché, as it does, for example, in "A Marriage Song" from *Entries,* but Berry is more willing to take this risk than to fall into the opposite danger of obscurity. Connections made in such "community" poetry are of a different order than the associative "leaping" favored by Bly, at once less extravagant in language and less exploratory in nature, clearly involving conscious selection and analysis. As with Snyder, Berry's poetry has been criticized as didactic, attempting as it does to communicate ideas he would like the reader to adopt. Lionel Basney notes the practical, instructive nature of Berry's poetic connections and how the didactic quality of his writing tends to put him at odds with contemporary notions of literature, since "'Didactic' is today a term of automatic disapproval." But such an a priori dismissal of didacticism as "an aesthetic fault—preachiness, doctrine worn on the sleeve. . . . has begged the question traditional didactic critics, Horace, Sidney, or Johnson, put at the center of their understanding of poetry: the question of what art contributes to a people's way of life" (175).

Christopher Clausen observes that twentieth-century poets, following Modernism, are characterized by a failure to share "with their public a common devotion to . . . landmarks—geographical, religious, and historical" (96), and he blames the isolated condition of poetry on this failure. Berry accepts the pertinence of traditional forms as "landmarks" and, more so, the underlying values that form embodies in poetry—care, clarity, community, and tradition—claiming, in "The Responsibilities of the Poet," that "any poem worth the name is a convocation" existing "literally, by calling past voices into presence." He states that "poetry can be written only because it has been written," [17] and he goes on to say that a poem not only calls to mind the poets and poetry of the past but also "may remind poet and reader alike of what is remembered or ought to be remembered," concluding that "By its formal integrity a poem reminds us of the formal integrity of other works, creatures, and structures of the world" (*What Are* 89). To borrow Edward O. Wilson's term, the poem's formal integrity is "consilient" with these other forms.

The fourth poem from the 1988 Sabbaths sequence enlists the formal elements of poetry in a way typical of Berry's formal verse:

> The world of machines is running
> Beyond the world of trees
> Where only a leaf is turning
> In a small high breeze.   (1–4)

The poem identifies and rhetorically relates two "worlds." The "world of machines" appears to be both separate from and more substantial than the "world of trees." But the poem's formal construction belies its assertion. The poem is unbalanced, with only the first line dedicated to "machines" and the other three to "trees." Furthermore, the exact rhyme between "trees" and "breeze," a rhyme that certainly falls into the category of community, even hackneyed, language, is enacted entirely in the "world of trees." A second, weaker rhyme contrasts the two worlds, the linear "running" of the machines leading them virtually out of the stanza, while the "turning" suggests both the seasonal rhythms of natural cycles and the upcoming completion of the "trees/breeze" rhyme. As Jeffers did, Berry uses the formal elements of poetry as a means to communicate ideas. The ideas do not take the form of provisional assertions functioning as parts of a self-contained system of poetic forces. Berry's poetry uses form to reinforce ideas he earnestly wants his readers to adopt.

Berry's rejection of the "machine world," implicit in the stanza, is a reminder that, although he defends certain figures and ideas that Bly associates with the "Old Position," Berry is not a believer in any notion of a clockwork universe. Berry's defense of Pope stems, instead, from his unwillingness to cast other poets and their methods in Bly's rather simplistic "us and them" terms, which Berry reserves for his political and social divisions.

Berry's "Reinhabitation" of Western Traditions

The central role of day-to-day autobiography in Berry's work marks him as a contemporary poet. Like Bly and Snyder, Berry has attempted to reconcile the individualistic basis of contemporary poetics with the public responsibilities he grants the poet. If Bly has, in effect, and Snyder has, explicitly, sought a position from which to address public concerns by adopting the persona of a poet-shaman, Berry has developed a different approach. Berry, like Snyder, has expressed admiration for both Native American and Asian ecological principles (*Long-Legged* 182). However, whereas Snyder came to his particular form of spiritual bioregionalism by what Patrick Murphy calls "a web of paths" ("Penance" 65), with Zen Buddhism and Native American lore as his foremost sources of instruction, Berry seems to have been led directly, like Andy Catlett in *Remembering,* not only back to his geographical birthplace but also into his own culture, specifically into the agrarian and Christian religious traditions of the West.

Berry seeks to "heal" his culture by rehabilitating its basic principles and ideals and by endorsing and fostering "an art that heals and protects its subject" (*What Are* 7, sec. 3). As "a farmer of sorts and an artist of sorts" (153), and because he sees the two occupations as fundamentally related, both providing a kind of nourishment, Berry has sought, in the history of Western agrarian thought, the kind of base that Bly finds in Romanticism and psychology and Snyder finds in Native American and Asian ideas. Not surprisingly, Berry advocates the traditional agrarianism of Thomas Jefferson and Sir Alfred Howard, whom Berry calls "the great British agricultural scientist" (*Unsettling* 46) and whose formulation of the Wheel of Life reappears embodied in Berry's *The Wheel*.[18] Berry believes that Western agrarianism, as he says in "Discipline and Hope," forms an imperfect but valuable tradition that could serve, if developed and nurtured over time, as a source for a truly "indigenous" relationship between people and the natural community (*Continuous* 102).

Berry admits that farming societies have been destructive of soil and general land health, a situation that has left agriculture suspect in the eyes of many environmentalists. In *The Dream of the Earth,* for example, Thomas Berry cites the development of agriculture as the beginning of the process of damaging the relationship between humanity and the natural world, though he admits that the damage was localized and probably not irreparable (7). Even Snyder, with whom Wendell Berry shares considerable common ground, prefers the model of the hunting and gathering society to that of the agrarian. Wendell Berry is not blind to the shortcomings of American agrarianism in practice, but he tends to view abuses as historical in nature, mistakes that could, under other circumstances, have been avoided, and not as manifestations of an essential flaw in the agrarian philosophy itself. In *The Unsettling of America,* he admits that agriculture "was never, in America, sufficiently thrifty or sufficiently careful of soil fertility" but argues that "It is tempting to suppose that, given certain critical historical and cultural differences, they [American farmers and communities] might have developed sufficient thrift and care" (32).

Berry's argument here illustrates his tendency to substitute acknowledgment of a problem for solution of it. In *The Hidden Wound,* for example, Berry describes in detail the falsification of slave owners' ideals and religious beliefs implicit in the slavery system, yet his own fiction, as Hamburger observes, virtually ignores racial inequality in its southern setting (84–85), and his lionization of Jefferson is apparently unaffected by Jefferson's well-known ambivalence concerning slavery. The same criticism could, however, be applied to other agrarians, perhaps to anyone who attempts to explain the failure of the ideal to translate into practice. Berry's characterization in

The Unsettling of America of the potentially independent and self-sufficient agricultural community based on the "collaboration of household and farm" (32) but seduced by the abstractions of advertising and industry echoes Jefferson himself. As the historian Forrest McDonald explains, Jefferson envisioned a society where "Relationships were based upon agriculture and its 'handmaiden' commerce, upon ownership of land, honest labor in the earth, craftsmanship in the cities, and free trade between individuals" (19), but this community was eventually subverted by "money—not 'real money,' gold and silver, but artificial money in the form of public debt, bank notes, stocks, and other kinds of paper—the acquisition of which had nothing to do with either land or labor" (19–20). In "The Mad Farmer Manifesto: The First Amendment," Berry first quotes Jefferson in an epigraph and then paraphrases him in the poem.[19] Significantly, it is the same force of disembodied capital that undermined Jefferson's yeomanry that the Mad Farmers must reject by declaring their freedom from "*ignorant money*" (3.1), which is

. . . driving
us into the streets of absence
stranding the pasture trees
in the deserted language of banks.   (3.2–6)

Also clear here is Berry's belief in the common interest connecting human and nonhuman ("the pasture trees") members of the rural community.

Berry's belief that adherence to "Adams, Jefferson, and the principle of 'usufruct'" (Elder 53) leads to stewardship or "kindly use" serves the same purpose as Snyder's adoption of Zen and Native American ecological principles. Despite its historical failings, agrarianism offers an alternative to the ecologically and culturally destructive impulses that drive contemporary culture. In *The Unsettling of America,* Berry claims that:

The old [agrarian] idea is still full of promise. It is potent with healing and with health. It has the power to turn each person away from the big-time promising and planning of the government, to confront in himself, in the immediacy of his own circumstances and whereabouts, the question of what methods and ways are best. It proposes an economy of necessities rather than an economy based upon anxiety, fantasy, luxury, and idle wishing. It proposes the independent, free-standing citizenry that Jefferson thought to be the surest safeguard of democratic liberty. And perhaps most important of all, it proposes an agriculture based upon intensive work, local energies, care, and long-living communities.   (14)

Like Bly and Snyder, Berry sees the desacralization of nature as a fundamental problem of Western civilization and seeks in his poetry to reassert the religious significance of the creation. Typically, though, he has sought to reinterpret, rather than reject, Western traditions. In the ongoing debate about the Judeo-Christian religious tradition's role in creating and maintaining the perceived qualitative difference between human life and the nonhuman, Berry has found himself on the opposite side from Bly and Snyder. Bly maintains that "The Church at the start of the Christian era didn't know whether to accept the ancient view that we shared consciousness with nature, or to declare a new era" (*News* 9), but it ended up rejecting the sacredness of the natural world because "The Church Fathers were afraid to open the door to too many visions for fear the ancient world would simply flood the Church" (9). Snyder basically agrees, as Steuding recognizes when he says that "The poetry of Snyder, like the works of Thoreau, is preeminently anti-Christian, even pagan" (117). Snyder himself, in "The Yogin and the Philosopher," goes as far as to say that Western poetry, in identifying the Muse as a personification of common ground between humanity and the natural world, has been involved in a "long 'pagan' battle . . . against state and church" (*Old* 13, reprinted in *Place* 51). In *Earth House Hold,* Snyder calls Jehovah "a projection of the gathered power of anti-nature social forces" (124). Religious historian Catherine Albanese sums up the effective diminution of nature in Christian history: "Through out the history of Western culture, at least, religious reflection has been preoccupied with three great symbolic centers, two of them more persistently, especially in certain forms of Protestantism. The three are the familiar trinity—God, humanity, and nature—and it is, of course, God and humanity that have been more pondered and nature that has formed the third and less noticed center among them" (7).

Critics of Christianity such as Lynn White Jr. have claimed that the privileging of human concerns over the rest of nature is inherent in Christianity.[20] Albanese posits that neopagan "nature religions" seek to restore nature to a sacred status by rejecting this Judeo-Christian history. She cites Starhawk, a "contemporary American witch" (180) as "Castigating the Judeo-Christian view of the world" (181). But Berry, again respectful of the living traditions of his culture, attempts to find ground for the resacralization of nature within the Judeo-Christian context; Roderick Nash calls him one of the "environmentally conscious modern Christians" (110–11). A recurrent theme in Berry's essays has been that the Bible's directive to subdue nature should not be blamed for the arrogance of Western cultures toward the environment. The real problem, he argues in "The Gift of Good Land," is not the text itself but a misreading of it. Berry reiterates this idea in "Poetry and Place" from *Standing by Words,* in which he refers to "Genesis I:28, a text much hackneyed lately by 'ecological' condemners of Western culture" (142), in "God and Country" from *What Are People For?* and again in "Christianity and the Survival of the Creation" from *Sex, Economy, Freedom, and Community.* In "God and Country," he asks, "Is this state of affairs caused by Christian truth or by the failures and errors of Christian practice?" (98). As with agrarianism, Berry's answer is that the problem is not in the essence of the doctrine but in the practical application, concluding that "The ecological teaching of the Bible is simply inescapable" and posing the question, "If God loves the world, then how might any person of faith be excused for not loving it or justified in destroying it?" (98).

It could be said that Berry's contention that humans are the world's "stewards," placed in charge by God, in effect evades the difficult task of becoming what Leopold called "plain member and citizen" (204) of the natural community, instead casting humans as God's agents in conducting the affairs of the earth. In the central position it affords the human, Berry's agrarian stewardship differs from the New Age sense of humanity as pilot of "spaceship earth" only in its contention that human direction is not an end to itself. But the advantages of Berry's formulation are inescapable. Rather than importing ideas and beliefs from other cultures and thus becoming marginalized, as in Snyder's case, Berry attempts to find depth ecology principles within, even at the core of, Western civilization. If, like Snyder, Berry sees the current Western society as an aberration, his response has been a kind of "reinhabitation" of the culture itself. In so doing, Berry avoids both the vagueness of Bly's synthetic mysticism and the cultural imperialism risked by Snyder's incorporation of indigenous and "foreign" beliefs. Yet Berry's enlisting of Christian vocabulary and symbols in support of his principles can be quite subversive, and Berry has not been blind to the potential practical worth of his effort. In the Sabbaths poems, his series of religious meditations, Berry enlists traditional Christian imagery to establish the sacredness of the natural world, as when he asserts that:

> . . . Resurrection
> Is in the way each maple leaf
> Commemorates its kind. . . .   (II, 1979 series, 10 –12)

Triggs observes that the poems are "sprinkled with references to Resurrection, Creation, Paradise, Heaven, Eden, the forfeit Garden, the Lord, the Maker, God and His sepulcher, and of course Sabbath" (198). The religious references remain nondenominational, even unorthodox, constituting "not a conversion to orthodox theology, but the acceptance of a traditional, Christian vocabulary" (198). The uses of this shared vocabulary include the didactic, as Berry adds his own take on what Christian faith might translate to in human action. In Sabbaths VII (1979), for example, the awareness of the "disharmony" (5) of "the peopled dark / Of our unraveling century" (8–9) charges poet and reader alike with a new commitment to rebuild:

> A harmony between forest and field,
> The world as it was given for love's sake,
> The world by love and loving work revealed.   (14–16)

Wendell Berry, in his reinhabitation of Jeffersonianism and Judeo-Christian religion and his further grounding in English poetic traditions and Thoreauvian simplicity, is at once less contemporary and more contemporary than either Bly or Snyder. As a contemporary, his poems are clearly about himself. A careful reading of Berry's poems reveals more about his daily activities and surroundings than is the case with either Bly or Snyder. Yet, by figuring himself as a kind of Jeffersonian everyman, Berry has attempted to form, in his own life and the lives of his neighbors in Kentucky, a rehabilitated version of Western civilization. He does not totally succeed. To return to David Perkins's glib but not inaccurate remark about Snyder, "most readers of poetry live in cities." [21] Although Berry may have succeeded in re-creating or furthering a rich cultural tradition for himself and those whose lives are roughly similar to his, the lives of most late-twentieth-century Americans are not appreciably closer to the Jeffersonian yeoman than they are to Snyder's Buddhist settlers on San Juan Ridge. At this time, as Thomas Lyon points out, "The prominent American attitude toward the small family farm, which might be termed the 'Currier and Ives' view, remains alive in the urban-industrial era, but is rendered sentimental and more or less irrelevant by demographics" (*This* 86). This is why Berry's poems tend so frequently to elegy. As he says in "Requiem,"

> Though the green fields are my delight,
> elegy is my fate. I have come to be
> survivor of many and of much
> that I love, that I won't live to see
> come again into this world.   (1.6–10)

In the "*East West* Interview," Gary Snyder tells Peter Barry Chowka that Berry demonstrates that "There was something like the Oriental wisdom here all along, wasn't there?" (*Real* 124). But as Berry himself explains, the agrarian way of life he represents is being overwhelmed by what Snyder calls the "Growth Monster" (*Practice* 5). Although Berry's thought originates at the core of Western civilization, he represents traditions that have become marginalized with the ascendancy of agribusiness, urbanization, and industrialism. His responses to this situation are incisive and penetrating but usually offer little hope. What Berry does offer, though, is the sense that, at least theoretically, Americans could have developed a sustainable relationship between culture and the natural order. By illustrating this possibility in his life and in his writing, Berry has gained a widespread and durable appeal among readers driven by environmental concern to seek alternatives to the commodification and domination of nature that has characterized late-twentieth-century American life.

6 · The Contemporary Poet as Environmentalist

The Place of the Poet

BLY, SNYDER, AND BERRY are certainly not the only contemporary poets with a deep interest in nature, defined in the vernacular sense as the "other" that is "not us." They are also not the only poets who, like Fritzell's self-conscious nature writers, have struggled to come to grips with their state of being both a part of and apart from their surroundings. In fact, the struggle to incorporate the inner world of the self into the larger sphere of the self's environment, and the reverse, has been the central theme and project of contemporary poetry.

In part 4 of *News of the Universe,* entitled "Poems of Twofold Consciousness, 1945–1979," Bly gathers a group of poems from roughly the same post–World War II period that, following Breslin and others, I have been considering as contemporary. Bly includes in this section of his anthology all of the poets covered in this study except Jeffers, who is represented by three poems in the previous section, "Poems of Twofold Consciousness, Early Twentieth Century." Along with Roethke, Snyder, Berry, and Bly himself in part 4 are other contemporary American poets who often focus on the nonhuman and its relationship to themselves as individuals and to humankind in general, among them Galway Kinnell, Denise Levertov, Mary Oliver, William Stafford, John Haines, and Kenneth Rexroth.[1] In his introductory essay to part 4, Bly links these contemporary poets with what he has envisioned throughout *News of the Universe* as a tradition that, though it has sources in earlier European cultural history and analogs in other cultures, basically shapes itself in the wake of European Romanticism. According to Bly, "My main point is that the Novalis-Hölderlin-Goethe tradition, associated with Middle Ages alchemy, respect for the integrity of the natural world, respect for the night-intelligence, and careful observation of detail, is alive in recent poetry, much more alive than the average reader is aware" (132).

Despite the obvious differences in their views of literary and cultural history, Wendell Berry comes to a parallel conclusion in "A Secular Pilgrimage," in which he claims that "One of the most exciting and vital kinds of poetry being written now in this country is nature poetry," in which "there is a sustained attentiveness to nature and to the relation between man and nature" (*Continuous* 3). Any of the poets listed above, plus many more, such as A. R. Ammons, whom Berry discusses along with Levertov and Rexroth, could be considered in this study.[2] I have chosen Bly, Snyder, and Berry because of the wide range of their styles, literary sources, and approaches, and because they have been so consciously involved in the role of the poet as a public figure or, as Snyder has it, a "spokesman."

As might be expected, other contemporary poets have a considerable range of responses to this politicized notion of the poet's role. William Stafford's distaste for the idea of the poet as spokesperson is reflected in his claim that Snyder's earnest didacticism has sometimes interfered with the open-ended process of composing the contemporary poem, in which "intention endangers creation" (qtd. in Nordström 153). Nevertheless, it is clear that many contemporary poets have felt the desire to make some sort of public statement in their poems. Kinnell and Levertov, for example, are among the many poets who wrote antiwar poems during the Vietnam conflict. Adrienne Rich has perhaps done more to redefine the relationship between poet and audience than any other poet of the contemporary generation; it is no coincidence that she is both beloved by her readers and excoriated by critics such as Harold Bloom for valuing political over aesthetic elements in poetry.[3]

Concern for the troubled relationship between American society and the earth itself has spurred other poets, in addition to Bly, Snyder, and Berry, to make public statements about environmental problems. In "Among

Wind and Time," an article she published in *Sierra,* Mary Oliver, for example, while echoing Stafford's concern about the dangers of "intention," speaks out against the notion that poetry is a specialized, self-contained activity and discusses her concept of the responsibilities of the artist in a time of ecological crisis:

> To me it is madness to set art apart from other social and spiritual endeavors. Writing that does not influence the reader is art that sleeps, and misses the point. Not infused with conscious intention, nor built upon polemic, a poem will inevitably reflect the knowledge and the outlook of the writer. Before we move from recklessness into responsibility, from selfishness to a decent happiness, we must want to save our world. And in order to want to save the world we must learn to love it—and in order to love it we must become familiar with it again. That is where my work begins, and why I keep walking, and looking.   (34)

"Think globally, act locally" is an axiom among environmentalists, signifying that, although in a time of environmental crisis it is appropriate and necessary to keep one's attention on such large-scale concerns as biodiversity and climate change, the most productive action is often taken on a local level, where issues tend to be more palpable and the effects of one's actions clearer. Furthermore, as Berry suggests in "Think Little," communities are composed of individuals, and so change, in order to be meaningful, must occur on the individual level. According to Berry, "If we are to hope to correct our abuses of each other and of other races and of our land . . . then we are going to have to go far beyond public protest and political action. We are going to have to rebuild the substance and the integrity of private life in this country" (*Continuous* 79).

For Oliver, an important part of the process of enriching what Berry calls the "substance of private life" depends on rediscovering the ability to "become familiar" with the natural world. Like Berry, she recognizes that the individual must be the starting point. By shifting from the plural "we" to the singular "I" of "I keep walking and looking," Oliver implicitly acknowledges that, even before acting locally, one must first "rebuild the substance" of one's own self.

The attempt to firmly anchor a poem so that it is at home in one's own life has been central to contemporary American poetry. From Frank

O'Hara's "lunch hour" poems to Bly's "inwardness" to Robert Lowell's attempt at a "breakthrough back into life," a characteristic, even diagnostic, desire of American poets writing since World War II is to begin with their own lives, sometimes, as described in Bly's "Leaping Up into Political Poetry," explicitly attempting to reach more encompassing, communal levels of meaning. Whether the contemporary poet explicitly seeks political or social relevance or not, an underlying assumption of contemporary poetry has been that one kind of universal meaning or another can be found through a close scrutiny of what is near at hand.

Earlier in this discussion, I mentioned the Modern poet William Carlos Williams as an influence on Snyder and Berry and suggested that the change from late Modern to contemporary poetics was accompanied by a shifting toward Williams and away from what Breslin calls "a particular phase of modernism—that identified with Eliot and the New Criticism in America," which "had achieved a powerful hegemony which successfully domesticated modernism" (13). Certainly there is much about Williams to recommend him to contemporary poets. He had a blend of grudging respect and personal and aesthetic distaste for Eliot's poetics and for Eliot himself, whom he calls, in "Prologue to *Kora in Hell*," "a subtle conformist" (21) and, in a 1940 letter to Reed Whittemore, "the concepts that walk around as T. S. Eliot" (237). Williams also championed the evolutionary notion of poetic development. Breslin tells of a 1948 conference in which Williams, at sixty-five, "advanced the cause of innovation" (28) by insisting "on the evolution of new poetic means that are organically related to contemporary American experience" (29). Because of his typewriter-based concept of organic form, Williams also offered an important model for the skills of line breaking and free verse music that would prove to be so useful to poets attempting to escape the autotelic formalism of the New Critics. But perhaps the most significant factor leading to the ascendancy of Williams as an influence on contemporary poets is Williams's immediacy. Of all the Great Moderns of early-twentieth-century America, Williams is the most obviously and intimately present in his poems. Wendell Berry, in his "A Homage to Dr. Williams," presents Williams in almost Whitmanesque terms, as one who "In his poems . . . did not speak as a poet but as a man" (*Continuous* 58). Berry asserts that a poet such as Williams, when deeply committed to "the art of writing as an instrument by which a man may arrive in his place and maintain himself there" (56), accomplishes "a sustained and intricate act of patriotism in the largest sense of that word" (57). Berry finds in Williams "the excitement of the awareness that poetry, as much as the axe or the plow, is a necessity of discovery and settlement, and of the husbanding and neighboring that must follow" (56). In short, Williams's poetry, as Berry sees it, thinks globally but acts locally. Berry concludes his "homage" by acknowledging Williams as a mentor whose "work seems to keep ahead of me, like a man's shadow when he walks eastward in the afternoon" (62).

In designing this study, I chose to include Robinson Jeffers as a representative of the early-twentieth-century age of Modernism that the contemporary poets followed. I chose him because of the obvious ecological "message" in his poetry and because of his importance to environmentalists today. Williams, however, has been a much more central influence on the development of contemporary poetics in general. And contemporary poetics itself, with its grounding in the quotidian experiences of the poet, has helped bring poets such as Bly, Snyder, and Berry to the same conclusion as that reached by natural history writers and later by environmental activists—that what one does locally, in one's own everyday activities, has global or universal ramifications and meaning. Despite the apparent isolationism inherent in contemporary poetics, environmentally concerned contemporary poets ranging from Bly to Snyder to Berry to Mary Oliver have not had to look far to find a principle to govern their activism. When Oliver says, "That is where my work begins," she is talking about both her work as a poet and her attempt to "save our world," in short, what Snyder might call "the real work."

The Quest for the Indigenous and the Literary "Frontier"

Perhaps the most important trend in American poetry and fiction in the past two decades has been the growing visibility of writers of diverse ethnic and racial backgrounds and the increasing use of literature as a source and reflection of ethnic identity. This is a complex development stemming from factors as diverse as the writers (and readers) involved and reflecting conditions in the larger sphere of American society. In at least some cases, however, the indigenous character, that is, the comparative "rootedness" of ethnic minorities, has been significant in their increased visibility, particularly in the extension of that visibility beyond the primary audience that shares their ethnic identity. The desire for rootedness has produced, even among majority white Americans vaguely disconcerted by their lack of a deep connection with their surroundings, a sense of fellow feeling with ethnic minorities whose writing reflects a "diaspora" or other disenfranchisement and a resultant intense longing for a lost homeland. The Hispanic notion of Azatlan is one example of an imaginative response to such a longing.

Berry's *The Hidden Wound* argues that, in the rural Kentucky of his upbringing, African Americans were more likely to have an intimate personal understanding of the land they sharecropped than were the white landowners, who saw their "holdings" in the abstract, as means to profit and status, and who, like Faulkner's Isaac McCaslin, knew that the claim of the descendants of the slaves as true inhabitants of the land was more earned and rightful than their own. Various observers from Amiri Baraka to Houston Baker have claimed that African Americans, because of their fundamental and inescapable involvement with the realities of American life, have developed a more genuinely American culture than have the "dominant" whites. The difficulties involved in African-American identification with the American landscape are self-evident and have often been discussed; they form a part of the thematic underpinnings of works as varied as Frederick Douglass's *Narrative,* Jean Toomer's *Cane,* and Toni Morrison's *Beloved.* It is unquestionably easier for a white writer to admire African-American connectedness than it is for African Americans to live that connection, but there is almost a kind of envy in works like Faulkner's *Go Down, Moses* and Berry's *The Hidden Wound,* or at least a sense of longing for what is seen as the hard-earned African-American rootedness in the American soil. But Berry realizes that this rootedness is also falsified by the history that has prevented African Americans from fully asserting their claim to the American earth. In his poem "My Great Grandfather's Slaves," Berry shares in the slaves' historical relationship with "the same fields that I have gone / long days over" (3–4), but the experience of this shared history is marred by the lingering presence of the slave owner, "whose blindness is my brand" (13). Ultimately, the poem comes to the realization that neither the descendants of slaves nor the descendant of their owner can ever be "free of one another" (41). For each, the sense of belonging to their ancestral farm has been damaged, and neither can be truly at home.

Certainly, the most obviously indigenous ethnic groups in America are American Indians, and Native American writers, often working in both poetry and prose, have been an important part of what could be called the recent ethnic expansion of American literature, so much so that critics such as Kenneth Lincoln have posited that a "Native American Renaissance" has occurred in the last decades, as poets such as Ray Young Bear, Joy Harjo, James Welch, Louise Erdrich, Linda Hogan, and Duane Niatum have formed what Brian Swann, in his introduction to *Harper's Anthology of Twentieth Century Native American Poetry*, calls "one of the most lively developments on the American art scene" (xvi). The recent upsurge in interest in American Indian writing is particularly significant to this study because of the importance of Native American cultures to Gary Snyder and also because of the widespread perception that Native American sources can provide a key to the development of a more balanced and spiritually based conception of nature, essential for continued human well-being in a time of ecological crisis. Christopher Vecsey believes that much of the recent interest in American Indian society and literature is based on concern for the environment, a conclusion with which Lars Nordström agrees. Snyder, also, clearly believes that Native American traditions, anchored on the American continents, offer potential ways to address environmental concerns. If the normally genial Snyder has been uncharacteristically sharp in his responses to Native American criticism, his reaction indicates the depth to which the transformation of the European continent of North America to the "old/new" Turtle Island is dependent on traditional Native American concepts and lifeways.

In the conclusion to his study of Northwestern poets, Lars Nordström notes that "Northwest School" regionalism has been characterized by Carol Jane Bangs as stemming from a "primarily male preoccupation." Although conceding that "This might be true," Nordström questions its validity when applied to the "ecological metaphor," which, he says, is apparent in poets such as Vi Gale and Ingrid Wendt as well as in male poets. However, his book belies this point by focusing on Theodore Roethke, William Stafford, and Gary Snyder; and even in the discussion of "Some Additional Northwest Perspectives" (141) at the end of the book, more space is given to Richard Hugo and David Wagoner than to Gale and Wendt. The predominance of male writers in discussions like this one is too complex to address sufficiently in a book about something else, but it is certainly related to a similar imbalance in the history of nature writing. The tradition of the American literary voice of the wilderness has often been figured as a lineage linking such male writers as Thoreau, Muir, Leopold, and Edward Abbey, who conveniently excises his wife from *Desert Solitaire,* perhaps to purge his experience in the wilderness of any distracting domestic associations. In Thomas Lyon's chart "Writing about Nature: A Spectrum" (*This* 4), all but two of the representative works are by male writers, and the two exceptions, Ann Zwinger and Beatrice Willard's *The Land above the Trees* and Annie Dillard's *Pilgrim at Tinker Creek,* were both written after 1970.

This historical thread is clearly oversimplified, and writers such as Susan Fenimore Cooper, Mary Austin, and Rachel Carson have been significant contributors to the tradition of American nature writing. But in the formative years of the generation of poets defined as contemporary in this study, the old correlation of masculinity and wilderness, femininity and domesticity, was an underlying part of what might be thought of as an operant mythology, evident not only in contemporary poetry but in works as disparate as Jack Kerouac's *On the Road* and Saul Bellow's *Henderson the Rain King,* as well as in Roethke's citing of "Muir and Thoreau and Burroughs" (*On the Poet* 4) and Snyder's citing of Ernest Thompson Seton as shaping influences in their own conception of the relationship between the individual and nature. The land itself may have been seen as feminine, but the journey into it was a male prerogative.

The emerging canon of American nature writing in all genres has been revealed to be more complicated than the lineage cited above. Furthermore, among contemporary nature writers, there are many prominent women who explore various forms of wilderness experience, among them Anne La Bastille, Gretel Ehrlich, and Ann Zwinger. Arguably the most widely known living American nonfiction writer whose work exemplifies the traditional concerns of the nature writer is Annie Dillard. Dillard is paralleled in poetry by Mary Oliver, perhaps the leading nature poet to emerge in what might be called the "late contemporary" period. Oliver's poetics are not especially different from her contemporary predecessors, but in seeking meaning in her direct individual experience of wild nature, she incorporates a perspective and addresses themes that seemed inexorably bound to the male writer as recently as the 1950s and 1960s.

In her essay "Letting Go Our Grand Obsessions: Notes toward a New Literary History of the American Frontiers," Annette Kolodny, who as a major critic of American concepts of nature and wilderness occupies a position in criticism more or less parallel to that of Dillard and Oliver in their respective genres, posits that the seminal American notion of the frontier should be reconsidered not as a border line but rather as "the Borderlands" (9), an area of "permeable margins" (2) between human individuals, human cultures, and the physical land itself. Kolodny's suggested redefinition provides another way of considering the work of the three poets central to this study. Bly, Snyder, and Berry have found themselves somewhat isolated from the mainstream of American life because of their attitude toward nature and because contemporary poetry does not offer the poet an authoritative public position from which to speak. What these three poets have attempted to do to mitigate their isolation is to expand the field they explore, emphasizing ideas, techniques, and themes linking their own contemporary experience to neglected corners of American cultural history, in Berry's case; to the European past, in the case of Berry and particularly Bly; and to Asian cultures, most obviously in the case of Snyder, although both Bly and Berry have also acknowledged Asian influences.[4] Each of the poets has also been aware of Native American conceptions of the sacredness of nature, and one, Snyder, has consciously sought to bring Native American ideas and materials to the attention of his readers. Also, each poet has attempted to create or further connections among various forms of human endeavor—science and art, religious and practical life, culture and agriculture. Finally, each has attempted to extend the "zone of interpenetration" to include the nonhuman, both the living creatures and the natural processes that Kolodny calls the "physical terrain."[5] Seen in this light, the interpenetration of prose and poetry in Bly's prose poems, in Snyder's direct instruction, and in the two "meditations" that open Berry's *What Are People For?* are logical expressions of the poets' attempt to create an inclusive, ecological, and reader-friendly synthesis.

Each of the three poets has found that the fundamental individualism inherent in contemporary poetics has limited the success with which any poet practicing this poetics of immediacy can reach beyond the individual level of meaning into the relationship between public readership and sub-ject matter. Bly's, Snyder's, and Berry's attempts to influence their readers' response to the natural world also illustrate that it is easier to criticize the fundamental beliefs of one's culture in the detached manner of Jeffers than to free one's self, individually, from those assumptions. Bly finds himself advocating "twofold consciousness," which, despite its intentions, not only establishes a division between human and nonhuman but in practice cre-ates a hierarchy. Although Lyon finds Snyder's poetry to be "fundamentally nondualistic" ("Twenty" 46), Snyder admits in his prose that nature as a separate "other," the "outdoors," appears "even here" (*Practice* 9). In "this poem is for bear," his individuality, asserting itself in the last lines, breaks up the field of "interpenetration" set up through the course of the poem and calls the poet back to his own perspective, from which he "couldn't hit a bear in the ass / with a handful of rice" (54–55). Berry, too, retains a division between human and nature in his use of the metaphor of marriage, through which the poet-farmer becomes, as Jack Hicks says, "Husband to the World" (118). And, like Bly's formulations, Berry's metaphor tends to reinforce sexual stereotypes, with the male "husbandman" tending and car-ing for the feminized natural landscape.[6]

Bly, Snyder, and Berry: Some Conclusions

The development of Breslin's "poetics of immediacy" (70) was a reaction to Modernism's apparent loss of what Bly might call "wildness," as a result of the hegemony of New Critical assumptions and prescriptions. Contem-porary poets each sought to "break through" what they saw as a kind of tyranny and to re-create themselves aesthetically through radical changes in style and focus. William Carlos Williams, in the preface to his *Selected Es-says,* claims that "The processes of art, to keep alive, must always challenge the unknown and go where the most uncertainty lies" (9). For Bly, Snyder, and Berry, the uncertain path away from the hegemony of late Modernism led, in Perkins's phrase, "Against Civilization" and through the realm of nature.[7] For Snyder, the journey away from "civilization" has at times been quite literal, bringing him to remote locations such as the fire look-out tower at Sourdough Mountain. For Bly, the wilderness road is more often experienced as psychological metaphor, leading down the suppressed "wild" road of "association," utilizing and exploring the nonrational and less controllable channels in the mind. Berry's journey has been more sociological, examining his culture's values in the light of what he learns from natural processes and cycles, and looking for alternative interpretations of American principles and lore in forgotten corners or margins of American life. His path, therefore, has included the intersections where his own culture has encountered natural systems and where Western peoples have attempted to live in harmony with them. In his support for nonindustrialized farming and equally nonindustrialized poetry, Berry's cultural and agricultural Jeffersonianism constitutes what Lawrence Buell calls "an insurgency of the disempowered" (14), far more radical and inclusive than Jefferson himself had in mind but grounded, again, on basic "near at hand" processes such as soil conservation and the maintenance of stable food supplies through the practice of sustainable lifeways.[8]

Throughout this study, these poets have been compared to what Fritzell calls self-conscious nature writers, those who pay attention not only to nature as a collection of valuable objects of study but also to their own complex and unavoidable connection to what is studied. In short, these writers of natural history attempt both to study nature as "other," distinct and discrete, and therefore not dependent for worth or identity on human consideration, and yet at the same time to cultivate the psychological and spiritual awareness of their own involvement, as both organism and observer, in the functioning of the "natural world" that they experience. Self-conscious nature writers are in the precarious position of reaching across the gap between human and nonhuman nature by recognizing their own participation in the processes they observe, including observation itself, while maintaining an uncompromised belief in the integrity of nature as an independently functioning totality.

Bly, Snyder, and Berry find themselves inexorably linked to a culture whose relationship with nature they do not approve of but at the same time cannot escape. Moreover, each is tied to a philosophical dichotomy between human and nonhuman nature that they all believe to be fundamentally false and harmful. But to give up this division would mean risking the self-absorption Bly claims to find in Pope's statement that "The proper study of mankind is man," a kind of societal solipsism that eventually denies the inherent dignity and worth even of most humans. Thus, to Berry, "green revolution" agribusiness's denial that nature has value apart from human measures of worth results in the inevitable consequence that small farmers and whole rural communities, seen as obsolete, are sacrificed to the complex of vast impersonal economic forces that he believes to be anomalous, even monstrous.

As a living edge of literature, contemporary poetry has not had to wait for the resolution of academic issues regarding canon restructuring. As a result, contemporary American literature has become a kind of frontier or, to use a term Kolodny adapts from historical research, a "zone of interpenetration" where poets from a wide variety of backgrounds combine to create a complex texture ("Letting" 4). In this context, the attempts of three individuals of the same gender, age, and vocation and of generally similar heritage to share the meaning they have found in their own experience need not be, and cannot be expected to be, sufficient in itself. Kolodny, in speaking of the literal frontier in American history, claims that, when one considers the frontier as a zone of interpenetration, it follows that any particular point of view would be partial, since "What makes the paradigm so appealing . . . is that English texts, by themselves, could never constitute a sufficient history" (6) and must therefore be augmented by other viewpoints.

The measurement of the usefulness of a particular poet's work, always difficult to assess, becomes even more elusive when that poet is considered as just one interacting part of a vast zone of interpenetration. One important contribution Bly, Snyder, and Berry have made, though, to developing a more complete understanding of the zone of interpenetration that is the biosphere in which we all live is inherent in their attempts to "break through" not only into their own lives but from them into the lives of others, even into the life of the planet itself, the source of Bly's *News of the Universe*. If they have remained essentially committed in practice to the notion of the isolated contemporary "voice in the wilderness," Bly, Snyder, and Berry have at least listened seriously to whom and what they have found there.

What role Bly, Snyder, and Berry may have had in promoting a more sustainable and satisfying relationship with the natural world remains open to debate, especially since their poetic authority still generally rests on an individual rather than communal basis. But the characteristic contemporary concern for the quotidian experience of the poet himself or herself has led, perhaps inevitably, to an expansion away from that locus, as the poet seeks to relate individual experience to that of others, especially when pressured by concern for a shared subject matter, as is true of Bly, Snyder, and Berry. The distance traveled by these three from their "far fields" toward positions of public recognition and influence is especially noteworthy when one considers that, as poets whose primary source of poetic authority has been their own experience with their natural environment, Bly, Snyder, and Berry have been even further removed from the mainstream of urban and suburban America than most contemporary American poets.

Ironically, a change in public attitudes toward nature, once a contributing factor in their isolation, has finally helped Bly, Snyder, and Berry reach a broader audience. The natural imagery and "hinterland" settings that were sometimes a source of critical alienation for Jeffers and Roethke have become a source of popularity, if not with the established poetry audience, then with a more general readership, the kind of audience that Gioia says poetry must reclaim if it is to "matter." In his 1989 article "Poetry and Audience," for example, Bly notes that "Gary Snyder's books of poetry— to name one of our best contemporary poets—have sold a total of about two hundred thousand so far" (19), a total Bly contrasts with much lower sales figures for Eliot, Williams, and Stevens when they were alive. Though Gioia points out that sales figures may not really be an accurate measure of readership since many readers in the past favored anthologies or comprehensive collections (17), the fact remains that Snyder is likely to be among the first names to come up in arguments asserting poetry's popularity, and Bly's name would surely follow. Certainly Snyder's sales figures reflect, along with an often-neglected increase in the number of poetry readers in general, a considerable group of readers for whom, as ecofeminist poet Susan Griffin says, "nature has become a source of meaning again" (45).

Bly, Snyder, and Berry have each been committed to the belief that poetry can be useful for individuals and cultures seeking a fuller understanding of their encompassing environments. The resulting purposiveness, with poetry seen not so much as an end in itself but as a means to a more complete appreciation of, and perhaps even an altered relationship with, its subject, gives contemporary poetry an increased potential not only to broaden its readership but also to contribute in the more community-oriented way that Bly, Snyder, and Berry have hoped and worked for. By reestablishing poetry as an epistemological implement for understanding nature and for regulating the complex and precarious relationships between human culture and the natural world, all three poets have laid groundwork for an art that could help restore humanity's membership in the natural community of the earth. That would clearly be a poetry that matters.

Notes

Preface

1. Breslin identifies the source of Lowell's "breakthrough back into life" as "The Art of Poetry: Robert Lowell." The source is an interview with Frederick Seidel (19).

1. Contemporary Poetry, Nature Writing, and Nature

1. Fritzell separates prose nature writers from nature poets on the basis of the former's dedication to science and the objective scientific perspective (4), but poets have also made use of that perspective, as is established later in this book.

2. The term "natural history" is also used by Charles Molesworth in *The Fierce Embrace* to characterize the poetry of Theodore Roethke and Robert Bly. "In the poetry of natural history," says Molesworth, "the reader must often reconstruct the sequence of biologic events with a metaphoric bridge, since the poet, in his efforts not to betray the otherness of the observed world into blurring sentimentality, has had to guard himself against a reductive taxonomy" (26).

3. In *News of the Universe*, Bly offers this admittedly oversimplified definition of the Old Position: "Consciousness is human, and involves reason. A serious gap exists between us and the rest of nature. Nature is to be watched, pitied, and taken care of if it behaves" (8).

4. In *The Rape of the Wild*, Andrée Collard explores, from an ecofeminist perspective, the links between similar attitudes toward nature and patriarchal, "white-coated" scientists acting under Old Position assumptions.

5. The opposition between the wild and the domestic in Bly's writing is rich in association; he entitled his 1990 collection of critical essays *American Poetry: Wildness and Domesticity.*

6. Evelyn Underhill makes a similar point concerning individual illumination in her classic study, *Mysticism.* In Underhill's formulation, illumination,

defined as the act of seeing the divine in the natural, attaining "a radiant consciousness of the 'otherness' of natural things" (234), is not the end of the mystical process, although it does represent the final achievement of many artists (169–70). Mystics who go on to become "the giants, the heroes of our race" (446) must turn back to active life in order to do so.

7. An example of a work covering Roethke's sources on mysticism is Neal Bowers's *Theodore Roethke: The Journey from I to Otherwise.*

8. Harry Williams also comments on Roethke's role as a pioneer, particularly in his relationship to the poetry of the deep image (153).

9. Other critics who have commented on Roethke's failure to write about human social relationships include Ralph J. Mills Jr., who finds "Roethke's mystical perceptions . . . striking inward steadily with little recourse to external affairs" (qtd. in Harry Williams 24), and John Wain, who, in his essay "The Monocle of My Sea-Faced Uncle," pictures a Soviet critic perplexed by Roethke's seeming indifference to "the social realities of his day" (75).

10. In *News of the Universe* Bly critiques this line from Pope as a characteristic statement exemplifying the Old Position. After establishing a qualitative gap between human and nonhuman nature, the next step, Bly argues, is to turn attention away from the less significant nonhuman creation. Snyder warns against the danger inherent in "the mistaken belief that nature is something less authentic" (qtd. in Steuding 118–19) than humanity.

11. For an example of Berry's attitude toward the relationship between the present and the future, see chapter 5, "Living in the Future: The Modern Agricultural Ideal," in *The Unsettling of America* (51–79).

12. Heyen's articles ("Open" and "Host") are concerned with the possibility of human extinction. Merwin's piece ("Letter") is more topical and overtly political, complete with mailing addresses of appropriate Hawaiian and federal government officials.

13. See Carolyn Merchant's *The Death of Nature* for the history of organic and mechanical concepts of nature in Western civilization. Other useful sources here are Max Oelschlaeger's *The Idea of Wilderness* and Neil Evernden's *The Social Construction of Nature.*

14. In *News of the Universe* and elsewhere, Bly clearly favors continental European poetry and poetics over those of England. He also says that "the exploitation by some poets of American Indian religion seems to me disgusting" (130). In a 1978 interview, Bly dismisses primitivism: "Most primitive poetry is probably boring. After you've said, 'Here comes the otter, here comes the otter, here comes the otter. A woka-woka-woka! The bird flew down the sky. Dawn is coming, Wok-i-way, I'm alive.' You say that ninety-eight

times. . . . We live in an industrial society. I love the oral quality of primitive poetry, but how can a university be oral?" (*Talking* 307–8).

15. Despite his efforts to distance himself from "the exploitation . . . of American Indian religion" (*News* 130), Bly, like Snyder, has been identified by Ward Churchill as one who appropriates and distorts Native American beliefs. Specifically, Churchill condemns the men's movement, of which Bly is "The founder and reigning Grand Pooh-Bah" (368), and notes that it has also been criticized by Russell Means, Vine Deloria Jr., and Sherman Alexie.

2. From Jeffers to Roethke

1. Nolte connects the Inhumanist perspective to current environmental and ecological thinking in *Rock and Hawk: Robinson Jeffers and the Romantic Agony* (16).

2. The idea of the poem as a conduit is explored further in chapter 3.

3. Elder uses "People and a Heron" to illustrate that the presence of humans in nature violates Jeffers's "sense of nature as *other*" (18).

4. Two of the numerous anthologies including Roethke among contemporary poets are Poulin's *Contemporary American Poetry* and McClatchy's *The Vintage Book of Contemporary American Poetry*.

5. Jeffers's poem "Animals" was actually published in 1951, after Bly's division date, 1945, yet Bly includes it in the chapter in which he also includes other poets of the Modern period, such as Frost, Williams, Stevens, and D. H. Lawrence.

6. Parini, in claiming that "Only a poet plagued by guilt feelings" (75) could have seen in the gathering of moss an assault on nature, neglects that for Roethke nature was composed of the small individual expressions of natural life, as much as, or even more than, its total expression in, say, a landscape.

7. Peter Balakian believes that "Roethke's relationship to nature in 'North American Sequence' defines what I think can be called a postmodernist and post-Romantic situation" (136).

8. The opening of "Meditation at Oyster River" echoes these lines from the beginning of Eliot's "Marina":

> What seas what shores what grey rocks and what islands
> What water lapping the bow
> And scent of pine and the woodthrush singing through the
>   fog.   (1–3)

9. In "East Coker" from *Four Quartets,* T. S. Eliot writes that "Old men ought to be explorers" (5.31). Roethke's response is typical of contemporary

poetics. He turns Eliot's universal statement into a question and then individualizes it ("I'll be an Indian").

10. Another of the *Four Quartets,* "Little Gidding," is also strongly echoed in "The Rose."

3. Robert Bly

1. "Dawn in Threshing Time" is also the title of a different Bly poem, included in his *Selected Poems* as an example of his early writings. In this chapter, the title refers to the later poem, from *This Tree Will Be Here for a Thousand Years.*

Bly sometimes revises and republishes his poems. Unless otherwise specifically indicated, I have used the 1986 *Selected Poems* as the source for quotations from those Bly poems included in that volume, as it is the most recent comprehensive source and therefore represents most poems as they now stand (although Bly is currently working on a new edition of his poetry). Where the original source is noted in the text, the purpose, as elsewhere in this book, is to place the poem in its context as part of the poet's *oeuvre.*

2. Although he has been critical of Romanticism, and is so even in the following passage, Snyder does recognize the contributions made by Romantic thinkers and artists. In "Good, Wild, Sacred," he says that "The idea that 'wild' might also be 'sacred' returned to the Occident only with the Romantic movement. This nineteenth-century rediscovery of wild nature is a complex European phenomenon—a reaction against formalistic rationalism and enlightened despotism that invoked feeling, instinct, new nationalisms, and a sentimentalized folk culture" (*Practice* 80).

3. For more on the "three brains," see "Poetry and the Three Brains," originally written in 1973, revised and republished in Bly, *American Poetry,* pages 52–63.

4. The punctuation here is that of Bly's *Selected Poems.* In some earlier versions of the poem, such as the one in *News of the Universe,* the first sentence appears as follows: "My friend this body is made of bone and excited protozoa . . . and it is with this body that I love the fields" (174). These changes typify Bly's tendency to edit his poems between publications.

5. In the "Iron John" story as retold by Bly, the boy is directed by the Wild Man to take a key from under his mother's pillow.

6. Following Eugene Odom, Gary Snyder applies the term "biomass" to describe the kind of "intelligence" Bly attributes to nature, as discussed in chapter 1. Snyder returns to Odom in "The Politics of Ethnopoetics," classify-

ing "civilization" as "an early successional phase" when human intelligence is measured by ecological standards.

7. Sugg concludes that Bly sees the policies of the United States as reflections of hidden psychic impulses (39). Bly's thinking here parallels Snyder's in *Earth House Hold:* "The American Indian is the vengeful ghost lurking in the back of the troubled American mind. Which is why we lash out . . . at the black-haired young peasants and soldiers who are the 'Viet Cong'" (112).

8. Bly's thinking on the environmental consequences of developments in Western philosophy and science here parallels that of Snyder in "Good, Wild, Sacred" from *The Practice of the Wild* and elsewhere.

9. Ponge's attempt to redefine the relationship between the human and nonhuman recalls Aldo Leopold's famous statement that "a land ethic changes the role of *Homo sapiens* from conqueror of the land-community to plain member and citizen of it" (204).

10. Hall goes on to suggest that "information" can also be included in longer, more versatile lines. Bly comes to a similar resolution in his essay "Whitman's Line as a Public Form." He contrasts the short free verse lines of Hart Crane's "Pastorale" to what he calls the "Smart-Blake-Whitman line," concluding that "The Smart-Blake-Whitman line belongs in general to declaration rather than inquiry, to prophecy rather than meditation, to public speech rather than inner debate, and to rhetoric rather than exchange of feelings" (*Selected* 197). Although he says that this quality is the line's "major flaw" (197), he also claims to emulate it in his own public or political poetry.

11. Bly not only freely substitutes "we" for "I" in poems, but he also habitually uses the first person plural in his criticism. This constitutes a minor but persistent and obvious attempt to involve an audience in poetry and the reading of poetry and to create a sense of communion between himself and his readers.

12. See chapter 5, note 20, for Berry's idea of interrelationships expressed as concentric circles.

13. For a typical comment by Bly concerning poetry's audience, see "Poetry & Audience," a series of comments by contemporary poets in the September 1989 issue of *Hungry Mind Review* (11).

14. In his *Selected Poems*, Bly notes that he had been writing the poems eventually collected in *Loving a Woman in Two Worlds* since 1973 (172).

15. Bly has published several versions of "Fifty Males Sitting Together." Significantly different versions appear in *The Man in the Black Coat Turns*, in *Loving a Woman in Two Worlds*, and in Bly's *Selected Poems*, the source of the version discussed here.

16. Williams quotes the description of the three "worlds" from "Five Decades of Modern American Poetry" from the first issue of *The Fifties*, released in 1958 (39).

17. Dana Gioia discusses Bly's "careerism" in his essay "The Successful Career of Robert Bly" (165–82).

4. Gary Snyder

1. In this discussion of "Toward Climax," the original version in *Turtle Island* is considered. In *No Nature*, Snyder has separated the "Two Logging Songs" and included them as a separate poem, immediately following "Toward Climax." In general, however, *No Nature* is the source for versions of the poems referred to in this book, if the poems were published before 1992 and are included in *No Nature*.

2. There are many versions of "beautyway" poetry. For example, George W. Cronyn's influential *American Indian Poetry* has examples in the chapter titled "Songs from the Southwest" (60–125). See also "Eagle Poem" by Joy Harjo, in *In Mad Love and War,* for a contemporary reworking (65).

3. As Steuding points out, there are significant differences between Snyder and the European Romantics. He concludes that, in Snyder's generation, the combination of "vision and craft . . . is similar in many ways to Romanticism but is essentially anti-Romantic" because it is primarily outwardly, rather than inwardly, directed (36–38). Snyder himself considers Romanticism as an important historical development in "Good, Wild, Sacred" (*Practice* 80).

4. In *Understanding Gary Snyder,* Patrick Murphy considers the "field composition" poetics developed by the Beats and by Charles Olson's Black Mountain poets as an influence on Snyder (15–16).

5. Joseph Campbell, in *The Power of Myth,* classifies the functions of myth as *mystical,* providing an initiation into the wonders of the universe; *cosmological,* shaping the universe; *sociological,* maintaining an ethical social structure; and *pedagogical,* providing a standard set of examples and references (31).

6. Snyder draws on the terminology of Ray Dasmann, who distinguishes between *ecosystem cultures,* "whose economic base of support is a natural region, a watershed, a plant zone, a natural territory within which they have to make their whole living," and *biosphere cultures,* who "spread their economic support system out far enough that they can afford to wreck one ecosystem and keep moving on" (*Place* 131).

7. Snyder's list of enclaves, or "social and religious forces," includes "Gnostics, hip Marxists, Teilhard de Chardin Catholics, Druids, Taoists, Biologists,

Witches, Yogins, Bhikkus, Quakers, Sufis, Tibetans, Zens, Shamans, Bushmen, American Indians, Polynesians, Anarchists, Alchemists" (*Turtle* 100).

8. For more on the deceptively complex prosody of Snyder's early poetry, see Thomas Parkinson, "The Poetry of Gary Snyder."

9. Geoffrey Thurley finds that it is "a sense of being—or feeling that he is—at the centre of what is happening in the world . . . which distinguishes Beat poetry and prose not only from academic poetry and prose, but also from the consciously isolationist work of the Black Mountain school" (189).

10. Although he believes that Buddhism embodies ecological principles, Snyder is critical of the tendency he sees in Zen to become institutionalized and "professional," a province of specialized experts (*Practice* 152). More fundamentally problematical for Snyder is his sense that even the healthy mythologies of the Orient have not been as helpful as they should be in functioning as complex "depth ecology" systems. In a 1989 interview with David Robertson, Snyder says that he is working on a study, to be titled *The Great Clod*, focusing on "why Buddhist and Taoist worldviews are inadequate to halt environmental degradation in China and Japan" (259).

11. The notion that the North American continent has its own "areas of consciousness" recalls Mary Austin's idea that particular landscapes result in particular rhythms and poetries. Like Snyder, Austin saw Native Americans as an important base from which American society was developing and believed that rhythms employed by American Indians were "the very pulse of emerging American consciousness" (11).

12. Ginsberg himself appears in similar fashion as "A. G." in "Bubbs Creek Haircut."

13. For more on the role of shamanism in the rise and fall of Mayan civilization, see Schele and Freidel.

14. Here Snyder draws on his proletarian or populist leanings by echoing the language of the slogan of the IWW, or Wobblies.

15. Snyder has come to use the phrase "the real work" to indicate individual and community efforts to become aligned with natural processes. In the poem "The Real Work" from *Turtle Island*, the phrase refers to the necessary actions of waves, animals, and humans.

16. In "The Landscape of Consciousness," Snyder asserts that the purpose of poetry is "close to the ancient function of the shaman. It's not a dead function" (*Real* 5). In a 1982 interview with Joseph Shakarchi, Robert Bly recalls that, in *News of the Universe*, he identifies Snyder's idea of the poet-shaman as "the most helpful addition to thought about poetry in the past thirty years" (322).

17. In "Tawny Grammar," Snyder locates the interrelationship between human and animal as a function of shared experience: "Animals as characters in literature and as universal presences in the imagination and in the archetypes of religion are there because they were *there*. Ideas and images of wastelands, tempests, wildernesses, and mountains are born not of abstraction but of experience. . . . This is the world people lived in up until the late nineteenth century" (*Practice* 73). For another retelling of the same story, with commentary, see also "The Woman Who Married a Bear" in *The Practice of the Wild* (155–74).

5. Wendell Berry

1. Snyder and Berry, as different as they are in temperament and life experience, have demonstrated a considerable measure of mutual respect and personal affinity. Berry cites Snyder in his acknowledgments page in *The Unsettling of America* and dedicates *Standing by Words* to him. Snyder, for his part, has said that Berry's "poetry lacks glamour but is really full of nutrients" (*Real* 123). Each poet has written poetry about the other. See "To Gary Snyder" by Wendell Berry, from *A Part,* and "Berry Territory," by Gary Snyder, from *Axe Handles.* As Michael Hamburger observes, "That two remarkable poets so little alike in their starting-points and their ways could meet on common, central, ground, bears out . . . the centrality and universality of Berry's concerns" (88).

2. Bly's move from Madison, Minnesota, to the more northerly location of Moose Lake in 1979 is evidence of both the nature of Bly's sense of place and the problematical character of his relationship to his family history. Of this move, Bly says that "In a way it feels wonderful to be out of Madison. I had carried my grandfather and my father too long. Up in the North Woods it is a lot like Norway" (qtd. in Baker 67–68).

3. For poems published before 1982, Berry's *Collected Poems, 1957–82* is the source of versions referred to in this book. For the Sabbaths poems, *A Timbered Choir* is the source.

4. In comparing rural America to a colony, Berry aligns himself with much more obviously progressive, even radical, writers. Gregory McNamee says that, because of his ideas about agriculture, "Wendell Berry, by all accounts a soft-spoken soul with the conservative bearing of a Southern gentleman, stands among the foremost radical writers of our time" (90). McNamee goes on to compare Berry to the "Twelve Southerners" of Louis D. Rubin's *I'll Take My Stand,* noting the obvious similarities but cautioning that Berry's "penetrating condemnation of the racism underlying American history, *The Hidden*

Wound, forces a distance between Berry and those who yearn for the stars and bars" (100).

5. It should be pointed out, though, that Bly and Berry have a very different sense of the relationship between humans and the rest of creation. Berry is generally reticent about assuming an underlying psychological connection between human and animal or plant. Instead, as in "The Old Elm Tree by the River," human and nonhuman are connected by virtue of common experience. Bly's phrase "granting consciousness" itself assumes a kind of privilege, or at least a kind of intuitive knowledge, that Berry's concept of nature would seem to preclude.

6. In "Leaping Up into Political Poetry," Bly sees the "American psyche" as inside each American individual (*American* 246). In "Tracking Down the Natural Man," Snyder admits that "there's no way that any of us can keep ourselves pure" (*Real* 88) or separate from the excesses of modern culture. In Berry's response to the correspondence he received concerning his essay "Why I Am Not Going to Buy a Computer," he admits to his own involvement in what he sees as a dangerously destructive consumerism (*What Are* 177).

7. Along with elegy, Lionel Basney includes "satire, lyric, narrative, song (and hymn), epigram" among Berry's poetic modes (178).

8. For an example of the mnemonic relationship between a familiar landscape and a local culture, see Keith H. Basso's "'Stalking with Stories.'"

9. The many literary antecedents to Berry's country dance imagery include T. S. Eliot's more ironic treatment in "East Coker" from *Four Quartets*, in which Eliot's rustics are pictured "Lifting heavy feet in clumsy shoes" (1.37) and "Keeping the rhythm in their dancing / As in their living in the living seasons" (1.41–42).

10. It is tempting to see Snyder and Berry as contemporary versions of Muir, who lived, as Snyder does today, in California's Sierra Nevada, and Burroughs, who inhabited New York's Hudson Valley, a settled region of small hilly farms and woods, basically similar to Berry's surroundings in Kentucky. Moreover, whereas Muir became famous as a spokesman for wild nature, Burroughs, as Frank Bergon notes in his introduction to *A Sharp Lookout*, a collection of Burroughs's essays, "measured the wilderness in terms of what was familiar" (42). Bergon concludes that "Unlike John Muir, Burroughs was less interested in a sublime panorama of wild nature than in a more intimate and personal one" (43–44). Likewise, Berry's response to the Southern Utah canyonlands was to remark, "This is as far away from Kentucky as I have ever been. . . . As far away as I am ever likely to be" (Terry Tempest Williams 63).

11. Herman Nibbelink echoes Fritzell's division when he considers the dif-

ference between Thoreau and Berry as the difference "between naturalist and farmer" (141). However, he also points out that Berry has consistently expressed admiration for Thoreau (135–36) and concludes that, despite their differences, Berry's "*Clearing* is 'healthy speech,' as hopeful as Thoreau's dawning sun; it deserves space beside *Walden* in the register of our cultural deeds" (151). Nibbelink also notes that Jack Hicks has called Berry and Thoreau "psychic kinsmen" (135). Berry has published a series of biographical lectures on the avowedly Thoreauvian painter Harlan Hubbard in which it is clear that Hubbard and Berry share a considerable familiarity with and respect for Thoreau, and that, moreover, Berry's admiration for Hubbard is based on his sense that Hubbard improved upon Thoreau's vision through his more thoroughgoing application of Thoreau's principles (see *Harlan*).

12. By echoing Blake's "The Tyger," Berry lends a spiritual and archetypal quality to the opposition of husbandman to "long hunter."

13. Stegner sees Berry as "one of the most provocative and thoughtful essayists alive" (48).

14. In "Form That Is Neither In nor Out," Bly discusses form as a "wildness" (24) and as analogous to the body shapes of animals. In approaching form obliquely, through metaphor, he continues to consider form not in terms of shared traditions, as Berry does, but rather as dependent on psychic forces that are essentially mysterious.

15. In his criticism of R. Buckminster Fuller in his essay "Standing by Words," Berry links lack of grammatical and syntactical clarity with cloudy thinking, concluding that Fuller's lack of grammatical clarity reveals "a man for whom words have replaced things, and who has therefore ceased to think particularly about any thing" (*Standing* 54).

16. Examples of concentric orders are illustrated in Berry's "Standing by Words" (*Standing* 46–47).

17. Berry discusses how the "community of poets" manifests itself in his own work in "A Homage to Dr. Williams" (*Continuous* 56–62). For an example of an indirect allusion linking Williams and Berry, see Berry's "The Wild" and Williams's "Spring and All."

18. In "Wendell Berry and the Politics of Agriculture," Gregory McNamee places Berry in the context of American agrarian thinking since Jefferson. *Meeting the Expectations of the Land,* an essay collection edited by Berry, Wes Jackson, and Bruce Colman, is dedicated to the memory of Jefferson, Howard, and Aldo Leopold.

19. Basney points out that the Mad Farmer is "preaching" to Jefferson's "text" in "The Mad Farmer Manifesto: The First Amendment" (180).

20. Perhaps the most prominent of the sources linking Judeo-Christian traditions with the ecological crisis is White's essay, "The Historical Roots of Our Ecologic Crisis."

21. Perkins's reservations concerning Berry's attempt to define "truth" as "what happens on twelve acres of Kentucky farmland" are discussed by Basney (181). The wording here is Basney's.

6. The Contemporary Poet as Environmentalist

1. Like other chapters in *News of the Universe*, part 4, in addition to American poets, includes poets from other countries and cultures, among them Anna Akhmatova, Gabriela Mistral, and Tomas Tranströmer.

2. Some (but by no means all) other contemporary poets whose work is notable for its ecological content are William Heyen, Maxine Kumin, Antler, Pattianne Rogers, and W. S. Merwin.

3. Rich drew loud applause at the 1998 Modern Language Association convention simply by declining to comment on Bloom's reaction to her 1996 edition of *The Best American Poetry*.

4. In *News of the Universe*, Bly lists among the factors leading to the increasing presence of poems of twofold consciousness in the later twentieth century that "American poetry has finally begun to draw on the mood of the ancient Chinese poem" (130). He has translated poems by Japanese and Indian poets such as Issa and Mirabai. In "A Secular Pilgrimage," Berry lists "Oriental poetry," with "its directness and brevity, its involvement with the life of things, its sense that the poem does not create the poetry but is the revelation of a poetry that is in the world," along with Thoreau, as "influences [on American poetry] that I think have come to be strongly felt" (*Continuous* 27–28).

5. Ironically, even in her attempt to refigure the frontier in order to avoid simple divisions such as that separating individual from "physical terrain," Kolodny's terms indicate that the dualism is deeply embedded in the language she speaks.

6. Patrick Murphy notes that Snyder also "tends to conceptualize the Earth as female and to associate fertility with both women and nature" (*Understanding* 98).

7. "Against Civilization" is Perkins's title for chapter twenty-three of *A History of Modern Poetry*, in which he discusses Bly, Snyder, and related contemporary poets.

8. In "Writer and Region," Berry reacts to William Matthews's claim, in an

article on Marianne Moore, that the subject of a poem is less important than the artist's attention to it: "Mr. Matthews's trivializing of subjects in the interest of poetry industrializes the art. He is talking about an art oriented exclusively to production, like coal mining. Like an industrial entrepreneur, he regards the places and creatures and experiences of the world as 'raw material,' valueless until exploited" (*What Are* 83).

Works Cited

Abram, David. *The Spell of the Sensuous.* New York: Vintage-Random, 1997.

Albanese, Catherine L. *Nature Religion in America.* Chicago History of American Religion Series. Series Ed. Martin E. Marty. Chicago: U of Chicago P, 1990.

Almon, Bert. *Gary Snyder.* Western Writers Series 37. Series Ed. Wayne Chatterton and James Maguire. Boise: Boise State University, 1979.

Altieri, Charles. *Enlarging the Temple.* Lewisburg PA: Bucknell UP, 1979.

———. "Gary Snyder's Lyric Poetry: Dialectic as Ecology." Murphy, *Critical* 48–58.

———. "The Poetics of Personal Contingency in Plath, Creeley, and O'Hara." Conference Presentation. National Poetry Foundation Conference. University of Maine, 20 June 1996.

———. *Self and Sensibility in Contemporary American Poetry.* Cambridge: Cambridge UP, 1984.

Ammons, A. R. *Corson's Inlet.* Ithaca: Cornell UP, 1965.

Anderson, Chester A., ed. *Growing Up in Minnesota: Ten Writers Remember Their Childhoods in Minnesota.* Minneapolis: U of Minnesota P, 1976.

Austin, Mary. *The American Rhythm.* 2nd ed. Boston: Houghton Mifflin, 1930.

Baker, Deborah. "Making a Farm: A Literary Biography." Jones and Daniels 33–74.

Balakian, Peter. *Theodore Roethke's Far Fields.* Baton Rouge: Louisiana State UP, 1989.

Basney, Lionel. "Five Notes on the Didactic Tradition, in Praise of Wendell Berry." Paul Merchant 174–83.

Basso, Keith H. "'Stalking with Stories': Names, Places, and Moral Narratives among the Western Apaches." *On Nature.* San Francisco: North Point, 1986. 95–116. Rpt. as *The Nature Reader.* Ed. Daniel Halpern and Dan Frank. Hopewell NJ: Ecco, 1996.

Bergon, Frank, ed. Introduction. *A Sharp Lookout: Selected Nature Essays of John Burroughs.* Washington DC: Smithsonian, 1987. 9–64.

Berry, Thomas. *The Dream of the Earth*. San Francisco: Sierra, 1988.

Berry, Wendell. *Another Turn of the Crank*. Washington DC: Counterpoint, 1995.

————. *Collected Poems, 1957–82*. San Francisco: North Point, 1985.

————. *A Continuous Harmony: Essays Cultural and Agricultural*. Orlando FL: Harcourt, 1975.

————. *Entries*. New York: Pantheon, 1994.

————. *The Gift of Good Land*. San Francisco: North Point, 1981.

————. *Harlan Hubbard*. Lexington: U P of Kentucky, 1990.

————. *The Hidden Wound*. San Francisco: North Point, 1989.

————. *Home Economics*. San Francisco: North Point, 1987.

————. *The Long-Legged House*. New York: Harcourt, 1969.

————. *A Part*. San Francisco: North Point, 1985.

————. *Recollected Essays, 1965–1980*. San Francisco: North Point, 1981.

————. *Remembering*. San Francisco: North Point, 1988.

————. *Sabbaths*. San Francisco: North Point, 1987.

————. *Standing by Words*. San Francisco: North Point, 1983.

————. *A Timbered Choir*. Washington DC: Counterpoint, 1998.

————. *The Unsettling of America*. San Francisco: Sierra, 1977.

————. *Watch with Me and Six Other Stories of the Yet-Remembered Ptolemy Proudfoot and His Wife, Miss Minnie, Née Quinch*. New York: Pantheon, 1994.

————. *What Are People For?* San Francisco: North Point, 1990.

————. *The Wheel*. San Francisco: North Point, 1982.

————. *The Wild Birds*. San Francisco: North Point, 1986.

————. *A World Lost*. Washington DC: Counterpoint, 1996.

Berry, Wendell, Wes Jackson, and Bruce Colman, eds. *Meeting the Expectations of the Land: Essays in Sustainable Agriculture and Stewardship*. San Francisco: North Point, 1984.

Blessing, Richard A. *Theodore Roethke's Dynamic Vision*. Bloomington: Indiana UP, 1974.

Bloom, Harold. Introduction. *The Best of the Best American Poetry: 1988–1997*. Ed. Harold Bloom. New York: Scribner, 1998. 15–25.

Bly, Robert. *American Poetry: Wildness and Domesticity*. New York: Harper, 1990.

————. "Form That Is Neither In nor Out." Jones and Daniels 22–27.

————. *Iron John: A Book about Men*. Reading MA: Addison-Wesley, 1990.

————. *A Little Book on the Human Shadow*. Ed. William Booth. San Francisco: Harper, 1988.

————. *The Moon on a Fencepost.* N.p.: Unicorn, 1988.

————, ed. *News of the Universe.* San Francisco: Sierra, 1980.

————. "Poetry and Audience." *Hungry Mind Review* 11 (September 1989): 19.

————. *Selected Poems.* New York: Harper, 1986.

————. *The Sibling Society.* Reading MA: Addison-Wesley, 1996.

————. *Silence in the Snowy Fields.* Middletown CT: Wesleyan UP, 1962.

————. *Talking All Morning.* Poets on Poetry Series. Ann Arbor: U of Michigan P, 1980.

————. *This Tree Will Be Here for a Thousand Years.* New York: Harper, 1979.

————. *What Have I Ever Lost by Dying? Collected Prose Poems.* New York: HarperCollins, 1992.

Bly, Robert, and Deborah Tannen. "Where Are Women and Men Today?" *New Age Journal* January-February 1992: 28–33, 92–97.

Bowers, Neal. *Theodore Roethke: The Journey from I to Otherwise.* Seattle: U of Washington P, 1982.

Breslin, James E. B. *From Modern to Contemporary.* Chicago: U of Chicago P, 1984.

Buell, Lawrence. "American Pastoral Ideology Reappraised." *American Literary History* 1.1 (1989): 1–29.

Butterfield, R. W. (Herbie). "'The Dark Magnificence of Things': The Poetry of Robinson Jeffers." *Modern American Poetry.* Ed. R. W. (Herbie) Butterfield. New York: Barnes & Noble, 1984. 93–109.

Campbell, Joseph, with Bill Moyers. *The Power of Myth.* Ed. Betty Sue Flowers. New York: Doubleday, 1988.

Carpenter, Frederic I. *Robinson Jeffers.* U.S. Authors Series. New York: Twayne, 1962.

Churchill, Ward. *From a Native Son: Selected Essays on Indigenism, 1985–1995.* Boston: South End, 1996.

Clausen, Christopher. *The Place of Poetry: Two Centuries of an Art in Crisis.* Lexington: UP of Kentucky, 1981.

Collard, Andrée. *The Rape of the Wild.* Bloomington: Indiana UP, 1989.

Cronyn, George W., ed. *American Indian Poetry: An Anthology of Songs and Chants.* New York: Ballantine-Fawcett, 1991.

Davis, William V. *Understanding Robert Bly.* Understanding Contemporary American Literature Series. Series Ed. Matthew J. Bruccoli. Columbia: U of South Carolina P, 1988.

Devall, Bill. *Simple in Means, Rich in Ends: Practicing Deep Ecology.* Salt Lake City: Peregrine Smith Books, 1988.

Edson, Russell. "The Prose Poem in America." *Parnassus* fall-winter, 1976: 321–25.

Elder, John. *Imagining the Earth: Poetry and the Vision of Nature.* Urbana: U of Illinois P, 1985.

Elder, John, and Robert Finch. Introduction. *The Norton Book of Nature Writing.* Ed. John Elder and Robert Finch. New York: Norton, 1990. 19–28.

Eliot, T. S. *The Complete Poems and Plays, 1909–1950.* New York: Harcourt Brace, 1971.

Emerson, Ralph Waldo. *Selected Poetry and Prose.* 2nd ed. New York: Holt, Rinehart & Winston, 1969.

Estés, Clarissa P. "The Wild Man in the Black Coat Turns: A Discussion with Robert Bly." *Bloomsbury Review* 11.1 (1991): 12–13, 18.

Evernden, Neil. *The Social Creation of Nature.* Baltimore: Johns Hopkins UP, 1992.

Everson, William. Foreword. *The Double Axe and Other Poems.* By Robinson Jeffers. New York: Liveright, 1977. vii-xix.

Faludi, Susan. *Backlash: The Undeclared War against American Women.* New York: Crown, 1991.

Fritzell, Peter. *Nature Writing and America: Essays upon a Cultural Type.* Ames: Iowa State UP, 1990.

Frost, Robert. *Poetry and Prose.* Ed. Edward Connery Lathem and Lawrence Thompson. New York: Holt, Rinehart & Winston, 1972.

Gioia, Dana. *Can Poetry Matter? Essays on Poetry and American Culture.* St. Paul: Greywolf, 1992.

Griffin, Susan. *The Eros of Everyday Life: Essays on Ecology, Gender, and Society.* Garden City NY: Anchor-Doubleday, 1995.

Hall, Donald. "Some Ideas about Prose Poems." *Goatfoot Milktongue Twinbird: Interviews, Essays, and Notes on Poetry, 1970–76.* Ann Arbor: U of Michigan P, 1978. 102–3.

Hamburger, Michael. "The Writings of Wendell Berry: An Introduction." Paul Merchant 81–89.

Harjo, Joy. *In Mad Love and War.* Middletown CT: Wesleyan UP, 1990.

Heyen, William. "The Host: Address to the Faculty at SUNY College at Brockport." *American Poetry Review* July-August 1989.

———. "An Open Letter to the Brockport College Community." *American Poetry Review* May-June 1989: 7.

Hicks, Jack. "Wendell Berry's Husband to the World: *A Place on Earth.*" Paul Merchant 118–34.

Hunt, Tim. Introduction. *The Collected Poetry of Robinson Jeffers.* Ed. Tim Hunt. Vol. 1. Stanford: Stanford UP, 1988. xvii-xxvii.

Jeffers, Robinson. *"The Beginning and the End" and Other Poems.* New York: Random, 1963.

———. *The Collected Poems of Robinson Jeffers.* Ed. Tim Hunt. Vols. 1 and 2. Stanford: Stanford UP, 1988, 1989.

———. *"The Double Axe" and Other Poems.* New York: Liveright, 1977.

———. *Not Man Apart: Lines from Robinson Jeffers.* Ed. David Brower. New York: Sierra-Ballantine, 1969.

———. *The Selected Poetry of Robinson Jeffers.* New York: Random, 1959.

Jones, Richard, and Kate Daniels, eds. *Of Solitude and Silence: Writings on Robert Bly.* Boston: Beacon, 1981.

Jung, Carl G. *Modern Man in Search of a Soul.* Trans. W. S. Dell and Cary F. Baynes. New York: Harcourt, 1933.

Kalweit, Holger. *Dreamtime and Inner Space.* Boston: Shambhala, 1988.

Keller, Karl. "Jeffers' Pace." *Robinson Jeffers Newsletter* 32 (July 1972): 7–14.

Kherdian, David. *Six Poets of the San Francisco Renaissance.* Fresno: Giligia, 1967.

Kolodny, Annette. *The Lay of the Land.* Chapel Hill: U of North Carolina P, 1975.

———. "Letting Go Our Grand Obsessions: Notes toward a New Literary History of the American Frontiers." *American Literature* 64.1 (March 1992): 1–18.

La Belle, Jenijoy. *The Echoing Wood of Theodore Roethke.* Princeton NJ: Princeton UP, 1976.

Larsen, Stephen. *The Shaman's Doorway.* New York: Harper, 1976.

Leopold, Aldo. *A Sand County Almanac and Sketches Here and There.* New York: Oxford UP, 1987.

Lessa, William A., and Evon Z. Vogt., eds. *Reader in Comparative Religion.* 4th ed. New York: Harper, 1979.

Lévi-Strauss, Claude. *Structural Anthropology.* Trans. Claire Jacobson and Brooke Grundfest Schoepf. Garden City NY: Anchor-Doubleday, 1967.

Lincoln, Kenneth. *Native American Renaissance.* Berkeley: U of California P, 1983.

Lyon, Thomas. "The Ecological Vision of Gary Snyder." Murphy, *Critical* 34–44.

———, ed. *This Incomparable Lande: A Book of American Nature Writing.* New York: Penguin, 1991.

———. "Twenty Years Later—A Coda." Murphy, *Critical* 44–48.

MacLeish, Archibald. *New and Collected Poems, 1917–76.* Boston: Houghton Mifflin, 1976.

Malkoff, Karl. *Theodore Roethke: An Introduction to the Poetry.* New York: Columbia UP, 1966.

Martin, Julia. "Coyote-Mind: An Interview with Gary Snyder." *TriQuarterly* 79 (fall 1990): 148–72.

Martz, Louis L. "A Greenhouse Eden." *Theodore Roethke: Essays on the Poetry.* Ed. Arnold Stein. Seattle: U of Washington P, 1965. 14–35.

McClatchy, J. D., ed. *The Vintage Book of Contemporary American Poetry.* New York: Vintage-Random, 1990.

McDonald, Forrest. *The Presidency of Thomas Jefferson.* American Presidency Series. Lawrence: UP of Kansas, 1976.

McKibben, Bill. *The End of Nature.* New York: Random, 1989.

McNamee, Gregory. "Wendell Berry and the Politics of Agriculture." Paul Merchant 90–102.

Merchant, Carolyn. *The Death of Nature.* San Francisco: Harper, 1980.

Merchant, Paul, ed. *Wendell Berry.* American Authors Series. Lewiston ID: Confluence, 1991.

Meredith, William. "A Steady Stream of Correspondences: Theodore Roethke's Long Journey Out of the Self." *Theodore Roethke: Essays on the Poetry.* Ed. Arnold Stein. Seattle: U of Washington P, 1965. 36–53.

Mersmann, James F. "Watering the Rocks." Peseroff 54–100.

Merwin, W. S. "Letter on the Wao Kelo O Puna Rain Forest." *American Poetry Review* March-April 1990.

Molesworth, Charles. *The Fierce Embrace.* Columbia: U of Missouri P, 1979.

———. *Gary Snyder's Vision.* Columbia: U of Missouri P, 1983.

Muir, John. *The Wilderness World of John Muir.* Ed. Edwin Way Teale. Boston: Houghton Mifflin, 1954.

Murphy, Patrick D., ed. *Critical Essays on Gary Snyder.* Boston: G. K. Hall, 1991.

———. "Penance or Perception: Spirituality and Land in the Poetry of Gary Snyder and Wendell Berry." *Sagetrieb* 5.2 (fall 1986): 61–72.

———. *Understanding Gary Snyder.* Understanding Contemporary American Literature Series. Series Ed. Matthew J. Bruccoli. Columbia: U of South Carolina P, 1992.

Nash, Roderick. *The Rights of Nature: A History of Environmental Ethics.* Madison: U of Wisconsin P, 1989.

Nelson, Howard. *Robert Bly: An Introduction to the Poetry.* New York: Columbia UP, 1984.

———. "Robert Bly and the Ants." Jones and Daniels 192–200.

Nelson, Richard. *The Island Within.* San Francisco: North Point, 1989.

Nibbelink, Herman. "Thoreau and Wendell Berry: Bachelor and Husband of Nature." Paul Merchant 135–51.

Nolte, William H. *Rock and Hawk: Robinson Jeffers and the Romantic Agony.* Athens: U of Georgia P, 1978.

Nordström, Lars. *Theodore Roethke, William Stafford, and Gary Snyder: The Ecological Metaphor as Transformed Regionalism.* Stockholm: Uppsala, 1989.

Oelschlaeger, Max. *The Idea of Wilderness.* New Haven: Yale, 1991.

Oliver, Mary. "Among Wind and Time." *Sierra* November-December 1991: 33–34.

Parini, Jay. *Theodore Roethke: An American Romantic.* Amherst: U of Massachusetts P, 1979.

Parkinson, Thomas. "The Poetry of Gary Snyder." *Southern Review* 4 (1968): 616–32. Rpt. in Murphy, *Critical* 21–34.

———, ed. *Robert Lowell: A Collection of Critical Essays.* Englewood Cliffs NJ: Prentice-Hall, 1968.

Perkins, David. *A History of Modern Poetry: Modernism and After.* Cambridge: Belknap-Harvard, 1987.

Peseroff, Joyce, ed. *Robert Bly: When Sleepers Awake.* Ann Arbor: U of Michigan P, 1984.

Peters, Robert. "News from Robert Bly's Universe: *The Man in the Black Coat Turns.*" Peseroff 304–14.

Pinsky, Robert. *The Situation of Poetry: Contemporary Poetry and Its Traditions.* Princeton NJ: Princeton UP, 1976.

Poulin, A., Jr. *Contemporary American Poetry.* 5th ed. Boston: Houghton Mifflin, 1991.

Richman, Robert. "The Book of Winter." *The Wilderness of Vision: On the Poetry of John Haines.* Ed. Kevin Bezner and Kevin Walzer. Brownsville OR: Story Line, 1996. 193–200.

Robertson, David. "Practicing the Wild: Present and Future Plans: An Interview with Gary Snyder." Murphy, *Critical* 257–62.

Roethke, Theodore. *Collected Poems of Theodore Roethke.* Garden City NY: Anchor-Doubleday, 1975.

———. *The Far Field.* Garden City NY: Doubleday, 1964.

———. *"The Lost Son" and Other Poems.* Garden City NY: Doubleday, 1948.

———. *On the Poet and His Craft: Selected Prose of Theodore Roethke.* Ed. Ralph J. Mills Jr. Seattle: U of Washington P, 1968.

———. *Open House.* Garden City NY: Doubleday, 1941.

Ronald, Ann, ed. *Words for the Wild: The Sierra Club Trailside Reader.* San Francisco: Sierra, 1987.

Rosenthal, M. L. *The New Poets.* New York: Oxford UP: 1967.

Schele, Linda, and David Freidel. *A Forest of Kings.* New York: Morrow, 1990.

Seidel, Frederick. "Robert Lowell Interviewed by Frederick Seidel." *Robert Lowell.* Ed. Thomas Parkinson. Englewood Cliffs NJ: Prentice-Hall, 1968.

Shaffer, Eric Paul. "Inhabitation in the Poetry of Robinson Jeffers, Gary Snyder, and Lew Welch." *Robinson Jeffers Newsletter* 78 (October 1980): 28–40.

Shakarchi, Joseph. "An Interview with Robert Bly." Peseroff 315–333.

Shelley, Percy Bysshe. "A Defense of Poetry." *English Romantic Writers.* Ed. David Perkins. New York: Harcourt, 1967. 1072–87.

Shepard, Paul, and Barry Sanders. *The Sacred Paw: The Bear in Nature, Myth, and Literature.* New York: Viking, 1985.

Sienicka, Marta. *The Making of a New American Poem.* Poznan, Poland: University tet Im. Adama Mickiewiccza W Poznaniv, 1972.

Smith, Dave. *Local Assays.* Urbana: U of Illinois P, 1985.

Snyder, Gary. *Axe Handles.* San Francisco: North Point, 1983.

———. *Earth House Hold.* New York: New Directions, 1969.

———. *He Who Hunted Birds in His Father's Village: Dimensions of a Haida Myth.* Bolinas CA: Grey Fox, 1979.

———. *Left Out in the Rain.* San Francisco: North Point, 1986.

———. *Mountains and Rivers without End.* Washington DC: Counterpoint, 1996.

———. *Myths & Texts.* 1960. New York: James Laughlin–New Directions, 1978.

———. *No Nature: New and Selected Poems.* New York: Pantheon, 1992.

———. *The Old Ways.* San Francisco: City Lights, 1977.

———. *A Place in Space: Ethics, Aesthetics, and Watersheds.* Washington DC: Counterpoint, 1995.

———. *The Practice of the Wild.* San Francisco: North Point, 1990.

———. *The Real Work: Interviews and Talks, 1964–79.* Ed. Wm. Scott McLean. New York: New Directions, 1980.

———. *Regarding Wave.* New York: New Directions, 1970.

———. *Riprap and Cold Mountain Poems.* San Francisco: Grey Fox, 1965.

———. *Turtle Island.* New York: New Directions, 1974.

Snyder, Gary, Lew Welch, and Philip Whalen. *On Bread and Poetry: A Panel Discussion with Gary Snyder, Lew Welch, and Philip Whalen.* Berkeley: Grey Fox, 1977.

Stegner, Wallace. "A Letter to Wendell Berry." Paul Merchant 47–52.

Stein, Arnold, ed. *Theodore Roethke: Essays on the Poetry.* Seattle: U of Washington P, 1965.

Steuding, Bob. *Gary Snyder.* U.S. Authors Series. Boston: Twayne–G. K. Hall, 1976.

Stevens, Wallace. *The Collected Poems of Wallace Stevens.* New York: Knopf, 1961.

Sugg, Richard P. *Robert Bly.* U.S. Authors Series. Boston: Twayne–G. K. Hall, 1986.

Sullivan, Rosemary. *Theodore Roethke: The Garden Master.* Seattle: U of Washington P, 1975.

Swann, Brian. "Introduction: Only the Beginning." *Harper's Anthology of Twentieth Century Native American Poetry.* Ed. Duane Niatum. New York: Harper, 1987. xiii-xxxii.

Tarn, Nathaniel. "By Way of a Preface." *He Who Hunted Birds in His Father's Village: Dimensions of a Haida Myth.* By Gary Snyder. Bolinas CA: Grey Fox, 1979. xiii-xix.

Thoreau, Henry David. "Civil Disobedience." *Walden and Civil Disobedience.* Norton Critical Edition. Ed. Owen Thomas. New York: Norton, 1966.

———. *Natural History Essays.* Salt Lake City: Peregrine Smith, 1980.

———. *Walden.* Ed. J. Lyndon Shanley. Princeton NJ: Princeton UP, 1971.

———. *The Winged Life: The Poetic Voice of Henry David Thoreau.* Ed. Robert Bly. San Francisco: Sierra, 1986.

Thurley, Geoffrey. *The American Moment: American Poetry in the Mid-Century.* New York: St. Martin's, 1977.

Triggs, Jeffery Alan. "Farm as Form: Wendell Berry's *Sabbaths.*" Paul Merchant 191–203.

Trimble, Stephen. "Introduction: The Naturalist's Trance." *Words from the Land.* Reno: U of Nevada P, 1995. 1–29.

Underhill, Evelyn. *Mysticism.* Cleveland: Meridian-World, 1955.

Van Wyck, William. *Robinson Jeffers.* Los Angles: Ward Ritchie, 1938.

Vecsey, Christopher. "American Indian Environmental Religions." *American Indian Environments.* Ed. Christopher Vecsey and Robert W. Venables. Syracuse: Syracuse UP, 1980. 1–37.

Vendler, Helen. *Soul Says: On Recent Poetry.* Cambridge: Belknap-Harvard UP, 1995.

von Hallberg, Robert. *American Poetry and Culture: 1945–80.* Cambridge: Harvard UP, 1985.

Wain, John. "The Monocle of My Sea-Faced Uncle." *Theodore Roethke: Essays on the Poetry.* Ed. Arnold Stein. Seattle: U of Washington P, 1965. 54–77.

Weinreb, Mindy. "A Question a Day: A Written Conversation with Wendell Berry." Paul Merchant 27–43.

White, Lynn, Jr. "The Historical Roots of Our Ecological Crisis." *Science* 155 (1967): 1203–7. Rpt. in *The Ecocriticism Reader: Landmarks in Literary Ecology.* Ed. Cheryll Glotfelty and Harold Fromm. Athens: U of Georgia P, 1996. 3–14.

Whitman, Walt. *Leaves of Grass.* Norton Critical Edition. Ed. Sculley Bradley and Harold W. Blodgett. New York: Norton, 1973.

Whitt, Michael. Foreword. *Point Reyes Poems.* By Robert Bly. Point Reyes Station CA: Floating Island, 1989.

Williams, Harry. *"The Edge Is What I Have."* Lewisburg PA: Bucknell UP, 1977.

Williams, Terry Tempest. "A Full Moon in May." Paul Merchant 61–67.

Williams, William Carlos. *Selected Essays.* New York: New Directions, 1969.

Williamson, Alan. *Introspection and Contemporary Poetry.* Cambridge: Harvard UP, 1984.

Wilson, Edward O. *Consilience: The Unity of Knowledge.* New York: Knopf, 1998.

Zaller, Robert. *The Cliffs of Solitude.* Cambridge: Cambridge UP, 1983.

Index